CHRISTOPHER DEVLIN

For Patrick

CHRISTOPHER DEVLIN

MADELEINE DEVLIN

MACMILLAN

First published 1970 by
MACMILLAN AND CO LTD
London and Basingstoke
Associated companies in New York Toronto
Dublin Melbourne Johannesburg and Madras

SBN (boards) 333 12143 0

Printed in Great Britain by
ROBERT MACLEHOSE AND CO LTD
University Press, Glasgow

CONTENTS

Introduction by Cardinal Heenan
Acknowledgments

Part One: *'Thursday's Bairn'*

1	The Background	1
2	Stonyhurst	13
3	Rome — Subiaco — Assisi — En Route for Manresa	21
4	Manresa	24
5	Heythrop	28
6	Rome	32

Part Two: *Wartime*

1	Liverpool and the Mountains of Wales	34
2	Beaumont 1940-1941	36
3	West Africa	38
4	Syria	46
5	North Africa	56
6	Greece	64

Part Three: *Peacetime England*

1	St Beuno's	88
2	Beaumont: *'Mundus Puerilis'*	94
3	Roehampton	100

Part Four: *Journey to Rhodesia*

1	The Way There	111
2	African Journal: 1956 Salisbury	117
3	Musami	119
4	Monte Cassino Mission	130
5	Harari Township and Musami	139
6	St James's, Gatooma	140
7	Mondoro, 1957	150
8	Musami, 1957	165

9   Musami, 1958   168
10   Musami, 1959   182

Part Five: *Home*

1   196
2   209

INTRODUCTION

'I'm condemned to death!' Those were pretty frightening words for a boy to hear spoken in a dramatic whisper in a dark school chapel. The speaker was Father Woodlock, S.J. He was illustrating a retreat sermon with reminiscences from his days as chaplain during the then recently concluded first world war. At the time I assumed the story must be true. Since then I have walked often in the company of retreat masters to discover that not all have the same standards of objectivity. Some regard stories as parables to be told as if they were historical facts — on the model of the good Samaritan or the prodigal son. To add verisimilitude to unlikely stories some preachers reject the journey of an unknown man going from Jerusalem to Jericho. In its place they tell the fictitious tale of themselves on a journey from Wigan to Blackpool. I cannot therefore say whether Father Woodlock's story was true or false. It was certainly a good story and here it is in more or less his own words.

A sixteen-year old boy ran away from his Jesuit boarding school — where I happened to be teaching — to join the army. He lied about his age — as many patriotic young men did in 1915. It was not unknown for recruiting sergeants to tell schoolboys of sixteen who gave their true age 'Come back tomorrow, sonny, when you are eighteen and old enough to join the army'.

This boy was well built and very intelligent. He was picked out, rapidly trained and given a commission. He was barely seventeen when he found himself in France, an officer in charge of a platoon. He was shocked by the casualties, the noise, the stench and even by the language of his men. He soon became dispirited and demoralised. So one day he attempted to give himself a wound which would not be dangerous but serious enough to take him back to Blighty. This was the soldiers' word for England, Home and Beauty. Unfortunately a Colonel was watching the boy's performance through field glasses. What he saw was pathetic. The poor boy had so lost his nerve that he hadn't the guts even to wound himself. He merely threw himself on the ground pretending to be a casualty. He deserted the men he was supposed to lead in the attack on the enemy trenches.

A subsequent court martial sentenced him to death. I was allowed to stay with him the whole night before his execution. It was the longest night of my life. We talked for hours of the old days at school. I promised to write to his parents and tell them that he had served Mass on the day he died and that he had met his death bravely. This comforted him greatly and, to my surprise and relief, he soon fell asleep as if he hadn't a care in the world.

As the hour approached when he must face the firing squad it was I who felt a coward. I kept postponing the moment when I must wake him up. At last I could put if off no longer. Feeling like a murderer I shook him gently and he woke up. When he saw me he thought for a moment that he was back at school. He smiled and greeted me. Then, suddenly, he remembered. An agonised look came over his face. He whispered 'I'm condemned to death!'

The point of the story was, of course, that we are all condemned to death although, unlike this boy, we know neither the day nor the hour. I was reminded of all this the first time I saw Christopher Devlin after his unsuccessful operation for cancer. He was much too intelligent to be deceived by compassionate doctors and nurses. He knew very well that he was condemned to death and that the call would come within a few weeks or months. Unlike the boy, however, he had no agonised look on his face. He was serene. He was determined to use whatever time might be left to him *ad majorem Dei gloriam*. The Jesuit motto was his rule of life. He, of course, would not have said so. He was reserved and sensitive. He wanted to cause the least possible trouble to his family and friends. He also hoped to keep faith with his publisher.

I asked him if there was anything I might provide to comfort him in his painful illness. He smiled as he made his request. He told me that his breviary contained the new psalter with its almost clinical translation of the Latin psalms. He longed for the familiar version in the old psalter which though sometimes meaningless was full of rhythm. It would be unfair, he felt, to ask his superiors to buy him new breviaries since he had so little time left to use them. If I cared to give him some discarded breviaries of mine he would die happy.

That seems to be a trivial incident but it gives insight into his character. He was a true poet. He could bear bodily pain bravely but aesthetic affront he could not withstand. He was also a man of prayer. Lesser men might have asked for some gift to assuage physical discomfort. Christopher sought help to remove distraction from his daily prayers. He was also a typical Jesuit — if such a being can truly be said to exist. I mean that he loved the Society and in a spirit of poverty wanted to make no extravagant demands upon its charity.

What is the most notable characteristic of the Sons of St. Ignatius? I would say it is their discipline. The order was originally called not the Society but the Company of Jesus. Their soldier founder pictured his order as a company of soldiers of Christ. For a soldier discipline is all important. Father Devlin died just before priests and religious began to become introspective. He had never considered what with clergy was later to become the obsessive question of his purpose and identity as a priest. He was also mercifully spared the current quest for maturity. His maturity had been gained on the hard way of the Cross. He knew his identity to be that of an alter Christus. However disappointed he had been when his superiors refused to give him the academic opportunities for which he was so eminently suited he did not rebel. He continued to act according to the spirit of his vow of obedience. Oxford or Africa, an army chaplaincy or the schoolroom — he cheerfully went wherever obedience might direct him. His friends fretted because he was not given sufficient scope to develop his dazzling gifts as a writer. Christopher Devlin did not fret. He found peace of soul in obeying orders.

In September 1969, Father Arrupe, General of the Jesuits, told all members of the Society of Jesus what was expected of them during these days of the Church's renewal. Having visited the communities of his order throughout the world he gave an account of what he had seen. Those who know only the Jesuits of fiction might imagine that the Father General would have listed the number of Jesuits in key positions directing public opinion or those in the highest scholastic posts. Instead he spoke of 'the majority of Jesuits who do silent but valuable work, without attracting the notice of the sensation-seeking public'.

Christopher Devlin was one of their number. He is remembered by historians and literati, by schoolboys and soldiers, by poor Africans, by priests and nuns who sought his spiritual guidance. To the sensation-seeking public he was unknown. I hope that this splendid account of his life will make him known to the many who often look in vain for the story of the spirit in a modern idiom.

December 1969   John Cardinal Heenan
                                                        Archbishop of Westminster

ACKNOWLEDGMENTS

Many people patiently answered questions about Christopher and so made it possible for me to write this life. I am grateful to every one of them but particularly I want to thank those who helped me not once or twice but many times. Amongst them are many of the busiest of Christopher's brethren:— Fr Desmond Boyle, so forgiving and generous; Fr Philip Caraman who gave me much material; Fr Thomas Corbishley who answered queries about the Society and checked quotations in three languages; Fr Terence Corrigan who explained Christopher's work in Rhodesia; Fr John Coventry who introduced me to many of Christopher's friends and pupils and gave me his earliest writings; Fr Martin D'Arcy for his wonderfully vivid memories of Christopher and his contemporaries at Stonyhurst; Fr Thomas Dunphy, Fr Robert Gorman, Fr John Harriott, Fr Peter Levi and also Fr Dermod Whyte who had kept for nearly 40 years the poems Christopher wrote at Manresa.

I gratefully remember the help given unsparingly by the late Fr Richard Clarke in tracing wartime contacts; the late Fr Cyril Martindale who did not want Christopher to be forgotten; and the late Fr Handley Lillie who gave me 'The Forgotten Fragment' to use.

I want to thank Charlie and Aileen Meade and all who gave me Christopher's letters including Rupert Hart-Davis and Miss Daisy Moseley; Francis Cowper who lent me the Stonyhurst magazines and told me of Gray's Inn in Penal times; Winifred Danson for descriptions of Christopher's first assignment; a number of people in the Ministry of Defence, particularly Mr C. J. F. Gilmore. He took much trouble and also put me in touch both with the Revd H. T. L. Lees with his splendid memories who allowed me to quote from his booklet, privately circulated 'for those who fought at Kiffissia', and the Revd George Church who allowed me to quote from the diary he kept in Greece. It was Mr Tom Harrison who gathered the Greek threads together for me and gave me a hitherto unrecorded story of Winston Churchill.

To Christopher's cousin Arnold Henderson I am indebted for information about the Crombie family tree — in particular for the name of Christopher's maternal great-great-great-grandmother.

I am grateful for the friendship of Veronica Wedgwood and Rupert Hart-Davis both of whom spared time to read the first draft of the typescript.

Finally I have been deeply dependant on the constant help and friendship of Nicolas Barker.

M.D.

PART ONE

THURSDAY'S BAIRN

1
THE BACKGROUND

Christopher was born on 30 May 1907; he was the second son and third child of William and Frances Devlin. Another daughter and another son were yet to follow to complete what would become a distinguished family. He was born at Chislehurst in Kent, then a growing village set round a common. His heredity was a strange intertwining of two cultures, not very remote but antithetic: the one Irish, the other Scottish.

His father stemmed from a sept of the O'Neill's, warriors in their day, who had settled probably before the eleventh century, in the hills around Lough Neagh, not far from Donaghmore, in County Tyrone, and there, at the beginning of the seventeenth century the Chief, the O'Devlin lived, and there the last trace of the Chief's immediate family is found in 1656, 'in a place one mile north of the breeding-ground of your great-grandfather'. So wrote Christopher to his elder brother Patrick in 1950. They were gentlemen, the American chronicler of the O'Devlins claims, but, he adds, if they had a coat of arms it was not the same as that now used by their descendants in the U.S.A. which is of nineteenth century origin. Christopher's great-grandfather was Matthew. He did leave his ancestral countryside and went to Glasgow, but his son Daniel, Christopher's grandfather, swiftly returned and built a house to live in at Ro-an, just on the edge of the old Devlin lands, south of Rochan. He seems to have had all the charm and courage as well as the disability for business affairs often associated with his heritage. He was a builder like his father, and made his own bricks on which he stamped his name in full. He bought a property in Coalisland half a mile from his new house, and tried to mine coal. There was none — except in the name —. 'A sympathetic guide-book records: "The winding-gear and pit-head machinery stand today in sad and silent testimony of the frustrated dreams of an enterprising industrialist." ' and, added Christopher, 'a good thing too, for it is a lovely countryside'. A view which his father, despite the comparative penury to which the failure gave rise, would have endorsed, but one which would greatly have shocked his mother's relations.

Christopher's mother, always called Fanny, was a Crombie, a family which in the nineteenth century had become influential and rich through trade. The connection grew large, large and wealthy enough to be a great force in and around the neighbourhood for over a hundred years, living for the most part in the town of Aberdeen, or on Deeside, or a few miles north, beyond Fintray, where John Crombie of the Old Manse, had started between 1802 and 1805, the mill at Cothall from which their fortunes came. His father was James Crombie of Fetternear, who had been a weaver and John had been employed in the cloth trade in the Buchan district before he came further south. It was his sons, James of Goval and John of Balgownie who had the drive and initiative as well as the good fortune to bring the mill successfully through the difficult years at the height of the Industrial Revolution. James had taken over the management in 1828; he was only eighteen and he became a partner in 1837, John who was nine years younger, had to wait till 1854 for his partnership, but it is he who is given most of the credit for the move to the large factory at Grandholm, nearer to Aberdeen. The move took place in 1859, a year after John of Fintray's death – he was eighty-six. The works are still there and flourishing, though no longer a family business.

But in 1837 skill, hard work and good judgment would not have been enough to weather the storms which had been blowing for a number of years. More capital was urgently needed. That year James married. He married Katherine Scott Forbes. She was the daughter of Theodore Forbes, a younger son of the Laird of Boyndlie. She had £10,000 which had been left to her by her father. 'It is oral tradition' wrote Mr Allan in 'The Crombies of Grandholm', 'that the money Katherine brought to the marriage helped to grease the wheels at Clothall at the very time when the tweed trade brought a great opportunity.'

Theodore Forbes was a merchant who lived and traded in Bombay. He amassed a fortune in a short time for he died at sea on his way home to England when he was thirty-three. But Katherine brought something more than her fortune, she brought new blood which was to make her descendants unusually interesting. Theodore had married at Surat, north of Bombay. His bride was called Eliza Khawur. Little beside her name is known about her. After her husband's death she came to Scotland with her daughter and a son, and lived – or was kept – in seclusion all her life. All traces of her, such as a portrait known to have been in an attic at Goval at one

2

time, were carefully destroyed and it was not until her great-grandchildren were middle-aged that it was said aloud that she was Indian. And yet the inheritance Katherine passed on from her was precious. She brought, of course, dark colouring to some, exquisite hands to many; she brought a leaning towards mysticism which was played with by her grandson Theodore, and which became the heart of her great-grandson, Christopher. She may also have brought the streak of cruelty so noticeable in her son Black Jock, so noticeably conquered in Christopher that it became a virtue; certainly she brought Christopher high cheek-bones and a wide generous mouth.

Her son, whose baptismal name was John, is described as being of a managing temper — a pleasing euphemism for choleric. His portrait which still hangs at Goval, the lovely house on the banks of the river Don, which he left to his unmarried sisters and after their deaths to his son John, shows him as having a black-bearded sinister sallow face. Mr Allan says he had 'magnificent almost oriental side-whiskers'. His behaviour to his wife and family was certainly almost like that of an oriental potentate of the eighteenth century. He had married, in 1865 Annie, a daughter of George Thompson of Pittmedden, of the Thompson Shipping Line, which traded until recently with the Far East. Of their four sons and four daughters (1) who dearly loved their mother, only two of them did not fear their father, Connie his prettiest daughter and his son John. Black Jock died in 1898, five years after Annie, and it was some months after that that Fanny, with her eldest sister, Grace went on the pleasure trip to South Africa on which she met William.

William had qualified in Dublin as an architect, he had been to the School of Art as well as to the College of Science and had been articled to Mr Walter Glyn Doolin. Then he left Ireland for good as the rest of his immediate family were to do — his brothers, Daniel and Matthew, and his sister Ellen (2), although Ellen did not leave until her father had died. She stayed at home looking after him until she was twenty-six, and then did what she had longed to do, she trained to be a nurse. She greatly resembled William in looks and character. He was a handsome man with an aristocratic mien and a high Irish pride. In London, since he was a fine draughtsman, he had no difficulty in getting a job; he was employed by the L.C.C. and worked there under the distinguished architect Reilly. He lived in a flat in Gray's Inn — the Inn of Court to which his son Patrick would in time belong, and where he, too, would have a flat which Christopher would visit.

(1) In order of age: James (Uncle Jim), Grace, Constance (Auntie Connie), Frances, (Fanny), Joan (Aunt Janny), John, George (Uncle George or Geo) and Theodore (Uncle Theodore or Theo),

(2) Aunt Ellie or Ellie.

William must have been going to South Africa for some reason connected with his work. Fanny's trip was partly to soothe her ruffled feathers; she had vainly imagined that Duncan Abel, a clever young barrister was courting her. Her pretty elder sister Connie was his quarry, but since during her father's lifetime no man was allowed to visit the sisters except when they were in each others' company the mistake could easily arise. It gave, however unfairly, added weight to her youngest sister's dictum NEVER TRUST A MAN. Fanny was to listen to this sister, Janny, all her life and usually she took her advice. So now, when on board ship William fell in love with her and she with him, she refused his offer of marriage. Perhaps he knew that her heart was not behind her refusal, for though he told her that he would never write to her, he added: 'If ever you change your mind write to me'. We do not know what address he gave her, whether one in South Africa or in England which might have been Gray's Inn Square — we only know that she wrote and that the marriage took place at the Episcopalian church in Queen's Cross, Aberdeen, in September 1900. Connie and Duncan Abel gave the reception in their house.

Fanny and William went south to Chislehurst and it must have been a halcyon period. William rejected the idea of joining a firm and set up with an office in the Adelphi, off the Strand in London, on his own. Fanny had sufficient money to keep them whilst they waited for work to come. Black Jock, having threatened to leave his daughters unprovided for, because, he said, 'they had left him to die like a rat in a hole', a fact they indignantly denied, had left them £12,000 apiece, two-thirds of the sum he left to each son. This was a goodly portion but all the money he left his daughters he tied up in a trust; the investments in railway shares they were not permitted to change, and so they were forced, as the years went by, to watch their fortunes dwindle away.

For four years William and Fanny had no children and then their first child, Joan Mary was born, to be quickly followed by Patrick, Christopher and Frances. Still the work did not come; they had waited hopefully for nine years but now they took the decision to go north to live amidst Fanny's relatives; it was fairly hoped that where he would be known William would get work.

The move took place in August 1909 when Christopher was two, Joan Mary was five and a half, Patrick within three months of his fourth birthday, — he and Christopher travelled barricaded onto the seat in the railway carriage behind their father's golf clubs, — Frances was not quite three months old. They went to rooms in Carden Place kept by a Miss McKay until they found a house in Forest Road and here in December 1911 their fifth child Billy was

4

born. Later they moved to 60, Rubislaw Den North. So from the first they lived in the heart of Aberdeen amongst uncles, aunts and great aunts, and cousins, near and remote, all of whom were friendly towards the Devlins even if they skirmished among themselves. Naturally thenceforward Christopher's home was to be predominantly Scottish and the Devlin children grew up with a secure background, sure of a welcome anywhere, which was very good for them and for Fanny too.

For William it was different. He must have gasped like a fish out of water. His obvious integrity and his charm of manner pleased Fanny's relations but there was no possible basis for understanding between him and the bluff pragmatic commerce-loving Crombies — except of course, mutual respect. Their thought was different and poles apart. William was an artist, delicately sensitive, which in itself would have made him incomprehensible to this generation of Crombies; in addition he was a catholic and his religion informed his thought. The 'connection', though not Fanny's brothers and sisters whose feelings about religion were as mixed as their own practice, was predominantly presbyterian. But since so many of the noblest families in the County had never lost the old faith, and were seen to practise it, there was no battle on that score; — though, it was said, that had Black Jock lived he would never have permitted the marriage, for he detested catholics. Of all his children only two remained faithful to the fold in which they had been reared; James, the eldest, an enchanting man but one who rarely came to Aberdeen, the place he loved, once his wife, whose slightest wish he thought a command, wanted to live in London, and John, who disliked catholics, if dislike is not too strong a word to use of so gentle a man, and whose views in any event in practice were softened by the kindly nature of his indomitable wife, Joan.

Of the others, Grace had no religion, only vegetarianism and taboos. She was a kindly creature and had migrated south and lived there for the rest of her life with a diminutive companion called May Robinson. All the Crombie uncles and aunts were consulted by each other — and Fanny was a great consulter — as experts on any matter on which any of them was thought to have had even the most fleeting and superficial experience. Because May Robinson had once met Sybil Thorndike, Grace became the acknowledged family expert on theatrical matters; she was consulted twenty-five years later when Christopher's younger brother, Billy, was beginning a dazzling career. She knew, she said, of a John Giel — something or other who had succeeded but for her part she could see no opening on the stage. She was consulted, too, on growing bulbs; her ideas were once more negative. She lived at the time on the Isle of Wight, where she

5

said the foreshore moved and any way the island faced north so her bulbs were disturbed and would not grow but perhaps elsewhere they might. Grace was, in fact, specially remembered for her excessive gloom and for singing sad songs, such as 'Strew on him roses, roses and never a sprig of yew', which several of the children, including Christopher, who could not sing at all, imitated with joy. She died in London at the height of the Blitz, leaving instructions that she was to be left alone in a darkened room for six hours after she was presumed to have died and then her heart was to be pierced to make sure that she had — and that her ashes were to be scattered from an aeroplane 'over some beautiful spot'. The first request could not be attended to since it took longer than that to discover that she had left her will in Aberdeen; the second, however, Messrs Barkers of Kensington quite easily arranged. The ashes were scattered over Dinnet Moor, some miles from Danestone, where her parents had lived and where she had been brought up.

Aunt Connie and Aunt Janny were both High Anglicans, though of different kinds so that they could never worship in the same church. Theodore, so named after his maternal grandfather, Theodore Forbes, was a Theosophist; George searched for faith all his life, now questioning Theodore and now Fanny who had become a catholic on the birth of Joan Mary. It was Connie and Janny with Geo and Theo, John and his wife Joan, who were now part of the every day life of the Devlins.

William took an office in the main street of Aberdeen, Union Street. Work did come to him through the 'connection' and in other ways too. Within the first three years he remodelled the inside of Goval for John, opening up the hall and designing a beautiful oak stairway and he built a country house, a school and a chapel. Later he built several little country churches. They stand today to show his excellence but, like his father, he lacked business ability and the idea of pushing himself was repugnant. It was a mistake that he tried to work on his own and it was only in the last years of his life when he had a partner and an office in Edinburgh too, that he made anything like enough money to keep his family in Crombie style, and, by then, the family no longer required keeping. The blood of the O'Devlins must have welled up in him as he accepted help all the while that his children were growing up.

Giving money to someone who is proud and sensitive is difficult; indeed the whole art of giving is difficult and Geo, the great bene-factor, had no idea of the art at all. The other relations, who had much less to give, gave with great delicacy. Aunt Connie was not at all well off; for her husband Duncan had died when he was very young leaving her with their son Dick to bring up. She would ask the

6

Devlin children to lunch whenever she thought Fanny looked tired, though, in doing this she had to take care not to over-work her maid Jeannie — indeed it was she who waited on Jeannie, rather than the other way round. Christopher, at a much later date, of course, told with affectionate amusement of a conversation he had had with his Aunt Connie, typical of many: 'Well come tomorrow there is a joint of beef waiting to be cooked and there is a pheasant — O, but I think the cold mutton will be best, don't you?'. Aunt Janny interspersed her advice with presents as often as she could. She was rather 'modern' with her red hair cropped, and she had a manly independence, not but what she would not have made some man an excellent wife had she been able to rid herself of her prejudices. Alas, Janny having got these originally from her father's cruelty to her mother — the cruelty which was alleged though never specified — was confirmed in them by the love affair of the friend with whom she shared most of her life. Lucy Newill, her companion, had been jilted — some said for a richer woman; however as soon as he had returned from his honeymoon Dr Kingdon had come to his former love to say that he now knew that he had made a terrible mistake. Lucy answered that there was nothing now to be done — he must lie on the bed he had made, but softening her words, she added that if his wife died, then he could come back to her and would find her waiting. And so he did. Janny gave not a sign of her feelings when forty years later he returned a widower and took his first love away with him.

As for Uncle Theodore's gifts they gave pleasure to everyone. He came back from India where he spent most of his time, loaded with presents. Janny treasured an amber necklace. Christopher remembered for years his disappointment the time Uncle Theodore came back *without* another brass elephant for him. If he gave a cheque to Fanny instead of a necklace or ornament no one could mind. He was a very generous man though not rich by Crombie standards and he had heavy commitments. He had brought two Indian boys to England to educate, an act ironically enough, frowned on by the 'connection'. Only Fanny kept in touch with them when they returned to India, but she agreed with the rest of her kinsmen in Aberdeen, that the marriage one of them made with an English girl could not turn out well. Theodore's visits to his family were gay affairs; he was less avuncular than Geo and more of a friend. Christopher found it exciting to make him tell tales of life in India, and when he was older, to get him to talk about theosophy. Fanny did not approve of such talk but Christopher wheedled it out of him nevertheless. He was a sweet man and not only Uncle George, with whom he lived when he was home, but all his family missed him greatly each time he went away to Bombay. And it is sad that he died in India, of a neglected appendix when he was fifty-six; he left his money to his Theosophist friends in India to help their work.

Uncle George had a genius for successful investment and a Croesus-like urge to amass money; the money Black Jock had left his sons he had not left in a trust and, with Geo's help, they were all able to increase their inheritance considerably. But the rest of them had more to spend their fortune on than had Geo. Within the bounds of comfort — a moderately sized house, a nice garden and a large staff uncle George lived frugally. Like Theodore, Grace and Janny he never married. He was a lonely man; many of the ingredients of pathos were there but he was not in fact pathetic. He played both golf and bridge for Scotland. He owned one of the first motor cars in Aberdeen and in the nineteen-twenties bought a Rolls which a decade later was still kept like a shiny horse by his chauffeur, Duncan, who whistled as he cleaned and polished it in the way ex-coachmen turned chauffeur did in the early years of the century. Duncan taught all the Devlins to drive, Christopher rather less successfully than the rest. Geo drove himself in a specially fitted Rover. It was specially fitted because as the result of a fever, from which he had suffered in the Navy, he had been invalided out in his twenties, with one leg rigid and shortened, from which he continued to suffer a certain amount of pain. Such work as he did thereafter he did from the comfort of his own study.

John also had early been attracted to cars. He had had his first Renault well before he married in 1912. After that date he had two — a purple landaulet and a smaller grey — but when he bought his first, a lean-to had to be attached to the garage of the house he shared with Geo in Rubislaw Den South. Since he was the elder brother it was his car that went into the garage proper and Geo's that went into the makeshift one. Yet seniority did not count when advice was sought. Geo was the family authority on cars, and on driving, as well as on finance and some other matters. And it was Geo who was consulted. Fanny took this so far that she scarcely felt safe when driven by anyone else. She loved it when he took her for an afternoon drive which in those days, besides being a novelty, was enjoyable. Christopher, Patrick and Billy were grown up when they discussed the matter for the first time and realised, with quite a shock, that even if the trams of the town, in front of which Geo would drive with verve, causing them to stop abruptly on their tracks, were always in the wrong, it was yet unlikely that the wall at Myrtle bridge would regularly present itself as an obstacle on Geo's oncoming homeward path from his club. No one had questioned — at least no one in the family had questioned Geo's manner of driving before — and so they kept their thoughts to themselves.

By the time the Devlin boys were in their teens Geo had sold the house in Aberdeen and bought Fairgirth a few miles away up Deeside, where he lived for the rest of his life.

As long as he had lived in the town and they were not away at school, the Devlin children had visited him after Mass each Sunday, for about half an hour, before they went home to lunch. They lunched with him on festive occasions and when they were older, it was customary to dine with him, along with the cousins from Goval, on Christmas night. Never until the last days of his life did he invite anyone to his house who was not either related to the family or connected with it. Only when he was dying and the doctor had forbidden all visitors did he cause his door to be flung wide open; and to all who came — and the word got round — in the name of charity, he left money in his will. He had very great difficulty in disposing of his vast fortune. His lawyer was in constant attendance taking instructions and having to bawl anything that it was needful to say through the ear-trumpet which Grace had left to George and to which now, in his extremity, he had turned.

He gave to boys' clubs and girls' clubs; he gave £500 here 'because his cathedral is so ugly'; £50 there, 'to each of the Sisters of Nazereth who buzz about here like bluebottles'; he gave £50 to any who had served him kindly in shops. This last was his sister Janny's idea, for everyone in the house was disinterestedly helping him dispose of his fortune. He did not wish to leave much to any nephew or niece in case he should be encouraging them to be idle. Despite all efforts and the fact that his lawyer discovered he had miscalculated death duty — mercifully another £20,000 could be got rid of that way, — there was still £30,000 or so unallotted when he wearied of trying to think of anything more to do with his wealth, so he left the balance to dear faithful Aunt Joan, John's widow, to spend on any charity of which she thought he would approve. One of the last things he attempted was to phone the undertaker to tell him not to charge too much. Fortunately in the middle, he forgot what he was doing. He certainly enjoyed his dying and there was a kind of nobility in the manner of it.

Such was the uncle who played by far the largest part in the lives of the Devlin children, visiting them every day. On the whole Fanny enjoyed his visits. She had an enormous respect for her brother and looked up to him. So in fact did Janny who exempted him, and Lucy's brother, who any way was an archdeacon, from her distrust of men. But Fanny must frequently have been hurt by him, must frequently have sensed and suffered for Willliam's pain; but gratitude and family feeling prevailed. On the surface she was a timid woman,

9

loathing cats, terrified of dogs and indeed of all animals, but deep down she had a calmness and repose that she communicated to her children. William *was* very fond of his brother-in-law but perhaps he was glad of those occasions when his visits coincided with office hours.

On the other hand, during their youth Christopher and his brothers and sisters found Uncle George's visits ordeals which had to be got through as best they could. He was, in any event, a truly terrifying figure to a child. He was gruff and growling. He asked questions at once tedious and alarming — 'Why', and 'What did ye say', and 'Speak up, can't you', for, alas, he was deaf. He had penetrating deep blue eyes, slightly rimmed with red, a ruby complexion, sandy hair and great sandy bushy eyebrows — enough to make any child quail, especially when he pointed with his rubber-tipped stick. They were fond of him — for indeed he was a loveable man and he mellowed greatly in later years — but in their nursery days they feared him and for good reason beside his manner and appearance. That he gave their mother a large cheque at Christmas, to bolster up the economy, they knew, and knew too that these subsidies were of vital importance and that they must always be 'polite to Uncle George'. They knew also that there were certain bills that he was willing to pay, though on one sad occasion one of these came back, with a cheque written out for a lesser amount, and an offending item crossed through in red. He would have paid for the boys to go to school at Uppingham, which, rather oddly, he thought of as the 'Crombie' school though the only members of his generation to go away to school had in fact gone to Clifton; he went there himself until he joined the Navy. He had nothing against Stonyhurst where Christopher and his brothers were to go except that it was unknown to the Crombies, and he could not conceive why his sister and her husband should want to send the boys to a catholic school ... When the time came for the University he paid for both Patrick and Billy — and, Geo having mellowed by the time he went, Billy did not have to account for his postage stamps. He would also have paid for Christopher, but Christopher as he recounts himself, refused on the first occasion the offer was made the reasonable condition inherent in it, and when Geo made the offer for a second time it was too late.

Uncle George got on better with Patrick and Billy than he did with Christopher. How could he rate a boy who, when asked what he would do with a five pound note, said he would make a boat and sail it on a pond? It is only fair to add that this was during Christopher's Shelley period.

Because of his manner, the restrictions imposed, the calling-to-account, they knew rather than felt that their uncle was good to them. It was not until they were grown up that they came to realise that Geo had given them money not only from a generous sense of duty but also because his chief interest and enjoyment lay in the triumphs of his nephews and nieces, and that even the restrictions he made he made because he saw himself as a father figure and acted in the only way he knew a father to behave.

However hurtful at the time no permanent harm was done. It is true that Christopher had a stammer as a child but it has never been suggested that this was due to Uncle George's exhortations to speak up; indeed these exhortations may have been of benefit for Christopher did well at school in elocution. The stammer when he grew up became a slight and attractive hesitation. Even the fact that all the children realised that they were the poor relations amid the rich troubled them not at all. Indeed it was extraordinary that, living as they did amongst the clan, they walked almost as untouched by the ideas of their Scottish relations as if they had been living on the shores of Lough Neagh. Especially is this true of Christopher. It was the moors and hills, so easily within reach, which had a lasting effect on him and coloured his thought throughout his life:

The purple moor with its green blaeberry tufts and the silver birch between the shadow of Morrone and the sheen of the river Dee.

Had Christopher been an only child the vagaries of the grown-ups might have been more oppressive but the five children were close friends and were to remain so. Christopher once wrote of Patrick as 'the adored companion of my pre-conscious years'; Billy, who was especially dear to him always, was Frances's boon companion; Christopher loved her hardly less and, as the youngest, Billy also enjoyed the special protection of his elder sister. Joan Mary alone, since she was a girl separated by five years and Patrick and Christopher from her sister, was the odd one out — but she was closer to her father than the rest of them. They all played absurd family games together, with their own kingdoms and domains and shops, and names, which never fell into abeyance and echoes of which were apt to crop up in Christopher's letters throughout his life. When some childish disaster occurred their mother would blame the oldest son — it was all the fault of 'Pat and his silly games'— The phrase became a slogan, but it was quite as often, in truth, the fault of Christopher and his! They all remembered these games amongst the happiest of childhood memories.

Very high up amongst these memories, too, was that of their mother reading to them. Fanny read to them frequently and exceptionally well. Christopher wrote about it long afterwards

11

carried on a human voice before the art of writing had revealed itself. They came from a book I was read to out of. It stood on a shelf along with Beatrix Potter and Hans Andersen and others whose titles I cannot remember. My brother had another book of the same edition, the same shape and colour, but subtly different; the first book was *my* book. It contained the story of St Christopher, my patron, of St Wenceslaus the King, of Alexamenos who worshipped God, and of a certain St John who caught a fly in church and carried a sword when he was a man.

But St Christopher was the first and his story had taken shape in my memory before I learnt to read. St Christopher had a muscular neck and a grim scornful face; he made a vow not to serve anybody who could not prove himself stronger than anybody else, and so he went on his way rebelling against various masters until he found one who was quite unconquerable. The daring and logic of this enterprise became a sort of 'axioma' in my private consciousness — one of those possibilities, like myths, which are too comprehensive to be actual in any time or place. Another such 'axioma' for me was the Scottish nursery rhyme for my birthday; 'Thursday's bairn has far to go'. Neither of them had any factual application that I am aware of; the only time I tried to go far, I was led back, howling miserably, by someone else's nursemaid.

He remembered too stories from the Bible:

I remember Old Testament ones better, especially the one about Ruth gleaning; perhaps that was because I had a cousin called Ruth who had corn-coloured hair.

He read for himself quite early and still when he was very small he went daily with Joan Mary and Patrick to the Convent of the Sacred Heart at Queen's Cross, whose chapel his father had designed. He was there when World War I broke out:

The age of seven opened the first fully conscious chapter of my life. It was marked by 'Tipperary' and the swing of kilts and the thirst for glory which is still my dominant if dormant passion.

His cousin Dick Abel was his hero at this time; he was then at Uppingham. He became head boy, won a scholarship to Oxford but he never took it up. In 1916 he went straight to the Front and was killed in 1918 during the last german offensive. His name can be seen on the Corpus Christi War Memorial.

A month after the War had broken out Christopher was separated from Patrick for the first time; Patrick went to Hodder, the preparatory school for Stonyhurst, in Lancashire. It was a difficult journey from Aberdeen in war-time and before Christopher was of an age to join him there, a preparatory school was opened in the town by a Mr Crichton. To this in 1916 Christopher was sent. The only remembered incident at this establishment is of Christopher being beaten for punching a very much larger boy on the nose and making it bleed. At the Convent the boys' departure was a relief to the nuns for the brothers would lie in wait for them in the garden with their water pistols — (a discreditable fact which would have been forgotten had not Christopher himself recalled it when, many years later, he revisited the school as a priest, and was over-pressed by some of the same nuns to give an edifying talk to their pupils.) In 1919, the year after the War ended Christopher, too, went to Stonyhurst and a new era began. Home was unspeakably dear, the holidays greatly to be prized but school was the battlefield on which to win his spurs.

2
STONYHURST

'There is no part of Stonyhurst which I like better than the Fells' Christopher wrote when he had been there for two years.

Perhaps that is only because it recalls to my mind the heath clad slopes, the blooming heather and the bleak hills which I love so well.

All the same he does not appear to have been in the least homesick. He soon emerged as a leader and threw himself with zest into many things. The interests which he had brought with him he did not abandon. He had begun bird-watching before he went to school by searching the hedgerows for nests and collecting eggs, and from this beginning the fascination of birds never ended, and later they were to have a mystical significance. There never was a time when he did not write about them in verse or prose or just in letters. At school he was noting their habits and storing their songs in his memory:

Tic-tic-tic-tui-tic, sings the Robin as he perches on the old dyke. His mate joins him and discloses a nest in a crevice between the stones. . . . A wood is a mysterious place, full of sights and sounds. I could hear the Wood Wren's twittering song like a shilling running down a plate.

He was in charge of the school aviary but it is difficult to imagine that he would care for birds in cages and there is a hint of boredom in the colourful notes which he wrote for the school magazine in the summer term of 1921.

To relieve the monotony of the usual Aviary Routine a blood-thirsty rat provided us with a most thrilling hunt. It had descended . . ., on the innocent birds and in one fell swoop 'necked' firstly the wounded lap-wing . . . secondly the Reeve, which has since proved to

13

be a Ruff, and finally a prize canary, worth £5. The President and a sleuth-like member . . . tracked the monster to his lair . . . With a horrible look of rage and agony on its whiskered countenance, the blood-thirsty buccaneer succumbed. Grimly we stretched him by the corpses of his butchered victims.

During the holidays which followed that term the family went, as they usually did each August, to a cottage on Deeside. Christopher described how he walked to the top of a high hill and prayed for a sign that the dream world of the future he had built for himself would come to pass.

There was no sign; and I swore an oath that I would dream no more, let the romantic future of gaeldom and monarchy go hang, and carve for myself instead a real living paradise out of the schoolboy world of rugger and games and rags and dramatics and debates and vigorous intoxicating friendships. Which I did to the full.

Christopher's many friends were as different as his interests which ranged from literature and history to games and the O.T.C. but in using the word intoxicating he was thinking of one friendship in particular. Intoxicating is the only word which describes the effect Henry John's friendship had on those to whom he gave it — whether boys or masters. He was a rare person, the son of Augustus John, and he had been brought up by his mother's sister, Miss Nettlefold. She was a catholic and sent him to Stonyhurst where he became one. He had inherited his father's genius; he did not paint but he wrote both verse and prose with extraordinary distinction, and whatever he chose to do he did brilliantly. He did not carry off every prize every year; several of his fellows were to become distinguished men and quite often wrested them from him, as Christopher did in English and History, but taken all in all he burnt like a candle in their midst and his flame shot up brightly above their heads. His poetry, perhaps, will be published one day; at the moment, it is in the tender care of Francis Cowper, his chief friend at Stonyhurst, who wrote fine verse, too, at school, though he is now known for his prose. He acted well, he read widely and he talked brilliantly. Where their paths coincided he was at once a challenge and a foil to Christopher.
Writing of this time, his fourteenth year, Christopher said,

Literature and Life were in separate compartments for me then, in Literature I was caught spell-bound in the faery-land of Yeats, in spite of the scorn of my friend Henry John who had discovered Chesterton.

In 'dramatics' Christopher acted in every production staged whilst he was at school — in 'Four Just Men', and 'Macbeth'; — he was Snout in 'A Midsummer Night's Dream', — and in 'The Merchant of

14

Venice' the critic said, 'Devlin's Jew had an impulsive humanity, quite a flash of genius; Henry John's Portia was a masterpiece when he came to the "quality of mercy", yet we still felt something large and noble in this passion of Shylock's'. This year, while Henry won the Elocution Prize for reciting 'The Hound of Heaven' 'as Francis Thompson would have loved his poem recited', Christopher was given a special third prize for declaiming 'The Battle of Lepanto' 'with the voice and bearing of an orator'. And their rivalry and friendship went on. But at the same time Christopher shared his brother's ploys. Brothers, in any case, walked together on Sunday mornings, but these two spent a good deal of time with each other and shared many things — including their cash prizes — the winner kept only three quarters for himself.

As soon as boys had passed Lower Certificate — this was in the days before 'O' and 'A' Levels — they were allowed to join the Debating Society which was run on parliamentary lines. Christopher joined as soon as he could, as the member for Donaghmore; in his first debate he supported Patrick, by now either Prime Minister or Leader of the Opposition, (to which high positions Christopher too, in due course, would rise) opposing the motion 'Prohibition would be beneficial to England'. They won but how much this was due to Christopher stoutly maintaining that it would be a farce to try to stamp out drunkenness in a world that had got drunk for six thousand years, cannot now be gauged. His first paper for the Popinjay, which was a fashionable society under the aegis of a master, of which Patrick was at the time Secretary, was on Shelley. Christopher was then fifteen.

Wordsworth came down to earth to deal with lesser things but Shelley rose up to a world above mortal conception. Nevertheless however high he rose he never rose high enough to reach God; therefore his word was false. But though his ideas were false that did not detract from the value of his poetry.

In the discussion which followed his paper, on 'whether truth is a necessary attribute of great literature', his view can be judged from the blunt opening of an essay of the year before:

This is an absolutely untrue statement, art does not preach virtue but good art is always on their side.

There is no record of Henry John having played any part in these activities nor in two more in which Patrick hardly shared either. One was games; Christopher became vice-captain of Rugger and was chosen to play for the Northern Public Schools at Twickenham; this was in 1925, when he was second head of the school. The rugger coach made a trite enough remark about him only somehow it accords with the rest of his life — 'He does not know what it is to be beaten.' The other activity was the O.T.C. and it is not surprising that he enjoyed this, since he seriously considered making the Army his career. He tremendously enjoyed the camps.

There are two kinds of camp. The first is the strenuous kind . . . All around you are the blares of bugles and the glares of the sergeant-majors; you feel the slightest mistake you make will be received as a deadly insult to all the traditions of the British Army. And so you stand straight and stiff like a ram-rod except that you sweat copiously and swear in an undertone . . . Personally I love that sort of thing; I am never happier than when I know that I, in my modest little way, am functioning perfectly, as a cog or a sparking plug or something small and insignificant, in the great machine of militarism, moreover I look such a frightful ass whenever publicly rebuked that I am sure every self-respecting sergeant-major must positively leap with fiendish joy when he sees me make a mistake . . . but . . .

I must plead guilty to a certain slinking fondness for the other kind of camp.

By the other kind of camp I mean the easy-going, happy-go-lucky kind, where it is always raining and everything is pervaded by a sense of sodden hilarity. Your soaking and lop-sided pack seems to gaze obstinately up at you and assure that you're both wet and in a disordered condition, but it doesn't really matter a —— because nobody minds. Moreover everything is delightfully topsy-turvy, and you encounter the most wonderful and undreamt of situations. I like that enormously. Any way we were accustomed to the martial realities of Aldershot and Tidworth so we marched out, ram-rods all, burningly eager ones . . . we marched out, I say, fiercely contemptuous in the knowledge that our drill was perfect and our marching even better and we landed with a 'splosh' of disillusionment in a district of mud, where the parade ground wrapped gently around your ankles, and everybody marched with their heads down against the wind and rain, and did arms drill with their groundsheets on.   .   .   .

The last day brought the usual expectations of a rag, but we were doomed to disappointment. I love a really good rag, but all that came to us that night was a series of resentful and dis-cordant cat-calls from some adjacent grammar schools. Serenaded to sleep by this, we awoke next morning and departed homewards, my only recollection of that period being a burning desire to get into a bath.

In his fifteenth to sixteenth year Christopher released himself from a vow he had made two years before. The period 1921—22 had been very stormy. Instead of being bored by the strict routine of Stonyhurst, which was only just beginning to differ from that set in 1794 when the School returned from exile — and that, in itself, differed little from when it had been founded in the sixteenth century, he was happily rebellious.

I made a resolution in the form of a vow; that whenever I was

16

rebuked by a master or a prefect, I would always answer back. Various complications resulted from a faithful execution of this vow.

But in 1923 Father Martin D'Arcy joined the staff to teach the scholarship class. He said himself that he was sent to Stonyhurst to teach three brilliant boys, Christopher was one, Tom Burns (3) and Henry John the other two. The immediate result was that Christopher now felt in touch

with Fathers of the Society whom I considered eminently humane and so released myself from the vow though the habit died hard and spasmodically.

Father D'Arcy's influence was of enormous importance to all of them and so was that of another equally 'humane' equally remarkable Jesuit Father, Father Cyril Martindale, who was nine years Father D'Arcy's senior. He did not teach at Stonyhurst and his influence began with his books.

The book Christopher 'had been read to out of' was by Fr Martindale and so were the stories from the Bible. In 1922 he appeared in person and preached the Good Friday sermon at Stonyhurst.

Its theme was the Courage of Christ. With the judicial impartiality of youth, I noted in my diary 'This is the only really good sermon I have ever listened to.' (For greater accuracy, the 'really' might have been put in front of the 'listened')

so wrote Christopher and thereafter, of course, he read a number of Fr Martindale's books.

But just at this moment the works of Martindale instead of germinating like seeds in my consciousness began to pepper me as it were from a pea-shooter. My friends, Henry John and Thomas Burns, were it appeared, in personal touch with Fr Martindale himself; they had become fired with apostolic zeal and were, I thought, rather annoying and Bloomsburyish about it all. These were the days of the founding of the C.E.G. at Stonyhurst. I hung about the fringe of the vortex, not liking it much.

The work of the C.E.G., the Catholic Evidence Guild, involved tub-thumping in Hyde Park and on Tower Hill, too. Henry John was very good at this,

Heckling fierce ... Voices like untamed fog-horns ... Huge crowd. Got most of my speech in before they got their eye in ... extremely exhilarating ... a trifle nerve-racking. Meeting not wasted. Answers to hostile hecklers not really given to them but to silent listeners — the latter we are chiefly out to help — the hecklers draw the crowd.

(3) Thomas Burns, writer, editor of The Tablet.

It was splendid work but it was never Christopher's way, neither then nor later.

For his seventeenth birthday Henry John gave him Fr Martindale's 'Lives of the Saints'. It was in several volumes and before Christopher had had time to read many of them Fr Martindale appeared again at school to arrange for a tour to Budapest.

Fr Martindale was in charge of it but it was Fr D'Arcy (and men have won a martyr's crown for not so much more) who actually took charge of us.

So far as Christopher and Henry John were concerned he did more that take charge. He had won a prize of a hundred pounds and had been given permission by the Society to do with it whatever he liked. He wrote to William to know if he might take Christopher on this trip; William gladly accepted and so Fr D'Arcy paid for both boys. Henry John wrote some notes on the expedition.

Budapesth: yellow trams and gorgeous markets, where we bought enormous pink melons . . . I myself all but drowned in the Danube.

Indeed he had — both he and Christopher wished to swim across the river; Fr D'Arcy forbade the dangerous undertaking. Christopher obeyed; Henry had not.

Refreshing zoo (baboons) . . . Gallery. Roundabouts, shawls, Oratory, Feasts, *Concert.*
Venice: Unctuous tradesmen occasionally picking mandolins, and steaming fraulein. Lido execrable. Creation, Flood, Saints, Peter and Bacchus mosaics in St Marks — unparalleled; ditto doors and floors and rooms of Piazza Ducale . . . Gloated over Charlie Chaplin, lost all our money and fought.

Coming home through Venice Henry had been in charge of all the money. It is easy to understand why Christopher thought of a martyr's crown for Fr D'Arcy. Christopher's own description of the tour is brief and vivid.

We saw the cuirasses glint and heard the halberds clash in the great cathedral, on the Feast of St Stephen the King And after that we went on to Venice.

Christopher now had one more year at school.

Next year I slipped back to a lower level of life, athletic and poetic in the sense of Rupert Brooke. I left school in the toils of this retrogression, wrapped in a yeasty and impenetrable steam of egotistic immaturity. My only ambition was to prolong this state of arrested development through three or four years at Oxford.

18

and then he added

Two things only did I take away from school, the friendship of a master, Martin D'Arcy and a boy Henry John.

In fact during the last year Christopher had matured rapidly. Up to this point nothing has been said about his religion — because there has been nothing to say; but to most born catholics there comes a time when, having taken everything for granted they have need to put away childish thoughts and consciously to accept or reject their heritage. This moment had been reached by Christopher during his last year at school. It is improbable that he discussed his faith with anyone. He wrote that, oddly enough, at the end of the turbulent schoolyear of 1922 he had got his 'First Vocation' but that then he put it aside in favour of more exciting dreams and more immediate hopes. He left Stonyhurst in July 1925, but in the month before, in June, he had had what he called his conversion. He said it was on the Feast of Corpus Christi and thereafter that day was especially dear to him. His conversion meant that he now knew that whatever he did, and there was great doubt in his mind as to what that was going to be, would be offered daily to God at Mass. For the time being that was enough for him to know.

The summer brought the usual visit to Braemar. Joan Mary had left home. She had entered the Convent of the Sacred Heart. This had been intended for a long while and caused no suprise. Patrick had just returned from a Cambridge University debating tour in the Mid-Western states of the U.S.A. Frances and Billy were still at school. With their parents and with William's greatly gifted pupil, Douglas Collie, there were long walks in the hills. With Patrick, Christopher went for longer ones still, when they slept at night in the open. To one of these Christopher attached great importance and it remained a vivid memory.

When they had started out and had begun to climb the day had been very hot, and so, impetuously, they had flung down their sleeping-bags intending to find them next day on their return. After coming down, though, in the evening from Lochnagar, a mist descended and they got lost on the Capel Mounth Pass which leads from Glen Muick to the Whitewater of Esk. Heather is said to be warm to sleep in but it did not seem so to them that night. Christopher, sleepless, thought of a book of Fr Martindale's, one in the series Henry John had given him. It was about the great mystic — Saint John of the Cross. His mind lingered sleepily on two pictures which it had conjured up for him, — one of a bride with flowers in her hair, going over the wilderness, over the bare hills, in search of her lover. The other was of the branched antlers of the

19

Kingly Stag appearing through the gloom at the end of the Dark Night. At last he drifted off to sleep and when he awoke the mist was still a thick curtain, but a grey-white one showing that the night was over. A dawn wind stirred it and it parted in wisps. And as it parted Christopher said he saw a deer looking at him. It looked gentle and noble but it had no antlers. He wondered whether after all it could be a mountain hare, magnified by the mist, or imagination, or even a rabbit — but, no, not at that height, no, most likely a deer — but who knows? Any way Christopher, whom Patrick remembers as wearing a red shirt, was filled with great courage and he awoke his brother. Together they set off to find the lost track. They found it at last and climbing down, watched the mist departing in the glory of the morning and saw the land rolling down and down two thousand feet to the shining water of Esk. Down in the valley in a croft called Braedownie, a dour-faced woman with a soft voice gave them hot oat cakes and fresh warm milk.

But the pictures and the deer remained firmly in Christopher's thought. In writing of this time he wrote,

of the memorable days and one memorable night with Patrick on the misty mountain passes round Braemar.

He referred to the incident of the deer, writing first that it had made no difference to his mode of life and then crossing this out and substituting

To this incident I attribute a silly but important and not ignoble, attitude which I thereafter adopted. The perfectly reasonable condition imposed upon my going up to Oxford was that I should announce what career I intended to adopt as a consequence. This I refused to do, saying that I wanted Oxford purely in order to see life and could not pin myself down in advance to any profession. This attitude lost me the long cherished dream of Oxford.

Uncle George who was so desperately anxious to encourage his nephews to work, though he had not done a hand's turn himself since his early twenties, could not believe that Christopher was ignorant of what he wanted to do. Christopher genuinely did not know then, though from the importance which he attached to the night on the mountain pass it is clear that he had an inkling of what it might be. However there followed a troublesome few months which Christopher described as 'a purgative period'. At the end of this time he did know, he had got his 'Second Vocation'. He shrank from it as he had shrunk from the first — but for opposite reasons. He spent some time thinking about it, telling no one. When he felt a little more certain he told his parents. The idea was a surprising one to them, they had expected him to choose the Army or the Civil

Service; he had given no sign of considering a life vowed to religion.

3
ROME – SUBIACO – ASSISI

To those who believe that God is dead – if indeed they believe that he ever existed, – the decision to lead a dedicated, – a religious life, is incomprehensible. Uncle George was no atheist, but he thought of material pursuits as the highest good and, on the whole had not much time for spiritual and philosophic thought. He was horrified by Christopher's announcement. What his nieces chose to do mattered little to him, his Devlin nieces (4) were in fact not so dear to him as his nephews or his Goval nieces (5) whom he watched grow up, – John and Joan's daughters, – but he had great worldly hopes of what his nephews, with all their talents, might achieve. Moreover he had a feeling of guilt – a feeling that he might have driven Christopher to this new idea by not having sent him to Oxford. The feeling, of course, was wrong. He was however filled with remorse and hoping it might make Christopher change his mind he offered him the money to travel abroad, asking him to defer his final decision. Christopher was very grateful. He did need to test the idea and to discover whether the Vocation was genuine. And if it were he still had to discover in which direction it lay. Years later he said that he never had any doubt that, if it was right for him to be a priest, he would want to be a religious, as distinct from a secular priest, but he did not know which of the Religious Orders he should join.

With the money Uncle George now gave him he decided to set out on a long pilgrimage through Europe. He planned to do all the interesting parts on foot and all the boring ones by train, third class. From the books he was reading and the places he planned to visit, it is easy to follow the direction of his thought. He was reading 'St Francis of Assisi' by Chesterton and 'St Ignatius of Loyola', another book of Fr Martindale's. Of what he learnt from them he wrote:

From the first I realised with a shock that it was possible to love God with vivid emotional reality, from the second that it was necessary to protect this love by tactics and discipline.

(4) Joan Mary became a nun in the English Province of the Sacred Heart Order. Christopher once wrote of her 'every girl I have met who has been under her always speaks with an affection and respect which I don't think was put on for my benefit. Her Vocation is a very positive one & she has never wavered in it for the nth part of a second.' She became a head mistress for a short time. Frances joined the same order but the Scottish-Irish Province. She went to Dublin University and did brilliantly but she died shortly afterwards. in 1937.

(5) Mary Lindsay (Merlyn), Anne and Felicity.

His route, and later, his writing, show that in addition to the Franciscan and Jesuit Orders he was considering a third possibility — the Benedictines. He went first to Rome, where presumably he was reassured about his vocation. The only memento of this visit, in fact, is the sestet of a sonnet which he wrote in praise of the fountains outside St Peter's

> 'As the hart panteth' can I really find
> In this gross church where no one seems to pray
> But push and grunt like pigs on market day
> And yet perhaps each one — pants as pants the hind
> And I the pig — with face thrust forward, blind
> Feeling the faintness of the furthest spray.

From Rome he walked fifty miles to Subiaco. This was where St Benedict had spent three years in a cave high up in the mountains before he gathered his followers. The Benedictines are a contemplative order. They teach and run parishes and missions but primarily their object as contemplatives must be to know and love their Creator.

A few years later Christopher was deluged with the recollection of this visit to them at Subiaco when he heard

a sound of singing not louder than the other birds but easily soaring above and penetrating through them, ringing all among the trees ... and just a certain little catch in one of the notes was a catch, too, to a door in (my) memory and (I) was back in a grey cloister looking straight down a drop of seven hundred feet, and over across at the mountain with an apricot moon above the pine trees. And then gently in the utter stillness, as if the moonlight had not yet its full meaning ... there came a little twang like a violinist tuning up, then true clear and sweet came the first note; and after that it was not so much a bird singing as the whole sleeping valley telling aloud the perfect dream ... The moonlight had found a voice and every pearly ray of her quivered and rejoiced.

Christopher had been waiting for Matins, the Church's early morning prayer; and as he stood there with the Benedictines, gazing out of the Monastery and heard for the first time the sweet song of the nightingale, he realised fully, what he had only apprehended before, that the pure contemplative's life was not for him. It is indeed not possible to doubt that when much later he described Robert Southwell's realisation of the same thing he was also describing his own

no doubt as a boy ... he had had the experience of rapt adoration of invisible beauty; and this experience informing the exercise of prayer and spiritual reading, seemed now a genuine attraction to the contemplative life. In fact the two are not the same — may even be mutually exclusive — but the borderland is hard to find and involves humiliation. (6)

That night in the moonlight he had found the borderland so when the 'old Monk' said 'Wouldn't you like to stay here?' Christopher 'had journied swiftly northward like the swallows to Assisi'. One can see him going, turning away with his shy smile, quickly, as though he might be tempted against his better judgement.

I walked there (Assisi) from Rome 1926 and had various adventures on the way. I didn't find the Franciscans at the lower church (Santa Maria dei Angeli?) so hospitable as had been the Benedictines at Subiaco — on both of them I inflicted myself as a pilgrim guest. It was in a lavatory at Subiaco that I left all my travellers cheques — having taken them out of the lining of my coat where Mother had sewn them. I discovered the loss when my loose money ran short somewhere around Foligno I think, and for a long time I could not remember where they could be. At last an inspiration came and I sent a most peculiarly-worded Italian telegram saying to send Poste Restante, Assisi. I came into Assisi with no money just as the evening Angelus was ringing, the air was full of bells and just before the Post Office shut, and at first they said, no, nothing, and then they said, Oh, yes. But the important thing was that on the way, when I was saying the Glorious Mysteries of the Rosary, I was suddenly enabled to pray for the first time in my life that it didn't matter about the money either way provided the will of God was done. I wrote a poem on the subject of which now I can remember only two lines:

'And so my head is ever high and so my arms swing easy
Vado — vado come un soldado — sempre a piedi ad Assisi'

So vividly did he remember the time that he could still write of it as in this letter of 4 October 1956, nearly 30 years later.

In Italy Christopher had been alone; now he turned towards France, and, having crossed the border he was joined by Henry John and they walked on together. Their objective lay in Spain; it was Manresa near to Barcelona. It was to this place that Ignatius Loyola had trudged when he set out on his long journey which was to end in the founding of the Society of Jesus. When he reached it in 1522 it was a little walled and towered town which the Romans had built on the river Cordona, and he crossed the river by the bridge they had made. But now it is a sprawling manufacturing town with very little left that he would have seen. However the cave to which he went when he wanted to be alone to pray, (7) and to practise his heavy penances, still stands. On top of it in the nineteenth century a chapel

(6) 'Life of Robert Southwell', p. 30.
(7) Unlike St Benedict, St Ignatius did not live in a cave; he lived in the hospital of the poor, St Lucy's and worked there except when he was ill and needed care himself. See 'St Ignatius Loyala', by James Brodrick, S.J., pp. 96, 97, Burns and Oates, 1956.

was built which has become a place of pilgrimage and devotion. This was Christopher and Henry's goal. They walked many many miles and very rapidly, such in those days was their urge to be there. When they reached the Spanish Frontier post Christopher was utterly exhausted but Henry was as fresh as a daisy. They looked ragged and unkempt and they were carrying suspicious looking rucksacks. The frontier guards at once arrested them and cast them into a cell. This suited Christopher admirably; he lay down on the cool stone floor and instantly went to sleep. 'I had hardly fallen asleep', he said with the utmost indignation, reliving his exhaustion as he told the tale, many years later, 'when I was woken to find we had been released; John, the damned maniac, had bribed the guards with cigarettes and we had to go on.' (8)

Alas, no other adventures can now be recaptured and none of their discussions, their songs, their quarrels or their laughter. Their pace slowed down and they spent several weeks wandering in the Pyrenees of Aragon and Val d'Aran always getting nearer to Manresa — but Christopher never got there. Perhaps it wasn't necessary to reach the town for he had already reached the answer he had sought. He wrote:

In the middle of Andorra I was suddenly assailed by a violent attack of nostalgia. I turned and rushed back through that lovely fairyland to the French frontier where I caught a bus for Toulouse and a train for home. Home appeared indescribably beautiful. I felt a surge of power to write. So improved was my behaviour that Uncle George offered to pay my fees to Oxford if I had given up the idea of religion.

But Christopher turned the offer down

Knowing my Vocation was genuine I finished my Manresa journey at Roehampton

4

You bring the lamp out of the Sanctuary
Or fetch the credence cards and candlesticks
And on the threshold there of mystery
You handle the ciborium and the pyx. (9)

MANRESA

Christopher entered the Novitiate of the Jesuit Order, which was then at Manresa House, Roehampton, on 14 August 1926. A Novitiate, he wrote

(8) The story was told by Christopher to Fr John Harriot, S.J.
(9) From a longer poem written by Christopher about this time.

consists largely as far as mere time is concerned, in a relentless rush from one duty to another, during which the vocal silence is counter-balanced by a good deal of noise from other instruments — knives, plates, broomsticks not to mention heavier objects . . .

and the novices

had to settle down to a humdrum rhythmic life: eating plenty, sleeping soundly, and achieving a smiling and modest efficiency at half-a-dozen tasks, among which those of scullion and pantry-boy loomed large.'(10)

Christopher managed to cram a number of other things in addition to the half-a-dozen tasks and household chores. He wanted to be a poet so it was natural that he should make a special study of the two members of his Order who had written poetry; he immersed himself in Robert Southwell's Elizabethan background; and he taught himself to analyse and imitate the 'sprung rhythm' of Gerard Manley Hopkins. He had known about Southwell and had written about him whilst still at Stonyhurst, but it was when he went to Roehampton that he was overwhelmed by Hopkins's verse; it was indeed new then and its merit was not yet fully realised; it had been kept hidden by the Poet Laureate, Robert Bridges in whose possession much of it was, and who only published it in 1918, nearly thirty years after the poet had died. For the present Christopher left the thought behind the poetry alone and revelled in the new rhythm. His imitations were not very successful. His best effort is a sonnet which begins

Glory to God for water humble useful and chaste
And the stoop of the sun wide-eyed; and the whole heart's leap

on the back of which he explained to his confidant of the time, his contemporary Dermod Whyte (11) who kept the poem, and a number of others, which Christopher had given him:

It is essential that the poem should be recited not read because the rhythm goes entirely by stress . . . The peculiar rhythm is copied from the only poet who has hitherto used it (viz a Jesuit called Fr Hopkins).

However it was not the Jesuit poet Fr Hopkins but the Jesuit Robert Southwell who was to be his lode-star from the first moment that he seriously set about trying to achieve the dual purpose of his religious life; that is to pay equal attention to contemplation *and* action.

St Ignatius sets a double object before his disciple: 'the love and the

(10) 'Life of Robert Southwell', p. 41.
(11) Fr Dermod Whyte, S.J.

service of God': and though objectively these two are inseparable, yet it is not long before his disciple is aware that in particular subjects they seem to part company. The soul would have him sit absorbed in the mirror of God forgetting and forgotten by all else. But the mind urges him to be up and doing and to exploit his talents to their best advantage. He must learn to keep trying to do both. His task is to keep his effective love of God at high pressure and at the same time to transfer all that latent energy into the daily activities of brain and volition. (12)

This quotation like the earlier ones are from the biography Christopher wrote of Robert Southwell. In this book when he described Southwell's early training, or wrote of matters common to them both, whether spiritual or factual, it is clear to those who knew him well that Christopher was unconsciously writing autobiography. In portraying Southwell it was as though he looked into a mirror and saw his own reflection. He would not have recognised it, he was far too humble, but others have no doubt of this, nor any doubt that when he used Southwell's notes he drew on the stirrings of his own heart to interpret them.

For example, when he was describing the moving force of Robert's vocation he was equally describing his own.

He soon discovered that the driving force of his vocation was not primarily a wish to build his character or to shape his career; it was a longing as the hind desireth the water-brooks for union with God in prayer.

and then, slipping into a general description of prayer, he writes of the method which, as a novice like Southwell he had been taught.

Southwell could now enter as of right into the Jesuit method of prayer. Not that there is or was then a special Jesuit method . . . But there is a general method commonly used in the Exercises, called active contemplation. It is roughly this: to soak the memory and the senses of the soul in the physical reality of Christ's words and actions, and then to let there be distilled, as it were, in the intellect a word of God, a confused apprehension of his divinity, to which the will 'with a blind and naked stirring' can adhere. (13)

So deeply did his study and research go whilst he was still a novice that the conclusions Christopher reached then and which were published in the Juniors' (14) magazine, 'Juvenilia' in 1929, he used to form the basis of his chapter on Southwell's literary apostolate in his biography. This book had world-wide recognition

(12) 'Life of Robert Southwell', p. 42.
(13) ibid., p. 43; for the Exercises see p. 88, n. 4.
(14) The Noviceship lasts two years; it used to be followed by the Juniorate which lasted two years also, or only one, as in Christopher's case, if scholastic achievement was high.

when it appeared in 1956 and these literary conclusions have never been challenged.

In the midst of this study, which ranged widely over the Elizabethan field — Christopher passed the first landmark of his new life. He took his First Vows; this was on 15 August 1928. Two days after he wrote to his parents.

The 15th was a lovely day for me — in three ways — firstly my Vow-Day, secondly as such a lovely feast day of Our Lady, and thirdly because I had the whole day to myself. I went for a walk with Brother John in the afternoon, and yesterday after dinner Fr Rector sent me off to see Joan (15) where I was longing to go: we had a very happy afternoon together and I saw all over the convent which is a very beautiful place, I thought, but I felt very deeply for you on those floors around the cloisters — it is all very well for those nuns in their carpet slippers . . .I had to leave earlier than I would have liked but on the other hand I wanted to meet the Juniors who came back yesterday evening as they are my new companions: they had been having a fine time at Hastings and were as brown as anything. By a great stroke of luck I met the first detachment of them rushing madly for the same bus as I was on, on Hammersmith Broadway, just after I had left Joan, so we journeyed home together and I got my fare paid. It is said you get anything you ask for on your Vow-Day so I begged for all blessings spiritual and temporal for you.

As usual his emotions were inward and he gave no sign of them. It would have been impossible for him to have done so at the time. But Robert Southwell had had no such inhibitions and, in Latin, he had written 'Thoughts on St Luke's Day, after my Vows,'

Crucifixo desposata est anima tua, unde et eam cum corpore crucifixam esse oportet. Sicut enim similitudo amicitiae, ita et dissimilitudo disunionis causa esse solet.

Twenty years after his own Vow-Day Christopher thought that these lines could almost slip accidentally into English verse. And so he 'slipped' them:

Unto the Crucified my soul is spouse, and she must likewise be, even with his body crucified. For likeness is the cause of love, unlikeness of disunity. (16)

and he amplified the meaning by writing further in his book,

The truth is that Jesuit discipline in the design of St Ignatius sets up an interior tension which can only be resolved by crucifixion. At the heart of it there is an element of supernatural wildness in his famous rule . . . 'to recoil from everything the world loves and embraces: to

(15) Joan Mary; at the Convent of the Sacred Heart, Hammersmith, London, W.14.

(16) 'Life of Robert Southwell', p. 46.

allow and long for with the whole heart whatever Christ Our Lord longed for and embraced'. (17)

5

HEYTHROP

When Christopher went to Heythrop College near Chipping Norton in the Cotswolds to do the next period of the long training that goes to the making of a Jesuit — his three years of Philosophy — which he began in September 1929, he set himself the task of gentling his nature to bring it more into accord with Southwell's courtesy and composure 'even in the strangest circumstances'. He was to have a hard time suppressing the terrifying heritage of Black Jock; for he had inherited a great capacity for violence and passion, for lightning outbursts of temper, for contempt, even for cruelty, and for pride and vanity. From the Ignatian Method of Particular Examen, by which at stated times of the day, like all his brethren, he would examine his conscience, he could tell how well or ill went the struggle of 'winning back from Lucifer'. The struggle tears at one's heart as it goes on and on and as Christopher noted it down. He was trying

> to embrace obscurity, monotony, and mediocrity.
> I must desire and foment the desire to be straightened
>   and smitten.
> My especial vileness is contempt for others.
> Vanity, intellectual and sensitive, surrounds me.
> My learning and my poetry are *FOR CHRIST* and not *for me*
>   in the eyes of others.

These phrases and others like them run through his spiritual jottings. Once there was despair,

I am tempted to give up my Vow as a bad job and go back to the world.

But swiftly this is countered,

I *said* I *would* and I *will*. The goal is CHRISTUS IPSE in the highest way.

In time he was almost entirely master of his passions and submissively could write,

> standing before Him in Naked Creaturehood
> I am compelled to the VOW OF POVERTY
> Then in return he reveals a glimpse of himself to me
> and I am compelled to the VOW OF CHASTITY

(17) 'Life of Robert Southwell', p. 46.

28

and in return His Thoughts grow in me
and I transform myself into them by the VOW OF OBEDIENCE.

And there was the further fight, the fight to train his mind whilst he longed for militant action in Christ's army.

John Dekkers, Robert Southwell's contemporary and 'confidant' wrote of Southwell as 'without a rival among his fellow students at the Roman College'. Southwell taught philosophy for five years beginning before he had finished his training and all the while he yearned with a deep eagerness to be sent on the English Mission. Christopher confided to his notes, 'How pleasant it is to come first in everything', and yet he too was subduing day-dreams of action, — subduing his longing to fight any foe hostile to the Faith — in Russia, for example — but he too worked on and even before he left Heythrop he was known as an authority on the mediaeval schoolman Duns Scotus. The truth is that both these men were cast in a common mould and, within their common vocation, beyond their chivalrous natures, the fact that both excelled in academic subjects concealed for a time that both at heart were soldiers. Despite their learning both of them would only reach the height of fulfilment in loving and serving God, in work far removed from a university.

Christopher had been at Heythrop just over a month when, on 3 November he addressed the Philosophical and Literary Society on the poetry of Gerard Manley Hopkins. He seldom wrote or lectured on him as a poet and he has been accused of being insensitive to his verse. On this occasion he couched his paper in terms just this side of idolatry — the lecture is hard to come by as it is only to be found in the Heythrop domestic magazine — 'The Blandyke Papers' — but in it he said,

Hopkins set himself with more deliberation than any other poet to find out how he could most faithfully translate the Harmony of Creation into human speech.

One way in which he achieved it, said Christopher

was by an exquisite arrangement of simple words ... But his chief device, and that by which he merits to live for ever in Literature, is his discovery of the one true rhythm which is native to the best English verse ... Finally and this is his crowning achievement, you may use what he calls 'outriding feet'. These as it were swing to and fro beneath the line, in another dimension: they do not interfere with the flow of the rhythm but act as a kind of backwater or lullaby wherein the soul may pause and cradle itself for a while, in contemplation of the thoughts conjured up by the words. *This is* his rhythm: it is the rhythm of Greek lyrics and the soft speech of country people, it is the rhythm of rivers, and of the flight of birds, it is the rhythm of freedom, it is the rhythm of order — it is called sprung rhythm — and Gerard Manley Hopkins discovered it and called it so.

But now studying at Heythrop, Christopher began to consider minutely what lay behind the verse, — and so found Duns Scotus, for it was on his philosophy that the words rested. His interest in Hopkins changed, his devotion to his poetry did not but he ceased to think of him primarily as a poet; he thought of him instead, as a fellow-religious whose mind had been illumined by Scotus. To his own thought Scotus became fundamental, and two years later, in 1931, he wrote in his spiritual notes: 'Renounced all intellectual obedience to Fr Geddes' (18) (who was teaching him) 'followed Scotus.' And from this Christopher never wavered. Intellectually the Faith was meaningless to him without Scotus, he explained twenty-five years later. (19) He was to become the leading British authority on this very difficult philosopher and much of his daring and original research was done at Heythrop whilst he was reading his Philosophy.

In 1932 the reward for all his labour — the long cherished dream of going to Oxford — seemed to be within his grasp. The Society had decided that both he and Henry John, — who had joined the Order a year later than Christopher, — should go up that autumn.

It was in February of 1932, on my wedding day, that I met Christopher for the first time. He stood at the foot of the altar having a minor part to play in the ceremony; he was still quite young but already he was a man set apart and dedicated. In May that year William died, and a month later, in June I saw Christopher again, for Patrick and I spent a sun-lit week-end staying near the College and walking with him in the Cotswolds. And then, quite shortly after that,

the sword of the guardian angel of paradise flashed out with unexpected cruelty. (20)

in Southwell's case this may have been 'to cut the bindweed of sentimentality'. The purpose this time seems to have been something quite different for the whole course of Christopher's life was changed.

It came about in so unheralded and unexpected a way that at the time no one seems to have realised what was involved.

(18) Only the doctrines of St Thomas Aquinas, enlarged and explained by later writers were taught, and through misunderstanding Scotus it was thought that his views were heterodox. 'Fr Geddes was a dear, but rigidly orthodox and was bound to view with alarm a young man who had the temerity to think for himself' Fr Boyle.
(19) See p. 126.
(20) 'Life of Robert Southwell', p. 32.

Christopher's friendship with Henry John had become very deep. Fr D'Arcy described it as a 'love-hate' relationship and Fr Martindale, who by this time knew Christopher as well as he knew Henry John, said

I am sorry that Henry John (though we were good and quarrelsome friends) influenced Chris, because Henry, I consider, spoilt himself by his idea that you could do nothing save by *violence*.
Frankly I thought Henry John was becoming so neurotic that his sanity was in danger. This is not impressionism — I had reasons.

One sultry evening at Heythrop, shortly after our visit, a fight broke out between the two of them; the sort of fight that could occur between two tense, hot-blooded men, within whose close friendship anything could happen. On this occasion one threw a book at the other and after this they came to blows. The two of them came down to supper in the refectory — one with a black eye and the other with a cut lip. This was noticed. They were made to do a refectory penance. The fight was not forgotten nor were other of their quarrels. It was thought that it would be as unwise as it would be distracting and disturbing to have them both together in one small house at Oxford, Campion Hall, the Jesuit house of studies. It was decided, therefore, that only one of them should go to Oxford and it would be difficult to dispute that the obvious one to go there was Henry John.
Of course nowadays Christopher would have been sent to get a degree somewhere else. The Juniorate was in fact abolished (21) so that all Jesuits can now get some qualification without necessarily lengthening their years of training. But in the third decade of the century the need for a degree, strange as that may seem thirty years later, was not obvious. The lack, in due course, gravely handicapped Christopher and caused him pain. Some indeed think it 'a waste of extraordinary talents' that he should not have had an academic training.
There is no word of frustration in any of his notes — spiritual or autobiographical; no pages have been torn out; no lines crossed through; no comment, nothing other than complete acceptance in tune with a note he wrote earlier during a period of interior struggle at Heythrop

I must be ready to abandon (not necessity, do it exceptionally) ordinary community enjoyments — Oxford.

. . .

In the struggle for self-conquest the figure of Robert Southwell emerged from the dust of battle with the plume of beauty nodding

(21) In 1958.

31

proudly and gaily above the helmet of righteousness (22)

Christopher's victory was surely no less complete. His normal training went on; for two years he was sent to teach, first at Stonyhurst and then at Beaumont. But in 1935 in his sparse auto-biographical notes there is a tragic epigraph:

I divided my pulpy young-old heart between God and men; and events cut in and tore it terribly. In 1935, Henry John — after the ruin of our fifteen year friendship but not because of it — left the Order and killed himself climbing down a mad cliff at Quantock. A fellow-jesuit showed me the headline in an evening paper. 'Well, he did not get much good out of leaving the Society, did he?' said this good religious. I went up to my room and looked wildly around me with clenching and unclenching hands.

This was the year when Christopher was due to begin his four years of Theology.

I got leave to go abroad for my studies — to Rome, the strictest of our houses; for after you have plumbed the depths of Rome, you must either leave the Church or cleave to it for ever.

The Fathers of the Society who dealt with such matters, were only too eager to grant his request to try to make up in any way they could for the bitter disappointment they knew he had suffered.

En route for Rome he came to London and his mother came from Aberdeen to see him off. I went with them to the Army & Navy Stores where she bought him a black rain-coat saying to me, 'when I can't, will you see that he always has what he needs.' Of this time Christopher wrote:

After I had watched my younger brother, Billy, triumph as 'Peer Gynt' at the Old Vic, I caught the night train to Harwich. For a week or two I wandered uneasily round old haunts in Italy, then braced my shoulders and entered the self-appointed prison that was to shelter me for four uninterrupted years.

6

ROME

Christopher went to Rome just at the beginning of the era of British Sanctions against Italy in her war with Abyssinia. Sanctions, as seem invariably the case, did little except engender bitterness. The hard life of the Roman theological student was added to by the anti-British feeling which naturally ran high in the city and penetrated ecclesiastical circles. Christopher's action in walking out of Mass on one occasion, because the Italian preacher denounced

(22) 'Life of Robert Southwell', p. 80.

32

England, had to be condoned, and it took quite a time before he made friends with his Italian fellow-students or they, for that matter, with him; yet later on he was able to look back on the time and on these friends with much affection.

His spiritual notes are full of his efforts to rid himself of the faults he found but, on the whole, to those with consciences less spiritually attuned, the faults were by now what seem to be the merest absent-minded peccadillos.

On 25 July, the feast day of his patron saint, (23) — the saint who had 'a muscular neck and a grim scornful face' Christopher 'passed through the great moment of his ordination to the priesthood.' He wrote at the time several short notes to his mother, telling her of the Masses he was going to offer for each member of the family and when and where he would do so. Then, ten days later, he wrote at greater length.

Villa vecchia, Frascati (24)   5th-6th August (1938)

Dear Mother,
    Please excuse pencil, but ink has run out and it is too late to get any more tonight
    I was in such a state of exaltation during the last week at Rome, that, blessedly, I hardly noticed the heat which was actually frightful. On the Feast of St Ignatius (July 31st) it reached 39 degrees — fever heat. The Ancient Fathers say it has never been so hot since 1923 — 15 years ago. I can well believe it!
    Here, of course, it is better, but still too much for any prolonged exercise. So I am just resting till the cooler wind comes. I have just been reading in the Breviary of to day, (5th) the beautiful story of how snow fell on the Esquiline on this day.
    You will excuse me not writing more. But nothing much has been happening and I have not had many letters. All my joy and excitement has been interior. And I cannot yet think of much except the Miracle that is to happen the next morning and every other morning for the rest of my life till the earthly altar suddenly becomes that of Heaven

Much love
Christopher

(23) It never ranked high in the Calendar & was abolished in 1969.
(24) The Jesuit summer villa.

PART TWO

WARTIME

1

LIVERPOOL AND THE MOUNTAINS OF WALES

The war clouds had gathered by the time Christopher's training in Rome came to an end. The final period still to come, which sums up the years of training and is a breathing space before Final Vows are taken, had to be postponed,

> I had just got down from the train at Victoria when someone laid a hand on my chest. It was Billy. A little further on flamed the red hair of Patrick. Then Madeleine, Pat's wife rushed up. Lastly I met Mary Casson, to whom Billy had just been married. They had guessed the train I would be arriving by. It was Madeleine's idea.

However, he had to leave his family in London for he was sent at once to the church of St Francis Xavier in Liverpool to which sixty years earlier – 1880 – Gerard Manley Hopkins had gone. But Christopher's work there was different from his. The school children of the parish had been evacuated to North Wales, and in the bitterly cold winter of 1939–40 Christopher cycled many miles, with a knapsack on his back, which contained not only his own possessions but also all he needed for saying Mass in the villages to which the children and their teachers had been sent. The villages were strung along the winding hill roads from east of Lake Vyrwny, through Llanfyllin, up to Llangynog by Penybontfawr and down to Meifod and on to Llanfair Caerinion. He had to sort out all the problems that arose when town dwellers were thrust amidst country-folk and sometimes he had to fight battles for them, battles for a little more coal or a little more room. He was, as Winifred Danson, one of the teachers, recalls – 'Not only our priest but our sole contact with home as well', for from time to time, presumably by cycling to Welshpool, and taking a train from there, he would visit Liverpool. It was all work after his own heart.

My work at first made me unbelievably happy it was divided between the slums of Liverpool and the mountains of Wales. When I fell for people now it was no longer sentimental vanity veneered with Catholic repository tinsel; but I saw them sharp and clean as symbols of God's Beauty and spurs to action. There were two especially.

Kathleen a girl of twelve from the slums of Liverpool
Aileen, in the Vale of Meifod, a lady of high degree.

Kathleen was a glowing sign of how Christianity can transfigure the vilest environment: she left the loveliest spot in Wales, before the Springtime, to look after her family.

> I wished to make the white and breaking bud
> Unite the slum-girl's broken hope, who stood
> Beside the brothel at the back-street corner,
> Kissing the scabied cheek of her baby brother,
> Virgin and mother, looking to the skies.

Aileen was the noblest figure of Virgilian paganism, standing blindfold in the glory of God's Grace; she washed and tended ulcerous, lice-ridden and ungrateful children — and then forgot that she had done anything in particular.

> I wished to walk through the world as thro' a wood
> In the early morning gently to surprise
> The shapes of thought that slip from half-awake
> Out of the undergrowth into the sunrise.

There is a second stanza to this poem which is called 'The Boy and Girl Evacuees' (1940)

> I wish to kindle in the boy's pale eyes
> The candle that cross-shadowed on the maps
> Of great adventurers those centres where
> The dove-wings droop and beat, the flashing reef
> Before the cold sea circles shudder and relapse

Otherwise nothing more is known of Kathleen and her brother; most happily there is of Aileen and of her equally remarkable husband Charlie. Christopher was billeted on Lady Aileen and Charlie Meade 'at the white house on the hill' at Meifod, and there at their lovely house of Pen-y-lan, they gave welcome not only to strange evacuated children but to this hitherto unknown quantity, a Roman Catholic priest.

Between Christopher, Aileen and Charlie the warmth of a wonderful and rare friendship grew up. No shadow ever darkened it. To the end Christopher thought of them and worried over their worries, and rejoiced when they were well and happy. Aileen said of him and he might just as well have said it of them:

He understands everything one could not express.

she added

his friendship was the most important thing in my life after Charlie.

2
BEAUMONT (1) 1940—41

The evacuees went home to Liverpool in March and at the end of the year Christopher was sent south to teach again at Beaumont. He was to spend most of his life teaching and much of it at Beaumont under a distinguished Jesuit, Fr Boyle, (2) who became Provincial of the Society. It was not dissatisfaction with Christopher's work which caused Fr Boyle to say, and to repeat several times, though never in Christopher's hearing, that

Providence and the Society between them had made a mess of Christopher's career, and that immediately after his ordination he ought to have been sent out to an unevangelized continent and told to get on with it!

Actually Providence had given the Society little choice and yet had the matter well under control.

Knowing Christopher well Fr Boyle sensed his malaise when he was sent from Liverpool to the school and knew that his work there was not satisfying him.

The glare of war, in the Battle of Norway and Dunkirk, laid bare my native misery. Explosives and incendiaries bursting around, but never near me, heightened the glare. Danger disdained me. I seemed doomed to live — to be died for — and to live. The ancient thirst for glory twisted my self-expression into ugly mouths of boastfulness, melancholy, cynicism and sloth. From a mind so defiled came work shot with vanity, impatience, faint-heartedness.

It was, of course the sedentary sheltered life niggling at his conscience. The soldier that he was at heart, all unrealised, made him long for action. But this was not at all his own diagnosis of his trouble and he buried deep his lack of patience.

Sometimes, too, I thought that thirst for glory was not the root trouble but itself only a compensation-disguise for unsatisfied sex desire; and this thought played like a dagger round the nerve-centre of my Faith. Either a hero or a hermit, — the old dilemma faced me. Either danger which would draw out the poison of my self-love, leaving firm clean scars. Or else prayer which would purify my heart's-blood more effectually from within. The easier way seemed closed, I must choose the latter. Impossible to be a proper hermit, but I could at least bury myself in my work, making snubs and

(1) Beaumont College, Old Windsor, Berks.
(2) Headmaster (Prefect of Studies) 1931-1950 and Rector as well 1947-50, Provincial (of the English Province) 1952-58. Now Rector of St John's Beaumont, Old Windsor.

discouragement the substitute for bombs and sand-storms.

I did; and was amazed how interesting Education became. Not to burden the memory, but to clear the ground for initiative and intuition and good impulse, to tend the growth of mind and heart: it became positively exciting. Fortunately I had a fine Headmaster (Fr Boyle) who, though intolerant of inefficiency, yet made no fetish of exam. results and was willing to risk reputation on the venture.

Never before had the delicacy and unerring aim of Christ's words and deeds in the Gospels, seemed so applicable to anything as to Education. 'Pie Pelicane, Jesu Domine' — the pelican of the legend who fed her starving young upon her own entrails. I thanked God for the Provincial's assurance that I should not be called up as a chaplain. How much better to be a builder of future citizens than a camp-follower in a dog-collar.

At our last meeting of the summer term, held in a grassy amphitheatre, after the Heads of Departments had congratulated each other, it was music to my ears to hear them add 'and of course we mustn't forget to thank Fr Devlin' —: I had taught them to teach themselves, without imposing my own personality. And next year there would be great improvements. I was to supervise the whole Middle School for games and studies and everything.

The summer holidays were filled with mission work; but I had arranged for a quiet last week in the lovely old parish church of Braemar, (3) among the Farquharsons and Grants and Macdonalds who had kept the Faith ever since St Machar brought it. I arrived in Aberdeen on 27 August. A battered looking missive, with a variety of labels and re-addresses arrived at the same time:

'Your application for a commission in the Chaplains Branch of the R.A.F.V.R.,'
'Has been granted. You will report at 0930 hours, 28/8/41, for medical examination at Adastral House, W.C. London.'

I laughed uneasily. A mistake of course. Next morning a misdirected letter from the Provincial (4) reached me; owing to unexpected demands he had sent in my name as chaplain to the Royal Air Force: he wished me God's blessing in my future work.

To avoid a further orgy of self-pity I will not describe my first twelve months as a chaplain.

Christopher wrote in a letter once,

In the rough and tumble of real life there is so rarely a clear field for reason; it is all a gamble or question of instinctive balance. So, naturally, instead of living from one moment to another, we hope and crave for a special predictable design of providence in our behalf; and we are not entirely wrong to do so. For 50% of the way it is forthcoming or for 70% or even for 90% — and then, wham! But I suppose the lesson is always the same: that we must not count on having things specially arranged for us; all we can *count* on is being subject to God's general providence, with a special intention for us

(3) So that he could see his mother. Fanny continued to live in Aberdeenshire.
(4) Fr Francis Mangan, S.J.

37

sometimes hermetically sealed within it. (5)

He had not yet discovered any 'special intention' for himself. Towards the end of his life Christopher said that he had several times attempted to resist God's will with dire consequences to his peace of mind. It certainly is a strange fact that every change in his life which can, in non-religious terms, be described as leading to his true métier, he initially resisted. This time at Beaumont, of course, he had firmly reconciled himself to teaching and now he blindly failed to recognise the summons to the R.A.F. as release for the action he had craved. Nor was it at first, for he was posted to Castle Kennedy in Scotland which seemed to him little more than a transit camp and there was not enough for him to do; after a little while he was moved to Sussex, to Tangmere with the fighter squadrons and that was better. Then came overseas posting – but this again was frustrating for it was not to an operational unit.

The first shock of finding it was West Africa and not Egypt was mitigated by the Staff Chaplain's assurance that very important things were going to happen 'out there'. Yes, of course, there was Dakar in the news, and Lake Chad and the Trans-Sahara route. We would come in on the flank and meet the Eighth Army (and Billy) (6) over Rommel's ruins at the gates of Tripoli. And any way there was Embarkation Leave.

I said good-bye to gallant Tangmere, and went off to stay with Aileen and Charlie in the apple orchards of Meifod. Thence to see my sister Joan (7) who was living on the top of a hill in Shropshire. I said good-bye to her and went on to Goval on the river Don, where my mother was staying and where Pat and Madeleine and their little boy (Gil) had come to stay for a fortnight. Pat and I went off for a few days to climb once more the mystic and aloof Cairn Gorms. Never since children had we been happier in each other's company. We laid elaborate and ridiculous plans for avoiding hotel acquaintances. Sometimes, as of old, we pretended to be elderly spinsters in distress; sometimes we exchanged chunks of experience from the unknown-to-eachother years that lay behind and between. Once more we knew the brief terror of being lost on a precipice in the impenetrable mist, and the apocalyptical thrill of seeing at last the mountain mist roll down the valley.

3

WEST AFRICA

Christopher had arrived at Takoradi in West Africa, in October

(5) Letter 18 June 1956.
(6) Billy had become a Major in the Provost-Marshal's Corps, having changed from the now unhorsed Wiltshire Yeomanry, and had been posted to N. Africa in 1940.
(7) Joan Mary had been evacuated with the Convent School at which she taught in Roehampton.

1942 and once more had found himself with too little to do; he at once set about remedying this but it took a little while.

He described the place where he was stationed in some detail:

West African Command uncoils in the shape of an elongated letter S its head flickering out over Dakar in Senegal and its tail tapering away somewhere around Pointe Noire in the Congo. Between the end of Senegal and the beginning of the Congo there are four thousand miles of coast. Here and there are buttresses of rock and alcoves of steep hills which have a shadow of beauty. There are creeks and inlets and lagoons. There are two English towns which are respectable, Lagos and Accra; there are French towns which are picturesque in their martial simplicity, like Conakry and Abidjan; and there are nondescript coagulations of 'coast scum' like Freetown and Monrovia which are neither picturesque nor respectable. But all these are only occasional incidents in a stretch of four thousand miles. For most of the way, sometimes dead-straight like a Roman road as far as the eye can see, the South Atlantic lies, in a sheet of surf along a line of langorous palm-tufts with a lingering hem of sand. Grain Coast, Ivory Coast, Gold Coast, Slave Coast — there is nothing much to distinguish one from the other.

But if you stoop low over one particular point you would see — behind one particular cornice of palms, a golf course. Above the golf course is an Officers' Mess and a huddle of other R.A.F.ish buildings. And beyond that, as everywhere, there is the swamp and forest changing into scrub. The forest-scrub goes back and back for five hundred miles till it fades into the Sahara.

Northward of this point is Timbuctu; interesting, but hard to get to. Westward Monrovia and Freetown; — Eastward, — the long air-routes and the waiting peoples. (8)

There was an R.C. chaplain here when I arrived six weeks ago and as he showed no signs of moving I got a fine job going up and down the air-routes and ministering to the British and American catholics in the bush stations and to the natives also where there were no missionaries. But now I am back here and I hope to keep the other job also. It was very interesting especially looking after the natives who were christians from South Nigeria, migrated into Mohamedan areas to work for the R.A.F. At one place I had four hours confessions. The Irish missionaries have done a marvellous job instructing them. After that I went 350 miles in a truck over quite wild country, sleeping out, to another place. It was such an out of the way place that I had to go to Khartoum so as to get a plane back. (9)

December 1942

He did not tell Fr Clarke that it had taken him three or four

(8) from 'A Forgotten Fragment'. See p. 40.
(9) December 1942, to Fr Richard Clarke, S.J., for 'The Chaplain's Weekly', the news bulletin which Fr Clarke ran for many years until he was forced by ill-health to give it up in 1965. He died in 1969.

weeks to arrange these expeditons, nor that during this time he had founded, at Takoradi, a native church, the success of which made him wonder whether, when the war was over, his apostolate might lie in the mission field. In these first months in Africa he does not seem to have written to us at all; but it was then that he wrote all the autobiographical notes which end with the description of his Embarkation Leave, and he began and wrote 250 pages of a novel, which he never finished and of which he destroyed all but thirty. These pages he called, when he prepared them for publication in a collection of wartime experiences which Fr Lillie, S.J., was editing, 'Fragments from a Forgotten Manuscript', (it did not arrive in time to be included). The thirty pages continue on the note of bitterness with which he described the time at Beaumont – save when he managed to wring satisfaction out of teaching – and which had returned to him when he found himself posted overseas 'but not to Libya as I expected'.

O God! Have you played me false, landing me in this nerve-sapping luxurious claustrophobic swamp; making me stand about in offices. shifting from one foot to the other till the twerp deigns to lift his mug; making my fingers twitch and my tongue stammer, 'Oh, yes, yes, I see . . . . Oh, well . . . . I'll call again' ('Yes, do!') as I fumble towards the door.

O God, give me a job that will shatter my inhibition, make me what I can be, stark and lucid, airy and penetrating, carven and serene. O God, make everything seem unimportant to me except to be in union with Your Will.

I prayed; and set out walking in the clammy dawn. As I walked, the sun broke like a bottle of Burgundy over Africa into the soaking clouds; above there roared a convoy of Kittihawks with a Blenheim escort. By the time I had said Mass, had breakfast and settled down to censoring letters, that convoy would be refuelling at Lagos, 350 miles away; – I had read the pilots' maps over and over again like a romantic school-boy. – And then they would take the route, the plunging Route that runs in double harness, swerving north and south till it clinches at Khartoum. The northern swerve goes eight hundred miles to the great walled native-town of Kano, then another five hundred east to Maiduguri and the shores of Chad, on the rim of the desert where lions couch and the veiled men come and go; then over the waste land of Dafur, by Geneina, El Fashi, Wadi Seidna, till the White Nile glimmers through the haze to join the Blue.

Or perhaps they would take the southern swerve, skirting the Congo over waves of forest where the ju-ju rules, by Makurdi and Yola where strange tribes dwell that file their teeth, then over the Mountains of Marra, by Nyala and El Obeid, to the cross-roads of Khartoum.

I know now why I want to go up the Route, – not primarily to be an apostle – for one can be an apostle anywhere – but to stimulate my own jaded energies, to revive my faith and self-confidence.

As an immediate result of this clarification, the Route became for me a matter of hum-drum policy. I go to the Embarkation Officer. 'Can you fix me a seat on an East-bound plane as soon as possible?' He replies, resting his fingers on the counter and with his head on one side, 'Certainly, sir. I'll let you know as soon as we have anything. By the way what is the nature of your journey?'

'Er — er — I just want to go and visit my chaps; I'm a chaplain, you know, see how things are going.'

'Ay see,' says the Embarkation Officer, 'Ay see.' No 'sir' now, and there is a look of relief on his face which adds, Well that's one sap I don't have to bother about. No trouble coming from *him*.

Walking away from the office, I curse and curse. Why didn't I say 'Temporary Duty. Authority; Staff Chaplain or Air Ministry' instead of that sloppy stuff about 'seeing the chaps'?

The trouble is that I haven't seen the C.O. yet

I go to the Adjustant's office again, and do some more foot-shifting.

'May I see the C.O.?'

'No I'm afraid not; he's busy.'

'Well, will you let me know as soon as he is free?'

No answer. The Adjustant goes on writing. I swallow hard and begin with a slight tremor, 'Will you — ' but the telephone goes, and the Adjustant begins a furious conversation. For all I know he may be deciding a crisis on the Station, suppplies to the Middle East, and the course of the whole war. My unworthiness pierces me like an icicle. Only as I trail out do I recognise that the conversation is about service transport to pick him up for a party.

A day or two later — back on trailing steps to the Adjutant. 'The C.O. was in this morning', with a gleam of triumph in his crab-like eyes. 'He won't be back for several days. You'd better see the S.Ad.O. . . . . He's out at the moment.'

The Senior Administrative Officer had a face like a mottled shark. 'I don't know why you're here at all. There's a chaplain here already. However the Air Ministry sent you here. So I suppose you'd better stay. There's plenty of letter cenoring to be done.'

'My Staff Chaplain at the Air Ministry gave me to understand he wanted me to look after the Stations up the Route'

'The job of looking after them means an attachment to Lagos'

'I have sent off a signal to ask about that — two weeks ago — they haven't answered that yet.'

'No I expect they have more important things to think of' Snap.

So I went back to the fan-less chaplain's office where the letters were piled, and the Other Chaplain sat — the one whom the Air Ministry had sent me to replace, but whom Air Headquarters had not authorised to go home. He sat quite still, except that occasionally he took out a handkerchief, wiped his arms and neck, and signed his name slowly on a half-read letter. He was a kindly man, older than me and very, very tired. So would you be tired if you had been a year in the Libyan Desert, and then a year on the Gold Coast without a day's leave in between.

At first he had urged me placidly to go up the Route: where I would find real work. But when I told him of the difficulties, he answered, spreading the palms of his hands upwards, 'isn't that what

41

I told you. That's just what you have to put up with on this Station. The climate tightened like a grey wet sack.

In that first dark fortnight it was walking to Mass that saved me. It meant that I was punctual, it meant that I was peaceful, it meant that I was certain of doing at least that much of my job. If the mottled S.Ad.O. were to say 'What do you do here?' I would be able to say, 'Well, to begin with, I get up two hours earlier than you do.'

Only four or five airmen attended daily. But there was Our Lord. Our Lord. Yes, Our Lord in the Blessed Sacrament. Of course. So altogether there were quite a lot of reasons for the two mile walk — two miles in West Africa equal five in England.

Afterwards, at breakfast, too, there is that washed-out, clear-eyed sense of resignation which makes an institutional breakfast so much less excoriating than it can be. Puffy-eyed people come in and bang and shout at the black boys, who blink their eyes in sorrowful perplexity, adding one more to the million unsolved mysteries mounting in their unconscious memory. Why should sausage with tomato be heinous sin in the eyes of one Massa, and sausage without tomato be mortal insult to another — or even to the same one on different days?

Like black Botticelli angels hover round me the faces of my three favourite boys, saying, 'Goomorfa' and bearing gifts beyond cavil — bananas not yet rotten, coffee hot with milk and sugar ready, toast with butter and melon jam planted at either elbow.

'Do not fraternise with the native.', says Station Orders — and rightly.

But oh, my little brothers, how can I forbear to love you when with such careful intelligence you bring my breakfast exactly as I like it!

Patrick with battered features and the so sad eyes, it is pain to see pleasure swim in them. Tall Theophilus whose dreamy ironic smile and long hair curling to the ears, remind me alternately of an Italian poet or a youthful don — but healthier and less opiniated, and Joseph, ah Joseph, he is frankly beautiful, and his beauty is almost immaculate.

From finger-tip to biceps, shoulder arch to jaw-angle, cheek-bone to eye-brow, the line and colour of his flesh and blood flow and glow like a rock-ribbed leaf-gold river when forest depths are opened to the unwinking sun. He is moulded on and whole, taut as canvas, clear as amber, firm as marble, fresh as a ripening plum. I multiply metaphor but I am striving to be accurate. The very staleness of accumulated metaphor embalms, as it were, a most consoling truth, viz: that in spite of the celluloid apotheosis by Hollywood fetishists of decaying flesh-bits, Man's Body can still be what it should be, the arch and paragon of created forms, requiring more than all other beauties to describe it.

'Goomorfa' thin' said Joseph, 'Mo' coffee, fa'? Yes, fa'.' His only flaw, a pleasant one, is that his gums shine cherry-red, almost transparent, all round his comical enormous smile.

These three are Nigerians, no 'coast scum' they, but Ibo, from the rich purple earth of Onitsha, — clean, well-bred, high-principled. I used to bring them with me in the car to Mass on Sundays. They made a great do of it. To watch them twitting each other about their best clothes submerged me in a wave of sentiment, reminding me how much I did, after all, love boys and schoolmastering, and how happy I should be to get back to Beaumont. I went out on to the terrace with my second cup of coffee, took a loaded pipe from my stocking leg, and sat looking at a view that might rival Miami, or any rate Torquay.

Two South African pilots of Communications Flight were sitting near me. I caught the word 'Accra.'

'Are you going to Accra, Barney?'

Barney looked up with the shade of friendly embarrassment that he had shown ever since he had confided his difficulties to me on board ship.

'Yes, Padre. Why? Do you want to come?'

'Yes, honestly I do — as long as it won't be a bore for you, I mean, as long as I won't be in the way.'

'Good Lord, no! But it's not really for me to say. I'll ask Hannah — Flight-Lieutenant Hannah — he's captain of the aircraft. I'm sure he won't mind. Look — he's over there! You go and ask him now!'

Hannah was a large Canadian with a face like an oak, and arms like the branches thereof. He glanced up at me through narrowed weather-beaten eye-lids.

'Why, sure. Glad to have you, sir. Come along.'

O splendid kindly drawl of the Dominions, thrusting like the sun through a vanishing miasma of administrative 'bull'! Why, sure, glad to have you! At those words I felt the aircraft rising like an ardent horse —

But will we ever take off? I won't believe it till it really happens.

But, by God, it did happen. The Hudson taxied, wheeled round, and stood thundering at the far end of the aerodrome. Port engine, O.K., starboard engine, O.K. She lashed the whole length of the runway, and rose, roaring full-throated out to sea. She swung round and rose again. The air-field became the size of my palm, the size of my finger-nail. We climbed to ten thousand feet, sweet agony in the ear-drums, and sped northward over the high mountains of Ashanti.

We were not going to Accra direct, but to a place called Tamale, a bush station three hundred miles inland. The First Pilot was a soft-eyed Englishman called Luckwell, with long Edwardian moustaches.

'Haven't I seen you somewhere before, Padre?'

'Thorney Island, maybe?'

'Thorney — that's it. Were you stationed there?

'No, I used to visit from Tangmere.'

He made a perfect landing considering how long a stretch is needed by a Hudson, on the small bumpy field that had only once been used as a landing-ground before. We ran in between two lines of leaping clapping tribesmen — Mossi Dagomba I think they were. The handful of officers and officials, defenders of our far-flung Empire, seemed pleased and proud to greet us in front of the enraptured throng of natives.

Very soon, the District Commissioner having been got on board and the bush-cows having been driven off the runway, we took off again.

And, after that on my return, I walked up to the Wing-Commander (Flying), and said:

'Good Morning, Sir. I very much want to go to Maiduguri, or rather to Lagos in the first place. Can I get a place on the next convoy going there?'

The Wing-Commander looked embarrassed and a little annoyed; but it was only a couple of years since he had been a fighter-pilot, and it takes more than a couple of years to change a fighter-pilot's attitude from 'Why, sure, come along' to 'Make your request through the proper channels.'

He hesitated between the two, and finally said, 'Well, I don't know; things are a bit sticky at present with this French flap on. I'll see what can be done.'

Fortunately the naval commander he was drinking with happened to be a catholic. The naval commander said, 'Why, good morning, father! Sit down and have a drink.' The Wing Commander started slightly, and added, 'I think we can manage something.'

He shouted across to the Squadron Leader of A.D.U., and in two minutes it was settled. A Blenheim tomorrow at nine o'clock, stopping at Lagos, and going up the route next morning with a convoy of Warhawks.

'How much luggage have you?'

'Just one canvas bag — so big.'

'Wiz-o. Actually *we* don't mind how much you take on the Blenheim. Only you'll have to come back by Pan-American and they are a bit sticky about weights.'

'If you're in any difficulty,' said the Squadron Leader, 'just take out the things and hold them in your hands: they'll count as your personal weight.'

'Yes, that's the score' said the Wing Commander.

I left them sooner than courtesy demanded. Swiftly, before my spirits should subside, I walked into the Adjutant's office.

'Where is the Movements Book, please? I am going to Maiduguri for a short period.'

There was silence while I began to fill in my name and dates. For the first time the Adjutant was giving me his undivided attention.

'Hadn't you better see the C.O. before you try to go off like this?'

I straightened up.

'Nothing would please me better. I've been trying to see the C.O. ever since I arrived on this Station.'

There was another pause. I completed my entry in the Movements Book, all except the column where it says 'Authority'. Finally the Adjutant said in an aggrieved voice, but with no apparent ill-feeling.

'He's been very busy of late, but I'm sure he would like to see you. I'll let you know as soon as he is ready'

I saluted and stalked across to the Chaplain's office. I told the Other Chaplain.

'So you are all set to go, eh? That's good, that's good!'

'Unless the C.O. tries to stop me but I shall tell him that it is not right that I should be kept here censoring when there's the whole of Nigeria without a single R.A.F. chaplain.'

The Adjutant entered, 'The C.O. would like to see you now'.

The Other Chaplain laid down his pipe. 'I'll come with you, Maiduguri and Yola are the places you want to insist on; there's not a priest within three hundred miles of either of them.'

I had imagined the C.O. to be a brusque bull-necked man with glazed eyes and a military moustache. Instead I saw a benign and knowing countenance, big bald dome of a forehead, enormous parrot beak of a nose, lustrous black eyes. He had a gentle bored voice and an attractive smile.

'Yes, I'm afraid I am a bird of passage, you have to catch me —er — where you find me . . . . . ' his voice trailed away.

The Other Chaplain was doing all the talking.

'Yes,' said the C.O. 'Maiduguri. No chaplain. Indeed. But, of course, of course. Yola – h'm – I don't know about Yola.'

He shot me a glance. 'How do you propose to get about from place to place?'

'I thought I could bum a lift on convoys as they came through.'

He opened his queer lustrous eyes and smiled dryly with his lips.

'H'm, I don't know about that. There's no air-route between Maiduguri and Yola. H'm. I don't know. Any way . . .' he was struggling against a descending cloud of boredom.

'You'd better see the Embarkation Officer. I'm sure he'll do his best for you. It may take some time, take a few days but, ...' The cloud of boredom had won; it enveloped him hand and foot. He leant back in his chair and smiled at us frankly and steadily, a smile which flashed the despairing message: 'Get out for God's sake.'

I saluted quickly and departed. Nothing had been said about the Blenheim. In the Adjutant's office, I wrote C.O. in the Authority column and blotted it with satisfaction.

With a terrific mental effort I remembered nearly everything it was necessary to take. Clothes: mosquito boots, long pants, bush-shirts etc. Mass things: wine, bread, candles, etc. etc. Toilet things and tobacco, in the fisherman's knapsack that Aileen had given me long ago in Wales. . . . . and the little travelling clock that Mother had given me before I left Goval.

Pilot-Officer Welch was a slim, pale mournful youth. It was three-fifty when I climbed up the wing into the cockpit beside him. The rest of the crew were a Sergeant-Observer in the nose and a Sergeant-Gunner in the rear — 'because we have to fly over Vichy territory.' I had to work a lever up and down (don't ask me why) for the pilot, as we took off, and then hold the maps and my little clock for him to see.

I glanced at the outline of this pilot sitting beside me, a little to the front. His wrist seemed very thin in the shadow of his heavy glove. But the gloved hand was very steady, the jaw-line firm and clean, the eye-lid unflickering. On the ground he had seemed a vague and absent-minded boy. In the air he was different. I had read and heard about the strange quality that pilots were said to acquire from the air, which set them apart from other beings; at first I had dis-believed it, but after a short time at Tangmere I admitted my mistake.

It is an air of finality – 'THIS IS IT . . . . . I'm looking for some-thing, waiting for something – *This is it.*'

The Pilot is so strung for Finality that he sees through the exterior obstacles imposed by 'various considerations' and interior obstacles which spring from doubt and timidity. He is impatient with anything that obscures for him reality; and reality for him is

45

strictly black and white, life and death, the probability of dying and the joy of living. To court death and to hang on to life, that is his problem; and the glory for him is not a glittering prize but a natural corollary to being left alive, just as daring and initiative are not virtues to him, but practical necessities like fuel and ammunition.

He is intensely personal, but utterly unmoved by sentiment unless it ministers to his physical needs; in him is none of the ideal tenderness which the soldier or sailor wraps around his regiment or ship; on the other hand, the pilot, who is nearly always married, however young, is not in the least reticent about how much his wife means to him. She means life. The air means death — sooner or later.

Such at the end of his 'Forgotten Fragment' was his tribute to the men of the R.A.F. who flew.

I have succeeded now in covering the whole coast of West Africa and a bit more, from 17 deg. West to 32 deg. East and from 20 deg. North to the Equator.

was what he wrote to 'The Chaplain's Weekly' in January 1943.

4

SYRIA

I

From the beginning of 1943 Christopher had to look after all the catholics, in both the Air Force and the Army, in the Gold Coast area but he still wanted to be in an operational unit. Air Ministry records show that in January he asked to be moved either to the Middle East or to Burma. No word of this request leaked out to his family then, though there is a cryptic remark in a letter of September 1944 (10) which probably refers to it but did not make much sense at the time. In April he heard from the Senior Staff Chaplain, Monsignor Beauchamp, that he would be removed as soon as a replacement for him could be found.

I expect to be moving from this colony before long: and indeed I hope to get to the M.E., shortly after my relief arrives. The rains are rising to the full flood here now, bringing with them clouds of mosquitoes and every variety of crawling insect. But so far I have kept in excellent health and have suffered from none of the current ailments, not even prickly heat.

I shan't be sorry to leave West Africa. It has been a good experience, but the climate, especially in this colony induces a terrible lassitude, particularly if one hasn't enough to do. (11)

(10) See p. 65.
(11) June 1943, to 'The Chaplain's Weekly'.

26 July 1943

Here I am back where I started from — except that I am now in No. 1. Mess — very respectable and stodgy — gliding noiseless black waiters, private bathroom, fathomless armchairs, club bores, etc. etc. It is quite pleasant after ten months of more or less bush life. What is going to happen now I don't quite know. I am supposed to be posted to the Mediterranean — but it is now three months since I was told by Mgr B. and nothing has yet happened. I would very much like to go north — to see Billy if possible — and to get to Italy to see Musso being chased along the streets of Rome. On the other hand this is a very comfortable place compared to the sticky misery of Sierra Leone and there is plenty of work to do and my native church which I started last November is going fine and I have taken it over again. It is very amusing — they are of all different tribes and the meetings take hours and hours with all the different interpreters etc. Last week the Bishop came up to encourage them — terrific to-do. An enterprising trader sold cloths with the Bishop's portrait in full robes. The mammies (native women) swaythed themselves in these cloths — and I dont know what the poor bishop thought — when he saw his own features peering benignly at himself from the backside of some enormous fat mammy.

I came by an 'object' (12) the other day which I am sending you (by one of my secret agents) but if you dont like it please sell, raffle or give it away or cut it up for dusters. (13)

31 August 1943

The Sierra Leone natives were of a very low type — most of them had worms — but in the Gold Coast and Nigeria they are very intelligent.

I have been exploring the ancient history of these parts, and it is much more interesting than I thought — at least in the northern territories around the Upper Niger and Lake Tchad. There are distinct traces of Christianity and also a kind of Judaism mixed with Isis worship, as early as the Roman Empire. It seems quite certain that there was at least one White Empire' — which soon got absorbed into black — on the Upper Niger about A.D.300 and considerable traffic from Upper Egypt (The Sudan) across to Lake Chad and even from Carthage over the supposed impassable Sahara down to these parts.

Yesterday a native driver came tearing out of a side road, saw that we were in his line, and forthwith jumped out of his car, leaving it to career along smartly till it hit our front wheel. By poetic justice he was the only one hurt — through jumping out — and I escaped with nothing but a bump on the head. I have to give evidence in a native court tomorrow.

We are still in the midst of our rainy season and it is wet and rather cold. (14)

19 October 1943

When your letter reached me, I was lying ignominiously in bed

(12) A red silk kimono, the silk and native embroidery are as fresh today as when he sent it.
(13) 26 July 1943, to Madeleine from Takoradi, West Africa.
(14) 31 August 1943, to Patrick, from Takoradi, West Africa.

with M.T. (malignant tertian) malaria. I was very lucky to have it here where there is a good hospital. It is quite a pleasant thing to have once you go to bed with it, and provides a most excellent rest.

I am resigned to remaining here till the end of my time. Rather confused news about Billy. In one letter Mother said he was organising troop-movements. But the other said he was touring with a company of actors so perhaps she meant troupe-movements Any way I am *glad* he is not in Italy. Another letter, just received says he has been down with malaria — by a coincidence at the same time as mine.

I am very anxious to see Dominick. (15) I cant imagine what he will be like. I have a ju-ju devil mask to present to Gil sometime. The pagans hang them in their houses to propitiate the powers of plague and darkness. Also some snake-skin slippers and a few other knick-knacks (16)

3 November 1943

I am writing this in the backwash of a farewell party at 11.p.m. — tomorrow at crack of dawn I depart for the Middle East (17) In my last letter to Patrick I said I thought I would not be going but soon after I had posted it the summons came. I don't exactly know where I shall be going after I reach Cairo — Italy I hope but it might equally well be Persia because the M.E. is a very wide area for chaplains. Still I have hopes of meeting Billy, as long as I can discover where he is.

Papers (i.e. Tablet) have come very late here — Sept 8 is the latest — so I have only just got details of the new education proposals of Mr Butler's White Paper. For the Catholic elementary schools it is disappointing but otherwise I am very pleased by the idea of the *Form-Master* — rather than melodramatic examinations, — deciding the capacities of the pupil. (18)

13 November 1943

I have been here (19) longer than I expected, but am definitely leaving tomorrow morning. I am not going to where Billy is — nor to the place where Aunt Ellie was in the last war — but somewhere in between!! (20) I shall be seeing something of Palestine on my way through, but alas, not enough. Still I may get a chance to go back and see it properly. I can hardly realise that I will actually be seeing it.

I didn't get to see the Pyramids here. They were out of bounds because some important visitors were staying near by. (21) The little

(15) Our son, Dominick, born December 1942 and our son Gil (Gilpatrick) born December 1938.
(16) 19 October 1943, to Patrick.
(17) The posting had been announced in London on 12 October and just after Christopher had posted his letter on 19 October, his relief Fr Finlayson, S.J., arrived at Takoradi.
(18) 3 November 1943, to Madeleine.
(19) Cairo.
(20) In the 1914-18 war Aunt Ellie had been in Arabia where she nursed Lawrence. She had many decorations including the Royal Red Cross.
(21) 'We all gather round the Pyramids' is the section-heading under which Churchill in the 'Second World War' (1st Edition, 1952, Vol. V, p. 287) describes his meeting there with Chiang Kai-shek and Madame Chiang. It was on 21 November 1943.

clock is still keeping excellent time. It will have seen a goodly portion of the world by the time it returns home. I shant be sorry on the whole to leave this city — the bugs are something awful, but I expect one has to put up with that, all over the Near East.

I am sorry you weren't able to get out into the garden during the summer. Of course it is winter now. I hope your room will be cosy enough against the cold weather.

Please remember me to Uncle George when he next calls, also to Auntie Janny and Auntie Ellie when you next write. (22)

13 December 1943
I have been seeing places since I last wrote to you. Travelling up here from Egypt I had a couple of days in Jerusalem and spent an unforgettable night on the shores of the Lake of Galilee, at the foot of the Mount of Beatitudes. One got the atmosphere of the Holy Land much better than at Jerusalem. After, there were the mountains of Lebanon — terrific bastions and gorges — and marvellous Roman and Byzantine ruins on the way through Syria. In fact the whole countryside is a paradise of ruins from the Hittite downwards.

The place where I am now (23) — it is where the rump-fed wych's husband went to (the master of the Tiger) — is full of interest — a cut above the usual Levantine city. Visiting some people the other day, I went thro' a maze of narrow dirty roofed streets, then suddenly through a hole in a great iron-studded gate, and up a flight of steps and into a dazzling mansion hung with Persian carpets and ancient scimitars — etc — Most Oriental.

In the town a few European and semi-European families are each a babel of about 5 different languages and faces.

Apart from the Latin Rite there are *FIVE* Catholic Bishops of different rites — Armenian, Greek, Syriac, Chaldean and Maronite — about which I will tell you a good story in my next letter. (24)

Alas, it was forgotten for in the next letter there was no place for a good story. Fanny had been living for some time in a country house-nursing home at Cults on Deeside, not far from Geo. She suffered from the dread Crombie disease of hardening arteries. It was as Patrick wrote to Christopher, a cruel fate that left her bereft of the company of two of her three sons in her last days. She died on 8 December, a great catholic feast day, the Immaculate Conception. Patrick cabled the news to Christopher.

16 December 1943
I had not long posted my last letter to Madeleine, when my back-mail arrived in a lump — some month-old letters from Mother and your two telegrams. I opened the first one first, so was pretty sure what the contents of the second one would be. —
I wonder whether you were able to get up there — or whether the end came unexpectedly. It seems that there was not much lingering

(22) 23 November 1943, to Fanny.
(23) Christopher had reached Aleppo during the last week of November.
(24) 13 December 1943, to Madeleine.

any way, which was surely a good thing.

It seems an evil twist of fate that she could not have passed her old age in more comfort and companionship. But even if she had been offered a magic carpet to transport her to a little cottage outside London, with a congenial companion and every possible convenience, I doubt whether she would have been happy to accept it. I really think that half of her died when Dada died, and she could not leave the scenes where they had lived. Morbid I suppose that might be called, but morbid or not, — to judge from history and literature, that is how faithful wives have felt since the beginning of time.

She had not the heart to embark on a new life in contrast to the old; and that being so, what with the failure of her limbs, and the absence of any home, and the inevitable loneliness, she had very little, temporally speaking, to live for.

It is only now that I seem to understand this hidden reason, and I am sorry that I did not see it clearly before.

I am sorry for Geo and Janny and Grace. In some ways it will be more of a distress to them than to us.

In her last letter — November 9th — written by dictation, Mother said that you had at last got a house, — in Wiltshire. I hope it is a success and look forward to a letter from you or Madeleine. (25)

II

Christopher, of course, was a Priest all the time, above all and in all; he was a Writer always, a Soldier, Teacher, Historiographer — all of these some of the time, but at Aleppo — the Hub of the Universe for him, where he was to be till the end of February, he was enabled to use all these diverse talents at once. And he had everything his heart most craved. He was in an operational unit — the craving for danger was part of his courageous Devlin make-up. It was not a desire for death — far from that — he never at any time at all *wanted* to die — there was always so much more that he wanted to do with his life. But his devotion to his country was intense, and he wanted to face the same perils as those who were fighting for her; not to shelter behind them because he was a priest. Here, at Aleppo, he was to have friendship; friendship which had mattered so much to him from boyhood mattered equally still, and in fact always would. He had a natural aptitude for it, and when he had become a priest, it was as though he engaged in a conspiracy to take those whom he loved along with him 'to his father's house' — the same feeling and intention as was expressed by Teilhard de Chardin when he wrote, 'The true union ... to be found not by going directly to them (creatures) but by converging with them on God sought in and through them.' (26)

(25) 16 December 1943, to Patrick; no address except '217 Group, R.A.F., M.E.'

(26) Hymn of the Universe. 'Pensees', pp. 1110-1111, Wm Collins Ltd, Harper Bros, N.Y., 1965.

Some of Christopher's friendships were life-long — as with Fr D'Arcy, and Charlie and Aileen, and Patrick and me, and, later, with Rupert Hart-Davis. Some, owing to circumstances, were brief but no less important. There was to be one, 'deep and brief' (27), to warm the cockles of his heart that strange, stirring, bitter winter, that he would spend in Syria.

Christopher had been posted to a Force of mixed R.A.F. and Army Units designed for Radar protection and waiting to move into Turkey as soon as the Turks joined the Allies which they were hourly expected to do. He was housed in a row of stables, in a horse box, with a blanket for a door. His neighbours were Richard Barnett, (28) acting as an Intelligence Officer with the Force, and his friend Flt. Lt. Wilfred Sloane.

I met and struck up a friendship with a most interesting and charming man. His name was Barnett; he was at Cambridge a little after Patrick and is a curator at the British Museum (now in the R.A.F.) and a practising Jew, a Sefardi.

We are living in Castle Kennedyish conditions not knowing when or where we may have to depart. I am finding the cold quite intense after West Africa and have bought an enormous sheep-skin coat, which will look quite handsome if I can get the outside decently lined. With this and the full allowance of blankets (5) I manage to keep warm at nights.

We have an airfield called Bab-el-Hawa on the Turkish border half-way between Aleppo and Antioch. You come from Aleppo across the wide plain and climb a little bony ridge; the airfield is at your feet, and beyond it two chains of pointe; hills with a gap between them; that gap is Bab-el-Hawa, the Gateway of the Wind. The modern road winds S shaped up and down the little ridge, but there is a Roman road there too, intact for half a mile. The Roman road cuts through the modern road like the stroke of a dollar, and leaps direct at the gap for Antioch.

I have to travel about quite a lot,· and the countryside has a dream-like, and sometimes night-mare-ish, appearance; immeasurable tree less plain broken by stark isolated rocks of mountain; the villages are all collections of huts.

The peasants wear very attractive clothes — the women favour red trousers. (29)

The troops were to spend three months in Syria, in great discomfort and freezing cold — over a cheerless Christmas, and New Year, too, and right through the early weeks of 1944 and nothing at all was done by the authorities to relieve their plight. Richard

(27) Letter from Richard Barnett, M.A., D.Litt., F.B.A., F.S.A. See note below.
(28) From 1932 he had been Asst. Keeper of Egyptian and Assyrian Antiquities at the British Museum. In 1955 he became Keeper, Dept of Western Asiatic Antiquities.
(29) 13 December 1943, to Madeleine; No address except H.Q. an obliteration, R.A.F., M.E.

Barnett and Wilfred Sloane were very distressed by this fact but at the same time they were impressed by the good behaviour of the men, despite their boredom, discomfort and homesickness when 'only Padre Devlin seemed to understand what they felt.'

Maybe it was not just neglect on the part of officialdom. They may have felt it was all too complicated to bother with – but if so they were wrong. Maybe any one taking any kind of interest in the men could have made them feel more at home. Christopher, however could help them in a way peculiarly his own. It was a far cry from his speciality – sixteenth-century England – but just as he could conjure up Shakespeare's London so that its streets, passages and houses became more familiar to his pupils than those of their own day so now he would bring alive the land of Genesis, the 'stamping ground of history', the land across which Abraham had gone on his journey from Haran to the Promised Land; the country through which St Paul had journeyed to Antioch. He could see the ruined cities well enough in his mind's eye as once they were, filled with gay and chattering men and women, and he could make others see them. He took his men to places where, when first they looked they saw nothing but a wilderness of boulders on every side but as they gazed he bade them watch

like grey smoke rising out of the ground, the ghostly cities of North Syria take shape. Go to one and two more will rise up to your right and left; go to either of these and you will see still another couple further on.

Babisqa – the wintry sun can only summon a feeble smile from the stones of Babisqa now – but it must have been a gay and lovely town, the queen of this region, when it was first built. Gracious little houses abound here, clusters of three or four, with their colonnades facing inwards on the same courtyard – as the old christian houses in Aleppo still do. Very deep cisterns explain how there was enough water at so high a level for the Public Baths which form part of the handsome Men's Club-house – this three-storied building with relics of stone couches, basins, drainpipes and stairways now all jumbled together.

Bear east by south-east from Babisqa and Baouda rises up. It is a market town and takes its character from its nearness to the Roman road; it is a stopping place for commercial travellers. It is full of hotels and shops but has only one church. The stone galleries which line the streets are the bazaars. The upper floors supported by architraves across the pillars, are where the shop-keepers live; their wares are displayed in the hollowed stones at their base.

And so Christopher dispelled some of 'the rock-bound silence' that arose from the well-preserved ruins of more than a hundred dead cities in the twenty mile radius round the airfield. There was no sound other than 'the tinkle of goatbells and the odd call of the

Bedouin shepherd' and the Bedouin shepherd was not calculated to make the British soldier feel at home.

An old man appeared between the rocks where the goats above meandered. He was dressed in the costume some of them still wear in these parts; he wore a high conical cap with a tassel of yellow, a kilt and shoes with curled up toes. He looked like a magician from a fairytale, or one of the seven dwarfs. Also he might have stepped out of the frieze of a certain Hittite slab in Aleppo Museum. For a moment he jumped so with my thoughts I wondered if he had, and whether he would hail us in the tongue of 'Tal-m'-sarrum: 'Be you some of these good-for-nothing seafarers that are come up from Troy? There's been no peace in these parts since they had the war up there.' I looked again to see whether he cast a shadow or no but he was gone.

As for the Bedouins: true they stabled their beasts in one of the loveliest and best preserved of the ruined churches and built a fire in the baptistry apse where the catuchumens sat for immersion. The offense is unintentional; they are the gentlest and most charming of hosts. I share my food and things with them; and they give me, not taking no, the delicious curds they call Leban, or in Turkish, Yaghourt; and coffee bringing it ritually three times to the boil and rapping the pot on the ground.

Then always trying to make things less foreign, he stressed the common heritage to be found; he showed them inside the churches the apses and the arches and the lacey carvings still remaining; and on the houses too were christian symbols, symbols which many of them could recognize from their parish churches back at home. The very architecture of their old churches and of the great cathedrals, with which at least some of them must have been familiar — were all inspired by these architects who had left Syria and gone to Europe — whilst Europe 'was stilled wrapped in the dark ages'. And as for Antioch, just across the Border where daily they expected to go — at Antioch the followers of Christ were first called christians, he told them,

I would have liked my companions — who had just got down from a three-ton lorry and were politely attentive — to realize, at one and the same time, how formidable are the centuries that intervene and yet how immaterial they seem.

Abraham and St Paul and the ancient road flying like an arrow through the loops of modern industry. That was the sum of what I wanted to say to my companions.

How many countless others have crossed this landbridge, lonely fugitives from the convulsions of nature or the corruption of man, perpetual wayfarers on the Sisyphean track between reconstruction and ruin; but the gardens of the ruined past also are transfigured by the rainbow of promise

Compared to the forest of milleniums that have trapped and tangled man's progress from the beginning up to the moment when

Abraham steps clear onto the Syrian plateau and into the light of promise it seems only a flash of time until St Paul journeying to Antioch declares the promise's fulfilment to all the world.

Another time he tried to convey his excitement to the others which came from climbing the steep track to Qalat Seman — the Castle of Simon:

You encounter an enormous porch which leads through three archways into a mighty echoing octagon. Five of its original eight arches still stand intact. In the middle of this octagon — courtyard, centre of all the rest, is the base of a great pillar; the pillar of Simon.
    Once it stood forty feet high and on top of it for thirty years lived St Simon the Stylite. After him the mountain range is named, and in his honour the monastery with its churches and the neighbouring town with its hotels, were built to house the host of pilgrims who used to come here from the confines of the known world.
    The outline of the building is like the outline of his life, terribly weird and strong, yet also touchingly delicate and graceful; but like the building his life has come down to us, chipped and desecrated by time. His life was written by contemporary historians in a world that was quite as civilized and sophisticated as our own, a world to which he was as well-known as, for example Gandi is to us — though for different reasons. St Simon's work was to spread peace.
    He has been called 'a diseased pervert' — Unjustly. His character seems to have been as sweet and simple as his manner of life was repellent and fakirish. His pillar, towering harshly outstrips and repels Western ideas; but his personality reaches sweetly out as far as Gaul and Britain.
    Feuds between Bedouin tribes, labour disputes at Antioch, international problems even, were solved by him from the top of his pillar. An enormous deputation of labourers came from Antioch to complain of starvation wages; by a mixture of prayer and threat Simon compelled the granting of the people's demands! His picture was found in the shops and factories of Rome. He was a power in the world — to whom the world meant nothing. We know his food was hauled up to him in a basket. We know, also, that a shelter was built for him when he was ill, and pulled down by him when he got better. Then how did he survive the blistering sun and the murderous cold?
    At first one laughs at him as at some fabulous freak. But when one realises that the facts are too well attested for him to be dismissed as a madman, one finds oneself with a shiver in the presence of the supernatural. St Simon is not to be imitated but his life points a lesson straight and simple as his pillar; the supremacy of spirit over matter.
    Per Ardua ad Astra.

And if sophisticated taste is tempted to laugh and think all this talk of ruined cities, saints and coffee, a waste of time and any way poor comfort to the men who longed for their own folk and fireside and football matches — the answer is that the men came asking for more. Because of this and because also of their own equal frustration in the highly peculiar situation, which had promised to be so very exciting and was by now obviously abortive, Christopher, Richard Barnett and Wilfred Sloane met together in one of their horse boxes, where they were joined by a splendid character, Père Taoutel, who was nearly twenty years their senior, and a native of Aleppo, based at the Jesuit house there. Together they planned a series of pamphlets that the men could use by themselves. The pamphlets covered such subjects as the history of Aleppo and its citadel, the churches and mosques, the dead cities, Islam, and manners and customs, and last of all, but not least in value, what to eat and where, and where and what not to eat.

Richard Barnett's knowledge was of course special but they found a surprising number of experts to help them. The pamphlets were an immense success but to Mr Barnett's continuing indignation, they got no official backing. So the horse-box quartet arranged for the pamphlets to be printed and the money they obtained from their sale they ploughed back into printing more. Eventually they bound all seventeen into a booklet and called it 'Aleppo and its Environs'. It sold like hot-cakes − the price was two Syrian pounds − (at that time two kilos of rich pastries cost three and a half) and it was accounted good value. Christopher first wrote of it in February 1944 when he also wrote of Richard Barnett

We combined to produce a sort of guide-book, there wasn't one in English. Sudden moves nearly spelt financial disaster. Quite apart from the writing it was most interesting getting it printed; I have learnt a lot about type-setting etc. It should be out in a few days and I will send you a copy by post if Security allows.

Père Taoutel, S.J., (30) who would sometimes invite Christopher 'prendre ses repas et fuisoner avec les Péres de la Résidence' may be a little prejudiced in the amount he ascribes to his fellow-religious. He says

J'estime que l'auteur principal de cet petit livre est bien le cher Père Devlin qui a stimulé le travail, recueilli les notes, et les rédigées définitivement pour l'impression dont il a financé l'impression.

Christopher in fact wrote three of the pamphlets. He had of course very much more money as an officer in the R.A.F. than is normal for a Jesuit to have to spend on himself. He was always very generous with his pay and on this occasion seems to have pledged every penny that he had. The Guide-book ignored by officialdom is

(30) Pere Taoutel is now 79 and prison and hospital chaplain in Aleppo. He wrote 'Je continue: . . . à accomplir mes fonctions sacerdotales . . . en attendant le jour proche des grandes rencontres avec nos amis, dont votre beau-frère, le Père Devlin, dans la maison du Père'.

now, strangely enough, the official guide in English in the Museum in Aleppo — the fruit of a delightful camaraderie.

In addition to such congenial company and such interests Christopher had other work to attend to.

I celebrated a marriage — having done my best to prevent it, they insisted that I put off my departure for a day or two in order to celebrate it. It was a most complicated affair from the point of view of both the Church and State. A girl of Syrian race, French nationality, and Maronite Rite, and a Protestant Officer of the R.A.F. They were married according to the Latin Rite in a church of the Franciscans by a Jesuit; in Lent with the organ blowing, and a Maronite Archimandrite attempting up to the last moment to take a 50% share in the Celebration. But all went off very happily and let us hope it will continue so. (31)

And there was welfare work, too, to be done

I came across the case the other day of an American soldier who married an English barmaid, and they had quadruplets. But unfortunately he was married already to a girl in America; when asked to divorce him she replied tersely: 'Let him sweat it out.' Welfare cases present a very depressing outlook. But, thank God, that is only one side of the picture. (31)

5

NORTH AFRICA

The Force which had been assembled on the Turkish Border was dispersed in February and Christopher went first to Palestine. He did not say so at the time but on one of his frequent 'hops' to his Headquarters which were in Cairo, he bought, second hand, a modern Greek Grammar. (32) On the fly-leaf he jotted down very roughly where he had been during the twelve months after he left West Africa.

I am covered with confusion what can I say except that this is the first letter that I have written this year and for some little time before. A partial excuse has been the 'situation' which was highly peculiar, promised to be very exciting, and then on the eve of the excitement relapsed into a dreary anti-climax of packing and unpacking and waiting around. I am not now where I was when I quoted Macbeth.

I had to go down to Cairo in the course of various movements and there I found (Feb 15) your parcel of books which had just arrived from West Africa. They could not have come at a more opportune moment because I got weatherbound for four days on the way back without any luggage but with this parcel of books in my hand.

(31) 17 March 1944, to Madeleine from Gambut.
(32) He gave it to Fr Peter Levi, S.J., who kindly gave it to me.

Is there any news of Billy, I wonder?

I must end this rather lop-sided letter; it is typed with a most peculiar machine, about the size of two pancakes. It was so handy that I could not resist buying it. (It is Italian loot from Eritrea) and I hope I will not lose it. (33)

I didn't know that Billy had changed to Broadcasting. I am very glad. I must write Mary and get his address so that I can get into communication with him as I am now approaching nearer to his sphere of activity. I have not actually reached the above place — Gambut — yet, but will arrive there tomorrow; it is near Tobruk. I am being sent there because it is on the way to Italy. I have spent the last month getting to various places with great efforts and patience and then finding I have to proceed somewhere else. Everything has been in a state of flux since I left Aleppo.

I wonder what will happen to Rome. The future is very mysterious. Reading between the lines, the raids on London, though small in comparison, seem to be no joke. A corporal here had his family wiped out the other day.

Address Gambut will reach me for some time I expect. (34)

Then, on 19 April, Christopher wrote rather an enchanting letter to his nephew, Gilpatrick, who was then aged five and a half and who, strangely enough, was to cover much the same ground some fifteen years later.

How are you? I hope you are quite well. I am now back in Africa where I used to be before, but in a different part. DA (35) says that you have a map of Africa. Before I was in West Africa, now I am in North Africa.

The first place you come to on the map, if you are coming from England is a place called St Etienne, on Cap Blanc, where Spanish Rio de Oro joins French Mauretania. It is all sand here, part of the Sahara Desert, with no grass or plants. You see many kinds of enormous fish along the shore. — Cuttlefish and Giant Rays washed up by the tide, and in the sea many porpoises tumbling up and down, and sometimes the fin of a shark. There are no animals except Camels and Hyena; I did not see the Hyena.

The next place further down, is a long deep, wide river called the Gambia. I sailed up this in a steamer one day and saw a Hippopotamus; only its top half and two big nostrils were showing above the water; it sank under with a lot of bubbles when it saw the steamer coming.

The next place is called Sierra Leone. I lived at the top of a creek behind a place called Freetown. This is not a good place; it is full of mud-swamps and flapping trees, and the natives are peculiar. I saw an enormous snake here, 7 feet long called a Green Mamba; it went tearing round and round the verandah until the natives killed it. And long after it was dead it went on coiling and uncoiling.

The next place is the Gold Coast. There are palm trees along the shore, and waves with white tops. Behind, there are forests, and I have seen crocodiles in the rivers there. I saw crocodiles in the Gambia and Sierra Leone too. Behind the trees there are rolling

(33) 26 February 1944.   (34) 17 March 1944.   (35) Patrick.

grassy plains where you can see many gazelles and antelopes, and behind the plains is the Sahara again.

The next place is Nigeria the biggest and most interesting of all; it is like all the other places put together; the natives are very nice there. I lived for a bit at a place called Maidurguri, near Lake Chad, and at another place further south called Yola. I saw a lion at Yola. But it was dead. It had been killed by a native with a spear — which was just as well.

If you draw a line north-east from the Gold Coast till it reaches the Mediterranean Sea, you will see where I am now, — near a place called Tobruk. There used to be a lot of Germans here, but they were all driven out last year by your Uncle Billy in his armoured car. It is a Desert place but not like the Sahara: there is quite a lot of grass. There is a lark which sings just outside my tent; it has got a nest there with three eggs. I live in a tent. At first it was blown down by a dust storm. But now it is dug three feet deep and the walls are lined with petrol tins full of earth so that it is half like a house. There are many birds in the Desert but apart from Camels not many animals. The rats and mice are much nicer than the English ones. The rats are more like chipmunks or squirrels; they are very tame. They rush about carrying bits of grass to line their nests, and stand on their hind legs and nibble. The mice are very tiny, but with long hind legs like tiny Kangaroos. There is a mouse in my tent which behaves itself very well. There is also an asp in my tent, i.e., a small snake which looks like a lizard. It gave me a bit of a turn at first, but it is also very well behaved; I give it bread crumbs. I hear that you went with Da to the Zoo and saw many animals. I would like to hear about them. I expect you have seen some interesting things too, at the farm at West Wick. (36) I will pay you a visit there as soon as I get back. (37)

And then, on 25 April in answer to a letter from home, he wrote

Yes, I am rather tired of trailing about the Middle East. But everybody now in the Middle East is afflicted with a feeling of anti-climax. It WAS so important and is now so dull. However I thank goodness I am not in Cairo or the Delta. The desert quite suits me. — though I have got the less interesting half of Cyrenaica to look after.

I have been correlating Prophecies about the War and the Middle East. One I got last winter in an ancient Syrian Monastery. Another (a prediction, rather) is one South Africans tell me General Smuts still adheres to, despite appearances to the contrary. The third is of shabby origin (The Pyramids). The Syrian monk says that there will be an armistice early in 1945, but the war (as it affects Syria, presumably, but of course he might save his face on the Japs.) will last in all ten years. Smuts is said to say that the final victory will be in the Eastern Mediterranean. The Pyramid one is a ridiculous hackneyed thing about Megiddo, near Haifa in Palestine (Armageddon) which can only compete as a long-shot guess. It is

(36) West Wick House, the house we had bought in Wiltshire, which Christopher mentioned in his letter on p. 50 and where he was to spend a good deal of time.
(37) 18 April 1944, to Gilpatrick.

58

funny how 'prophecies' never fail to rouse ones interest, however often they break down. (38)

7 May 1944

I have visited a most attractive ruined city in these parts. It is Cyrene. It looks out over the sea from the top of an escarpment a thousand feet high. It was built round the fountain of the nymph Cyrene (who was she?) which is a very cold and limpid spring jutting out from an over-hanging cave and making deep crystal pools in the rock floor; around this is the sacred part of the city, temples and baths and a marvellous amphitheatre which the Italians have excavated extremely well. On either side of these caves on top of the plateau, are the residential and industrial parts of the City; they manufactured and exported a drug called sylphium (?) which seems to have been very fashionable in classical times. One suffers terribly from having no books at all to read up about these places. The coast line is so like that of the Lebanon (Tyre and Sidon) that I guessed the Phoenicians must have stopped off to found a colony here on their way to Carthage. But apparently not. The first civilizers seem to have been the Greeks from the Aegean Isles who founded the city in the seventh century B.C. There are a lot of Greek inscriptions in which the city is written 'KURANA'. Down below is the Mediterranean, all purple and green, and Apollonia which was Cyrene's sea-port. All this country, from Derna to Benghazi, is called the Green Belt, and is in complete and abrupt contrast to the battle-littered dust-flayed wilderness which lies to the east and south. Unfortunately for me my pastoral care lies east of Derna. But along the whole coast line the sea is paradisically lovely, but difficult to get to. I now drive to the dissatisfaction of all of whom I have come in contact; but I am glad to say that such contacts are becoming rarer. I am becoming quite hardened now, but at first it was very nerve-racking: one spends most of ones time in mid-air, trying to avoid the next bump.

I have not lost all hope of seeing Billy but it seems harder for me to pass from the Middle East to North Africa, or Italy than for a camel etc.

What DID Lady Astor say about the Middle East? Shame and indignation seethe among the 'other ranks' in the desert, at supposed remarks of hers about Mediterranean holidays and venereal disease. Perhaps if the good woman had swallowed a dust-storm or two, she wouldn't have opened her mouth so wide. Many poor wretches feel that the attitude towards them in England is: they're having an easy time out there, no air-raids or restrictions; if somebody has to go to the Far East let it be them; they're half-way there already.

I must confess I am appalled when I reckon the equivalent of how many hundreds of pounds — in air-travel, petrol, sight-seeing etc — the War-Effort has expended on me, a religious, vowed to peace and poverty. My typewriter appears to share my emotion splutteringly — so must stop. (39)

---

(38) 25 April 1944, to Madeleine from Gambut.
(39) 17 May 1944, to Madeleine from Gambut.

14 June 1944

Terrific events! (40) First Rome and then the Invasion! No doubt there is more to come from other angles. I wonder if you are getting any repercussions where you are? I have just got my right arm out of three weeks of plaster of Paris which was put on to heal a cracked elbow joint (Head of radius is the correct term). It is gradually returning now to circulation with many agonizing creaks and groans. I can type quite easily with it but not write.

The cracked elbow-joint had in fact been very painful. It was set in hospital and he went straight out afterwards into his truck and began to drive away, when, fortunately he was seen by a doctor who noticed that he looked white and shaken and ordered him back into hospital for some days. Most of these he seems to have spent visiting friends in that hospital and in others near-by. He did not say exactly how the accident happened but from the rest of his letter it can well be imagined:

I got it on a most interesting trip into the desert about 100 miles south towards Jarabub Oasis. Two Boers had been out to salvage trucks and also to shoot what they called 'buck'; and they reported the presence of an unburied body or rather skeleton, which they had not investigated; so on their next trip they took me with them. We went in a German Mark III tank, and were out for five nights. It was lovely to get into the real desert which is incredibly fierce and clean, in contrast with this part of it which has got all frowstyish and mouldyish from long encampment, aeroplane dust, etc. It was also quite an experience from three points of view: 1. The Boers, 2. the gazelle, and 3. the body.

The Boers were the real thing; they were farmers and hunters in real life; they didnt speak much English but still got quite excited about Majuba and De Wet and the Great Trek. So I had to behave with great circumspection. They had a genuine instinct for direction and only used the compass to check up occasionally. We would go miles off our beat chasing gazelle — which of course I didnt approve of but couldnt help enjoying. The Basuto carrying the rifles would give a low cry and point; little figures would be seen flickering over the horizon on delicate legs. The tank would blare off sometimes touching seventy miles an hour, with us on top of it bouncing in the air when it hit a hummock. If the gazelle could reach a long hillocky belt it was safe; otherwise doomed; when it could run and leap no more, it would stand quite still looking straight at us with calm soft eyes. I could never manage to shoot one, even had I been able to aim straight from the rocketing tank, as the Boers could, but I cant without hypocrisy deny that I got a great primitive thrill out of eating it, holding a haunch in the red ashes, tearing off a cooked part with teeth and fingers, and putting the rest back to cook again. It sounds repulsive but it was most satisfying; and, curiously, seeing the thing skinned etc, only whetted the appetite!!

The skeleton was rather tragic because of a packet of letters from

(40) The Allied Armies had penetrated into the heart of Rome, the Piazza Venezia, on 4 June, and on 6 June the invasion of France had begun.

wife and mother which was nearby. It was of a lieutenant of the R. Dragoons, posted missing since June '42. However they will be glad to know that he has been found and buried in a proper place. From tracks, wrecks, etc, one could reconstruct some strange stories. Banal but ironic was the reflection that one might die here with all the ancient horrors of the desert — thirst, sun, glare, loneliness, etc, — and yet with all the most modern and expensive products of science within a handsthrow — shells, tanks, aeroplanes, etc.

Well I really do hope that nothing has gone wrong (I dont suppose it has for I got a letter from Aunt Ellie dated May 29th), and that I will soon be hearing from you. (41)

Christopher's next letter home was written three weeks later and told slightly disparagingly of a birthday present which clearly came to give him very great pleasure.

7 July 1944

In a weak moment I have just had wished upon me a puppy which was born on May 30th. (42) I call it 'Hi Tiddle' and it is a great nuisance and cause of economic and domestic upsets. Heaven only knows its species; it is white and looks like those little dogs you see frisking pointlessly about in mediaeval pictures. It appears to have monastic blood in it for it wakes me up regularly at 5.30 a.m. by gnawing my toes; then later on when I am miserably shaving, it calmly goes back to bed and sleeps till nine o'clock. I dont think I shall be able to stand it for long. For instance, just now when I was typing, a book of bar-tickets fell out of my trouser pocket. Tiddle was suspiciously quiet under the chair. I looked down to find him demolishing the last remnants of five shillings worth. However he has the great virtue of not being car-sick, and as he spends half his life bumping about on the seat beside me, that is just as well both for him and me.

I have got the east of Cyrenaica to look after — nothing but scrub, and thorn and sand. Westward there are dark green mountains two and three thousand feet up from the sea; with deep rolling valleys and white streaming water that never stops; in a week or two the vineyards will be thick with grapes up and down the mountain terraces, and the orchards with apricots, peaches, figs, dates and mulberries. Not to mention the most marvellously reconstructed ruins. The Italians have certainly made a good job of this Belt and it seems a shame to hand it back to the Senussi, who are well enough in the desert but who turn every house into a latrine and let their goats loose among the budding wheat. Swift, if I remember, has some words to say about the unimportance of political parties compared to the ability to make two blades of grass grow where one did before.

Hi Tiddle sends his love to Gil, Virginia, Clare and Dominick. (43) If he survives a week or two longer, I will try to get some photographs of him. (44)

(41) 14 June 1944, from Gambut to Madeleine.
(42) This, of course, was Christopher's own birthday.
(43) Our four children, Christopher's nephews and nieces.
(44) 7 July 1944, to Madeleine from Gambut.

25 July 1944

Yours of the 13th and 17th to hand (this morning). You are heaping coals of fire on my head; but I am very glad to get them for otherwise this has been a week of uninterrupted gloom. Nearly all the squadrons that I knew have moved on to Italy, but I am left here, deprived on some pretext or other of the galumphing truck which by subtle machinations I had acquired, and there have been dust-storms for the whole week without respite.

O that this blank blank Muddle East would melt,
Thaw and dissolve itself into a — grease-spot.

It is a pity, now, that we so cleverly captured the general commanding Crete, for he appeared to be a good fellow and might by now have surrendered the island, which would have meant a merciful release for us in this abandoned spot.

I am looking forward to seeing West Wick and all its inhabitants and environs. I dont know any of these Wessex towns or places.

Tiddle is growing into a great upstanding cur in tearing (literally) spirits. He capers around with arched back and dangling legs in the manner of a lamb or kitten. But in general outline he rather resembles a rat or foxikin. He has made quite a good impression on the various stations I have visited.

On the first he had a terrible adventure. Someone foolishly let him into the Officers' Mess. He had just had some milk and entered in high spirits, his tail up like a flag and beaming all round. Everyone said 'What a nice little dog.' but the C.O.'s cat (a whacking great ginger-black brute called Gremlin) unseen in a chair, uncurled itself slowly and — psst! like a doodle-bug, hurtled upon him. The poor little wretch rolled over and over shrieking his life out; and the cat even a second time heaved itself upon him. I got a nasty scratch hauling it off. The cat came to a bad end. The station acquired a kitten, and the cat attacked that and had to be destroyed. It was tied — horrible to relate — in a bag, and the bag was sprayed with a sten gun . . .

On another occasion by a coincidence, the owners of the three adjoining tents all had a puppy. In the morning, as was customary, a large plate of scraps was brought for the three. Tiddle surprised and pleased, rushed in with swinging hips and by a most extraordinary feat, in about five seconds demolished the whole plateful. He behaved very badly during the day and managed to get other unauthorized food. That night, at one o'clock, I was awakened by a loud tearing noise. Lighting a candle and looking under the bed, I saw Tiddle in a shrunken state gazing at me pitifully. Alongside him lay his entire breakfast, dinner and tea, quite undigested, just as it had gone in. Since then his table manners have improved — slightly.

On yet another station he was poorly received. They had a dog problem; 4 dogs; a large and savage police dog and his three wives. It was death, they said for any other male dog to appear. 'Better shut your pup up.' So I put him in the car but he got out. Later on a large crowd collected to see the police-dog rolling on its back in an agony of amusement, while Tiddle rushed in and out, snapping and shouting, and falling over himself with enjoyment. They went on like that for two hours. (45)

22 August 1944

I'm afraid I'm not able to proffer any reason or excuse why I havent written or received any letters since my change of address at the end of the month. (46) Indeed I don't feel equal to hazarding any information about myself at all, except that as far as I know I am not wearing a false moustache. So I had better pass on to a more fruitful topic.

Will you pass on my congratulations to Patrick. (47) I very much hope that now that August is here, he has been able to get away altogether from London. From what I gather about these flying bombs, the general menace is not so bad as the Blitz, but the effect of each particular one is much worse and more disturbing than the average 1940 one stick of bombs. The 'Bells of Ousely' — the fine old Inn (mentioned by Dickens) at the foot of the drive up to Beaumont — simply went for six, inhabitants and all. (48) Old Fr Geddes appears to have restored a restive congregation to calm and good order by his distinguished behaviour during a near miss. But I had better cease these second-hand, made-in-Birmingham bomb-tales; otherwise Patrick will refuse to read this letter.

I am still a thousand miles from the echo of bomb or bullet, and, despite my laudable intentions, likely to remain so. My whole career on 'Active Service' has been that of a Jonah in reverse. On no less than four occasions now I have arrived on a front where the war clouds were lowering, braced (decreasingly) for heroic deeds and each time my arrival has been the sign for the rumble to cease, the captains and the correspondents to depart, and the monotony of a peace-time station to resume its sway. My only hope now for a Kipling piece of ribbon to wear on my chest, is the institution of an 'Order of the Red Herring' for those who have suffered considerable sartorial and stomachic inconvenience through abrupt changes of climate.

Actually my work at present is not at all monotonous, and quite interesting and bewildering. I hope to write a more intelligent letter about it when I feel my style less cramped by censorship.

I had to part on leaving Gambut, with some sorrow, from Tiddle; but he on his side betrayed no undue emotion being still of the age when he can happily and swiftly switch his affections to any one capable of providing a square meal. Otherwise I was glad to leave Gambut. On my journey thither I was able to renew some old acquaintances and bestow my approval on a second, cheaper and more elegant and orderly edition of the Guide-book. (49)

(45) 25 July 1944, the sixth anniversary of his ordination, from Gambut to Madeleine.
(46) Written from Palestine.
(47) On the birth of Timothy, in July 1944.
(48) One of the earliest flying bombs fell at the Bells killing several people and shattering most of the glass at Beaumont on both fronts and the rose window in the chapel ... No one knew what it was, since the official news of the weapon had not yet been released. ('Beaumont', by P. Levi. p. 64.)
(49) 22 August 1944, to Madeleine, no address.

The Father Geddes of this letter is, of course, the Father Geddes of Christopher's days in philosophy at Heythrop. Though he 'renounced allegiance to him and followed Scotus' he still had a great affection for him.

4 September 1944

What a terrific crescendo of news! I cannot but suspect the hand of Churchill in the arrangement that sends each army back over the scenes of glorious disasters or triumphs: The Americans to Soissons and Montdidier, the British to Arras, the Canadians to Dieppe, the Highlanders to St Valéry. What a man! The end of October is the date favoured here for the end of the War, but I myself, after many discomfitures, have definitely retired from the prophetic racket. (50)

But not, it seems from prescience. In his book 'The Second World War' which was published in 1954 Churchill wrote:

The frontier towns so well known to the British Expeditionary Force of 1940, Arras, Douai, Lille ... were soon reached by Montgomery's Army Group, the 51st Highland Division occupied St Valéry, the scene of the tragedy to its parent Unit in 1940 ... Meanwhile the Canadian Corps moved swiftly to Dieppe where they repaid their old scores of 1940. (51)

But this was 1944 and a campaign, near to the heart of Churchill and one in which he made a dramatic intervention, was about to open, and in it Christopher was to play a part.

6

GREECE

This episode in Christopher's life is 'one of the rarest'. To appreciate the part he played his actions must be placed in their setting, in Greece shattered by war and enemy occupation, amongst Greeks who did terrible things to each other as well as to the noble British troops, all of whom, along with their leaders from the Supreme Command downwards and the statesmen who played their part, knew that they were fighting for something they all held dear; for democracy. They were fighting to bring it back to the city where it had been born. So this chapter has to be different from the rest. It is about this Greek adventure with Christopher caught up in it.

Towards the end of September Christopher wrote that we must

(50) 4 September 1944, to Madeleine, no address, except H.Q. Force 438 (R.A.F. Component), M.E.F.
(51) Churchill: 'The Second World War,' Vol. VI, Cassell, 1954, p. 167.

get Timothy baptised by someone 'locally'. He had, he said, just begun negotiations for returning home — and it had appeared possible that they would be successful

when I was offered the posting to this Force; (52) and as previously I had asked for the sort of thing it might turn out to be (if you understand me?) I couldn't very well refuse. (53) It looked as though it might be an interesting way of returning home. But now I am completely in the blue, though not entirely without hope, about the future.

A week later this hope could begin to swell; each day of the coming two weeks could be separately marked on the fly-leaf diary with a brief excited note.

On 1 October he left Cairo at 2 a.m. and, crossing the coast at 'Marble Arch' — still so named on maps of Libya — he flew to Malta. He arrived there at 12.30, midday, and left again for Bari some three hours later. Of what happened next he wrote in a letter of 4 October from Rome; that it was written from there, of course, we only learnt later; To me this letter still reads quite breathless with delight:

Here beginneth a travelogue. I landed at Bari at the end of·a 14 hour journey and after the usual 3 hours wait in a dripping hangar got a bus to the hotel where there was a serviceable telephone. With surprising and most satisfactory promptitude I contacted Billy, heard his incredulous yelp and found that his office was just a hundred yards or so round the corner. There he eats, sleeps and works in state, with a staff of two sergeants (Oxford), 3 privates (not Oxford) and a most excellent Italian cook called Liddio. He seems to have the most laborious hours, sometimes from early morn till midnight and hardly ever seems to leave the studio. But he obviously likes the work.

I understand from neutral sources that it is the best run broadcasting station in the Command. We spent the evening together and Liddio produced a special dish of spaghetti for my benefit. Next day having failed to find anyone to whom I could report myself I made arrangements for pushing on, and again spent the evening in the studio.

So, at last Christopher's great desire of finding Billy, — the moment for which he had been waiting ever since he had heard that he, too, was being posted to the Middle East had been fulfilled. He was satisfied and happy. Love of Christ was all to him but within that he held his family very dear. Rejoicing Christopher went on to his great adventure.

He left Bari for Rome on 3 October and flew by way of Assisi, Spoleto and Bolsena. 'This', he wrote, 'was irregular,':

(52) H.Q. Force 438 (R.A.F. Component).
(53) See p. 46.

H.Q. is not at Rome but I had made a vow to see Rome again and vows are not to be broken lightly. The second leg of the journey over the Apennines was very lovely indeed. We skimmed down deep valleys and circled towering mountains, under a ceiling of cloud; straggling wisps of cloud peeled off as we passed, concealing, then revealing, the fairy cities on the hilltops, with their walls of houses round, and a tower or spire in the middle, almost on a level with our wings. I saw Assisi plain as plain, and recognised with a stabbing shock, several little places, mountain passes and cypress avenues, which I had walked through eighteen years ago and have dreamt of ever since. Had I been holier I would have thought I was dead and on my way to Heaven. Picking up the Tiber we followed its course till the cupola of St Peter's from afar off announced the journey's end.

We landed at 11 a.m.; and this airport being run by Americans, found a bus ready waiting. Having fasted, I was just in time to say Mass at the altar of the Madonna of the Strada in the Jesuit church of the Gesu; and then repaired in a broken-down cab (all the taxis have been comandeered) to a hostel which is reserved for catholic chaplains. In the afternoon I contacted a number of my old companions and former fellow-students, and listened to all their stories. At present my sensations of Rome are too jumbled and probably censorable to describe.

On 4 October he had a Papal Audience and then on the 5th he wrote,

Conscience tore me away after one day and I hastened south to report to my H.Q. Here the wrack of war is far more evident than on the Adriatic coast and one was able to compare and confirm all one had heard about the difference between American and British bombing; their ideas in this matter are much more lavish and less precise than ours. Beautiful Velletri whose roofs and orchards, towers and terraces, rose and fell so graciously between the mountain slopes — is now a pock-marked shambles; and so with many another place. But the people seemed much happier than in Rome; a special type lives here, descendants of the Martii, not at all the typical southerner.

Christopher's flight had been from Albano by way of Velletri and then on to Terracina on the coast; then he had flown south again to Gaeta on the Gulf, and only then inland to Caserta, where he found his H.Q. and reported to it.

I received my destination vaguely. I will be off again tomorrow, W.P. and will probably see Billy again on the way. My address will be B.A.F. (Balkan Air Force) but I think it would be safer to keep it as it is: R.A.F., H.Q., M.A.A.F. I am sorry for all these fantastic initials; my mail is quite literally trailing across 3 continents now. But it will soon be all over now, please God.

While at Caserta he had also reported to the Senior Catholic R.A.F. Chaplain (54). He discussed with him a number of things, amongst

(54) The Rev. Patrick O'Connell, S.C.A., C.B.E., now Vicar for Religious in the Diocese of Portsmouth.

which was his strong desire to become a Paratroop chaplain. He had already applied for this to his Principal Chaplain in London; the application had been turned down as it was thought he was more needed where he was.

On 6 October the weather did permit and he flew to Bari and was able to see Billy again. On the 7th he took a train, which by this time was a novel way of travelling for him, and in this way he reached Taranto and his Unit. The 7th was a Saturday and nothing happened until the following Tuesday, the 10th. That day they were told that the Germans were pulling out of the Peloponnese and back upon Athens but since the Russian Army was sweeping round the Carpathians it would be impossible for the enemy to remain in the city and the Unit was given their objectives; (1) they were to occupy and service the big airfield near Athens; (2) chase out any remaining Germans, impeding their junction with their divisions still in the north of Greece; (3) at once to organise an air service of food and supplies to the Greeks; and (4) to keep order.

His Unit was part of the Force which was to come

Loaded with good gifts anxious only to form a united Greece which could establish its own destiny. (55)

It had been planned by Churchill and the British Cabinet with the approval of President Roosevelt, soon after they first heard in July, that year, rumours that the Germans had decided, because of hard pressure elsewhere, to evacuate the Peloponnese. The plans were for a small Force, of about 10,000 men to go mostly to Athens but some to Salonika, which was to be ready from September. When the time came it was smaller because of the demands of the Italian Front and no more than 5000 men were sent to the Athens-Piraeus area. The reasons for sending the Force were well explained in the objectives given to Christopher's Unit.

From the first Churchill had been aware of the danger that Communist extremists might try to slip into the Germans' places as they left, in an attempt to force their regime on the country, which, there is plenty of evidence to show, disliked communism. They were a minority but they were armed, for they were contained in the guerilla bands which had formed the resistance movement against the occupying Germans and in this they had been helped by the British with arms and with men, dropped by parachute. Their political wing was known as EAM — and very sick people were to become of the shout 'E— AM' as it echoed through the streets; the initials stood for National Liberation Front; their military wing was called ELAS, The People's National Army of Liberation, and when

(55) Churchill, op. cit., p. 259.

these letters were run together and shouted — ELAS — the name only needed the L to be doubled, and the sound remained much the same, for it to seem very like the Greek word for Greece. This was very helpful to their propaganda. During the German Occupation ELAS was known to have numbered six or seven divisions on the mainland alone and there was no reason to suppose their numbers had decreased.

To guard against the trouble he feared Churchill was anxious that there should be a strong broadly based Greek Government with sufficient authority to control the situation and which would be ready to go into Athens within two days of the entry of the Force. Since April there had been a Greek Government representative of all parties except the extremists, in Cairo, headed by Mr Papandreou who was strong and courageous; a man of integrity and as such he had the support of the British Government. EAM had been holding out for a weaker Prime Minister — so that they could twist him round their fingers, but late in August they finally decided to send six members to join him, all of whom managed to get over from Greece. Four of them were genuinely anxious for a strong government; they mistakenly supposed that they could control the other two who had joined only to test the British intentions and to see if they dare risk their own dictatorship. (56)

The King of the Hellenes, George II, was also at Cairo. When in September the Greek Government moved to Italy. This was in answer to a request from Mr Churchill that they should be near the Allied Supreme Command at Caserta and ready to move to Greece as soon as the time came, — timing was of the utmost importance, he had pointed out. — The British Ambassador to the Greek Government, Mr Reginald Leeper, (57) then had the disagreeable task of making it clear to the King that he could not share in the coming triumphal entry into Athens but must await the result of a plebiscite which would show whether or not free Greece wanted a king. Refusing to permit any kind of Regency to act in any way for him in Athens, King George went to London.

The Force for what was called 'Operation Manna' was waiting partly at Taranto and partly at Alexandria. It consisted originally of the 2nd Parachute Brigade, the 23rd Armoured Brigade, acting as infantry, both from Italy, administrative troops from Egypt, and 'whatever Greek Forces were at the disposal of their recognised Government'. (58) Then there was the 15th Cruiser Squadron, with mine-sweeping flotillas, together with American Transport, and four

(56) See 'When Greek Meets Greek' by Sir Reginald Leeper, Chatto & Windus, 1950, p. 69.
(57) Later Sir Reginald, C.B.E., K.C.M.G.
(58) Churchill, op. cit., p. 249.

British and three Greek Air Squadrons. A little later the 4th Indian Division was sent from Italy and went partly to Athens and part to Salonika, and must have felt the cold intensely; the famous Greek Mountain Squadron, which had fought with distinction in Italy, was added too, and instantly became a bone of contention between Papandreou, who had wanted it to come and EAM-ELAS who had not. The Force was put under General Scobie and all the foreign elements in it signed the 'Caserta Agreement', General Zervas signed for EAM and General Saraphis for ELAS and both declared that none of their men would take the law into their own hands or take any action in Athens except on the direct orders of the British Commander. Their pledges were worthless, but Allied Command could not know that owing to misleading information which was intended, as it did, to hide the strength and well-organised plans of the Communists. There were lesser troubles, too, and one really rather comic incident illustrates the sort of difficulties encountered in dealing with even those Greeks, who were, as the majority were, devoted to the British. The timing of this 'Operation Manna', was, as has already been said, all-important. The Supreme Command decided that the Force should arrive in Greece on 15 October, to be followed by the Greek Government on the 17th. The 17th was a Tuesday. Nothing of importance had been done on a Tuesday since 1453 for it had been on that day of the week that Constantinople had fallen to the final Turkish assault. To do nothing significant on a Tuesday was a widely respected Greek tradition: — 'Never on a Tuesday'!

Christopher's Unit had been given its objectives on 10 October. He spent that night in a Transit Camp and next day, after he had said Mass very early, he went on board the L.C.T. Samos. This form of tank landing-craft was an American invention of special value since it did not have to dock but could be beached. The Samos had on board the men and equipment needed for occupying the airfield. It was accompanied by another L.C.T. bound on the same kind of errand for the Piraeus Docks, and there were corvettes and other subsidiary craft with them.

On the first day they moved only from the Mare Piccolo, which, like some Scottish lochs, opens out to sea, to the Mare Grande which is properly in the Gulf of Taranto. On the 12th the news came through that Commando Units had gone into Southern Greece closely behind the retreating Germans. They had gone into Patras and were beginning to work their way round the southern shores of the Gulf of Corinth. This was followed by the news that the Germans were evacuating Athens itself. THEN the order for Christopher's Force to move was given. Greatly excited he noted that it was just 6 p.m. when

the great harbour gates yawned open and we put to sea, sailing
south-south-east by south at a slow six knots [an hour.]

The next day, the 13th, they headed due east having increased speed
to ten knots [an hour] and on the 14th they turned north. As they
passed between Crete and Cytherea — Cytherea the island where
according to legend Venus had risen from the sea — they sighted the
main convoy which, with General Scobie aboard, had started from
Alexandria. They joined it; and went on with it. There were four
cruisers, — one of them was the 'Ajax', of River Plate fame and
another was the 'Orion', — and there was a great array of troopships,
destroyers and minesweepers.

On the L.C.T. 'Samos' they were very crowded; six and kit in a
cabin eight foot square, 'but', wrote Christopher, 'in such conditions
one makes friends easily'. It was very stormy:

A severe gale blew up and the landing-craft wallowed as these things
do, from side to side disturbingly. I wondered if I was not over-
optimistic in announcing the time and place for Mass on the
morrow; the place was the only space available, the back of a
three-ton lorry. It was exciting to think that we were going to beach
instead of docking. I suppose the Crusaders were the last people to
beach their armour in Greece. For from the Middle Ages till today
beaching-in-force has been a lost art.

On the 15th the convoy sailed into the sight of Salamis — Salamis where
the Greek triremes, four times out-numbered by the Persians had
fought and won the great naval battle. Christopher, on the deck of
the modern craft gazed out, his thoughts turned back almost two
and a half thousand years. 'It was', he wrote,

one of those moments; one of the rarest of them. But it was
necessarily only a moment. The air was full of flashing signals. The
sea rocked with spasmodic explosions. A Heinkel swooped out of
nowhere on a daring reconnaissance over our landing-craft before her
guns could fire, and made off chased by two Spitfires from Araxos.
A tanker blew up alongside us.

Then the order came to turn and put back to the Island of Poros:

The islanders came swarming out in their little boats, shouting 'Io
Patriotes, Patriotes!' and our crew of the Royal Hellenic Navy ripped
open cases of rations and flung tins and cartons overboard. One or
two of the R.A.F. Officers said, 'There go our rations for a week';
but the men said, 'Let the poor — s have them', and threw down
cigarettes as well.

That same day but at 8 o'clock in the morning Leeper had also reached Poros and watched the same excited scenes. It was here that the Greek Government, whom up to this point he was accompanying, were to transfer to the Greek Cruiser 'Averoff', — she had been the glory of their navy many years before and was still sea-worthy; though slow, she could not make more than ten knots [an hour,] she had arrived in good time from Alexandria with orders to take on board the Government and to make the Piraeus so that the ministers could enter Athens on the 17th as planned. The morning drew on but the Greeks showed no sign of wishing to board her before they had greeted and responded to the greetings and enthusiastic welcome of all the notables who had come out from Poros. After lunch Leeper realised that Papandreou, unable to change the Allied Commander's decision that Athens should be reached on a Tuesday, had chosen this way of defeating the plan. The Ministers transferred to the 'Averoff' but, as it would soon be dark, and they would shortly run into the area the Germans had mined, they hove to. Next day, Tuesday, they followed the mine-swept, flag-marked channel and as that night fell the 'Averoff' waited a short distance outside the harbour, which of course had been cleared ready for the Government to make their triumphal entry into Athens; and make it they did on *Wednesday*, 18 October.

The 'Samos' had left Poros on the 16th and beached at Kalamachi on the same day. 'A ropey beaching', and Christopher stayed on deck all night watching the unloading. Next day, the 17th, he went into Athens. Strange things had indeed been happening there. On the 13th the last German officer to leave had taken down the swastika from the Parthenon and almost in the twinkling of an eye there came the first of the explosions Churchill had feared. Christopher after he had heard about it wrote,

The Athenians crouched in their barred and shuttered houses, felt gusts of bullets sweep the streets and spatter against the walls. An ultra-monarchist guerilla band was having it out with the guerillas of a communist band, the Ku-ku-ethes, for the control of Athens. Some dark deeds were done on that day and corpses found afterwards in wells and sewers which were only indirectly victims of the Axis.

The fighting had lasted for about twenty-four hours when rumours began to reach the city of events outside. First of all they came from Megara which lies between Corinth and Athens. There, and according to schedule, on Saturday, 14 October, the men of the 2nd Paratroop Brigade flew from Italy and in the teeth of the same vicious wind which was tossing the convoy, dropped on the airfield; their chaplain, Christopher noted, perhaps half-enviously, Fr Benedict Fenlon, dropped with them; they joined up with the

Commandos who had dropped at Patras, two days earlier and together advanced towards Athens; even before they had reached Eleusis which lies on the route, and long before, Christopher said, 'the hulls of the convoy had appeared above the horizon',

a mysterious telepathy ran through the silent houses of Athens. Windows were flung open, heads popped out and shouted across the streets; 'The English have come'. So many times the rumour had started; after the victory of Alamein, after the surrender of Italy, and after each one — another winter to face; so many times, so many wounds. But this time the rumour swelled and would not be suppressed. Then everyone from windows and roof-tops saw or heard of the blue flag hoisted on the Acropolis. The Khi-ites and the Ku-ku-ethes paused in their noisy debate, pocketed their weapons, and were swept, with mixed feelings, presumably, into the great massing concourse of the people, who sang and cried and danced — the taut, Greek, graceful dances — down the streets.

And this was the Athens into which Christopher went, in company with an Irish friend, perhaps one of those he had met, and made easily, when they were 'six and kit' to a cabin on the 'Samos'. He described their triumphal tour together:

We were on the back of an open lorry filled with an assortment of marines, paratroopers and airmen. The side-walks were thronged all the way with people and everyone waved and shouted greetings. Our welcome was the sort of thing you read about in the papers and don't believe. It was fantastic. Everywhere flew the flags of Greece, Great Britain and America. On some warehouses, ruined by our bombs, there were Union Jacks and the inscription 'Long live the R.A.F.'

My intention had been to visit the Archbishop and discover what army R.C. chaplains had arrived. But once dismounted from the truck it was impossible to move in any deliberate direction. The streets were dense and it was only the third day after the 'Liberation'. We were plucked at on all sides, and bidden to come in and drink a toast. Sometimes it was impossible to resist; but fortunately they were only thimblefuls; the Greeks are very abstemious; also though their effusiveness is often annoying, it is hardly ever impolite. The only thing was to cease feeling ridiculous and to enjoy it. My friend, who was from Kerry, kept shouting to me, 'I'm telling ye, Father, these people are *Irish*, they're Irish. He could not speak a word of Greek, but was conducting an animated, and apparently satisfactory conversation with an old man who could not speak anything but Greek.

I have forgotten all the people we met on that day or whether (as my friend would say) it was that day we met them. There was a party of workmen in the quarter beneath the Acropolis; there we drank 'retsina' and talked about the Germans . . . they tried to draw us on the political situation. They appeared to be E.A.M.ites & pro-British. Then there was a family of 4 generations, ranging from 2 to 70 & here there were tears as well as 'retsina'. Here we also talked about the Germans and touched lightly on the political situation; they were Venizelist Liberals. Finally there was a Colonel who produced, Oh dear, of all things, a bottle of John Haig. He said that he had kept it hidden in the ground for 3½ years, to drink with the British on the day of their glorious return. So — we talked about the Germans and touched lightly on the political situation. The Colonel was a monarchist and looked to the British to take a strong line in this matter.

We escaped back in the falling night to Kalamachi.

Meeting so many people with such differing views Christopher tried to draw his own conclusions about the political temperature of Athens; he was completely puzzled by the strange contrast between the ordinary people

who share the happy buoyancy of their golden dancing climate and the political parties who swirl around in mad witches tangle burning down each other's arches and building them up again at enormous cost of money.

He decided that probably the whole population was light-headed from long under-nourishment. He was writing home and having begun the letter on 15 November, he finished it on 20 November with the words,

no doubt things will take a turn for better or worse before Christmas.

In the month he had spent in Athens he had had much work to do. For quite some time he had been the only R.A.F. chaplain there. From the first there had been casualties. The first funeral stuck in his mind. He had known the pilot well and, after the burial, he stayed behind thinking that he was alone. He noticed the flowers some Greek women had brought from the graves of their own relatives to place on the British one; and then he saw that a Greek Officer, who was representing the Royal Hellenic Air Force, had stayed behind as well. Suddenly this man had saluted and cried out, 'Zito o Athanatos Iros — Long live the Immortal Hero.' This indeed was a normal ceremony, but Christopher was very moved.

.   .   .

British bombers were harrying the Germans still in Thessaly and the airfield had to be repaired for their use. In their retreat the enemy had not done more than was necessary to impede the liberating Force; — (this was Christopher's view though it was not Leeper's) — they had destroyed roads and bridges; but earlier on there had been destruction on a much larger and unforgiveable scale; Christopher wrote to us that he had seen, village after village where every single house had been gutted and smashed and where the inhabitants had spent one winter and would spend another in holes beneath the ruins.

By mid-November Greece was free — apart from a few islands — but everywhere there was heart-breaking poverty, misery and hunger. The British troops proved themselves superb at the task for which they had been assembled. They went on half-rations themselves to augment supplies of food. For some reason UNRRA did not come into action for several months so the troops not only repaired the roads and bridges making transport possible but undertook the transport themselves. They got on well with the people and so far it would seem that 'Operation Manna' was going as planned.

In this month, November, other chaplains arrived in Athens. Padre Church, (59) who had been at Patras, had observed that ELAS had played no part in taking the town but had organised vast victory parades and marched through the streets afterwards — the beginning, perhaps of their insiduous anti-British propaganda. He, after one or two other adventures with ELAS had reached Athens on 10 November. On the 24th Padre Lees had arrived; he noted in his diary, part of which was afterwards published in a little book for private circulation 'for those who fought at Kifissia', that when he got there he met,

a dare-devil R.A.F. Regiment Church of England Padre from the Middle East, Padre Church, as well as a charming Jesuit, Padre Devlin.

Padre Lees (60) was also Church of England and he and Christopher worked together at Kalamachi; he recalls in his diary how Christopher and he tried to find a house for a club.

The Jesuit Padre had heard of a house suitable for an airman's club and the two Padres paid a visit. The local police ... made no objection but did not seem able to obtain possession. The Padres were met by a deputation of suave Greeks who pointed out that the first floor had recently been taken by a babies' welfare society and the cupboards were stacked with baby clothes.

These, the Greeks remarked, could surely not be turned out? The cupboards, and in fact several rooms, were locked. The R.A.F. Padres had no order to search and though they knew ELAS to be in the neighbourhood they could not take the matter further. At a later date neither of them had any doubt that the rooms and cupboards were stacked full of arms and ammunition.

(59) The Rev. George Church, D.F.C.
(60) The Rev. H. T. L. Lees, 'Prisoners of E.L.A.S. Greeks', pp. 43 and 46.

Late in November Christopher flew with his advanced H.Q. to Crete. Crete was by this time two-thirds clear of Germans and so, the island, full of mountain ranges ideal strongholds for the Partisans, was only nominally in German hands. All the same it was an adventure which some of his friends among the paratroops, left behind in Athens, envied Christopher. The Cretans, politically, were broadly of two varieties, left and right, yet each variety consisted of every colour in the spectrum. They did not think of themselves as Greeks but as Cretans and each of them fought to get control of his own country. They fought each other whilst facing and fighting the Germans. In hatred for the Germans they were united and in one other thing besides — devotion to the British.

Christopher hardly mentioned his time on the island but writing from Salonika, a couple of months later, he compares and contrasts the attitude of ELAS there with that of the Partisans in Crete. Both of them seemed to him

to hark back to the century-old Macedonian idea that the test of your manhood was to take to the hills with a lethal weapon against the oppressor whoever he might be; they were a highly endemic fraternity whom you might as well ask to put their eyes out as to lay their guns down.

The Salonikans, he said,

were hostile to the British from the very start because we arrived professedly to keep order — (the Germans did not attempt to keep order, they garrisoned the region with a horde of Turkestan Tartars, deserters from the Russian army.) —
It is odd that in contrast we should have been so successful with the Cretan Partisans, who are just as brave and brigandish but at the same time quite passionately pro-British. (61)

On 6 December Christopher returned to Athens bringing back with him some bottles of Cretan wine for those friends among the paratroops whose envy of him had been unnecessary; adventure in plenty had been in store for them, during his quite brief absence, for an extraordinary change had come about in the city. At the end of November the Communists had become very active commandeering houses, making unlawful arrests, and, above all launching a determined campaign to change the friendly attitude of the people towards the British; amongst other things they gave out, though not all of whom they sought to convince believed them, that Great Britain was in no position to implement her promise to provide relief supplies. This was all part of the plans they had made to eject the British, seize power and torture or shoot, or both, all who disagreed

(61) 27 January 1945, from Athens to Madeleine.

with their views. ELAS had by this time sized up our Force and had decided that they could now act.

On 1 December all the EAM members turned against the rest of Papandreou's Government and resigned from it, leaving it distracted; from that time it lost such authority as it had had.

On 2 December a general strike was declared in Athens.

On 3 December Communist supporters engaging in a banned demonstration, collided with the police and civil war had begun. It was now abundantly clear that ELAS — EAM cared not a jot for the agreement signed at Caserta.

On 4 December ELAS attacked and captured all the police stations in the area 'murdering the bulk of their occupants not already pledged to their attack', Churchill wrote. (62) They then advanced to within half a mile of the Government Offices and quickly held the whole city except for the very centre.

The British troops showed that they had no difficulty in understanding the issues involved. Churchill knew of this from their censored letters home and was profoundly moved by them. And indeed they realised, also at once, the disagreeable fact that, despite the tumultuous welcome of six weeks before they now had to fight *some* Greeks', and, there, in the centre they fought, hemmed in and out-numbered by an enemy four-fifths of whom were in civilian clothes.

Two days later Christopher got into the city by the road from Kalamachi, which was described as insecure, all the rest were cut, and the Piraeus was no longer in Government hands; which meant, that in addition to the port being closed to them, the British could not reach many of their supply-dumps. Christopher described his bewilderment that day, as he found raging in Athens,

a battle of quite totalitarian ferocity. It came as a shock to most of us, because we had not been following the political situation but were chiefly concerned with getting food supplies going. A good ration for December was just about to be issued when all of a sudden this thing broke out and waves and smiling changed for no apparent reason into bullets and grenades.

Some time that evening Padre Lees managed to put a call through the Communist controlled telephone exchange at Kifissia; where he was at Air Head Quarters. Kifissia six miles N.E. of Athens housed at this time, in various hotels (for in normal times it was a much favoured holiday resort), all the H.Q. of the British Command. He phoned to tell Christopher of the excellent cinema show a sergeant from Welfare, Middle East, had put on for the men at A.H.Q., thinking that Christopher might like to get him to come over to the

(62) Churchill, op. cit., p. 251.

airfield and give it again. Ironically enough, Padre Lees had arranged that if danger threatened him he would phone so that Christopher could report the fact to the C. of E. Principal Chaplain at Caserta — no doubt Christopher had a similar arrangement with him. But Padre Lees was only aware of danger, when he was unable to phone again, a few hours later at 1.45 a.m. when both big hotels, containing various H.Q., the Pentelikon and the Cecil, were attacked by ELAS and, after 30 hours of savage fighting, were dynamited and a cease-fire was forced upon their defenders.

Padre Church had a very severe attack of jaundice; lying in a hospital bed opposite, unable to move, he was forced to watch his H.Q. go up in smoke. Padre Lees accompanied the wounded prisoners taken by ELAS and cared for them devotedly 'in the Bag'. Christopher of course heard about what he was doing in due course and no doubt he got a message through to Caserta but for a time any way he was alone in his work in Athens and in the Piraeus. At some date he was joined by another Anglican chaplain with whom he became great friends; one of their joint adventures he later described in a letter but the name of this friend cannot now, alas, be discovered. Padre Church was at work again at the beginning of January, although they knew of each other they never seem to have met, and Padre Lees, after his ordeal with the prisoners and hostages which ELAS had taken, was sent home that month to hospital.

To return to Athens on the 6th; that day re-inforcements arrived; part of one brigade of the 4th British Division was flown in from Italy in the bomb bays of seventy Liberator Bombers, an excessively cold way of travelling, and they were soon in action. On the 8th it was reported to Churchill that the 23rd Brigade had made progress in house to house clearing that afternoon and that the Parachute Brigade had cleared a further sector, but it was easy for 'civilians' to slip back again and resume firing from the houses in which arms were hidden — it was reckoned that there were fifty square miles of houses from Athens to the Piraeus; and so fighting went desperately on.

The Greeks, Christopher said, had an epic strain in the face of death,

I have seen an ordinary woman when a man was shot down in the street beside her, stand like some sybil or Cassandra; with blazing eyes, one hand pointing at the corpse and the other raised to heaven. Also I have noticed on more than one occasion when there have been fatalities, and when I myself was fussing around in a rather shaken manner, how some Greek man-in-the-street would take charge with a verve and incision utterly unlike their usual attitude of haphazard and ambiguity.

77

Soon he was made sore at heart by the deaths of several of his friends, some shot down in the streets before his eyes, and one, a doctor, by his side. One sees Christopher striding through the streets on his missions of compassion, thanking God after each hair's breadth escape; or at the wheel driving through the back streets of the city, the centre was impassable, in a battered car draped with a large red cross, which Philip Irwin, the M.O. and Raleigh St Lawrence, the Adjutant of the 1st Battalion the Parachute Regiment, whom he had known first when he was for a very brief time a master at Stonyhurst, had given him. Irwin had said that he did not suppose that it would make very much difference, and, sadly, he was right, for he himself was killed two or three days later when ELAS machine-gunned his ambulance as he went out to bring in a wounded man. Though their chaplain, Fr Fenlon, went out in an armoured car to bring his body in, it could not be found.

This kind of murder and the disappearance of all trace of the murdered man was commonplace at this time.

wrote Cornelius O'Beirne who was there and also a school friend of Philip Irwin's. 'You should have lived not I', Christopher felt as these young men were mown down, and so he expressed it in his poem the 'Seven Cities'. (63) Once, when he was in Cairo, Christopher had been caught in a street brawl, where knives were unsheathed — for a moment he had thought himself trapped; 'what a silly way to die', he thought — but the Egyptians let him go. Now in Athens he slipped from one danger to the next and still went unharmed. Once he escaped death by stepping into roaring farce. There was fierce fighting at both ends of the street; his only way of escape was to go through the door of a house; it opened to his touch and the noise of the fighting was blotted out by the noise of the gay party into the midst of which he stumbled. A glass of Ouzo was pressed into his hand and most warmly was he welcomed.

On 12 December Field Marshal Alexander took over as Supreme Allied Commander, Mediterranean Forces and went at once to Greece with Harold Macmillan who had been appointed his political adviser. He found when they touched down that the airfield was surrounded though it was not being attacked. It was of course in regular use for many operations but it was difficult for the air-arm to give much support to the troops fighting in the streets. The bombers could be used, though, against enemy machine-gun emplacements and also for dropping food and medical supplies. Particularly grateful were the prisoners and hostages taken by ELAS, some of whom were marched many miles in bitterly cold weather to be confined in

(63) A poem written after the war, at St Beuno's (see p. 89 ff).

78

a brewery near Mt Olympus, for the food and clothes and blankets that they dropped.

When Alexander phoned for a car to take him from Kalamachi to Head Quarters which were now in the centre of Athens the 'Communists obligingly' put through his call. An armoured car was sent,

We bought a lot of bullets on the 6—7 mile journey from Kalamachi but we were not stopped, we could hear them hitting the outside of my armoured car. (64)

He told Churchill of the plight of the troops and informed him that they had only six days rations and three days reserve of ammunition in the city.

I spent the night with the British Ambassador, who was pretty well besieged in his Embassy; in fact a bullet was fired through the window of the room in which I was sitting with Mr Macmillan and our Ambassador.

He might have added that Mrs Leeper and their daughter, as well as the Embassy staff were in the house too. He continued,

Next morning I left for Italy, leaving Mr Macmillan behind to sort out the political situation. It was necessary for me to get back as soon as possible to arrange a strong military set-up in Greece.

And he sent help of various kinds but he was convinced that unless the Front in Italy was to be seriously hampered, once Athens was under control, a political solution must be found for the rest of the country. From this time on the plan of asking Archbishop Damaskinos to act as Regent, — he had originally been suggested by Leeper but the idea had been firmly rejected by the King, and by Mr Papandreou, — would be strongly pressed by Mr Macmillan.

The street fighting went on but a little before Christmas the tide was turning in our favour and our troops began to have the upper hand in the Athens—Piraeus area. Churchill was of course receiving daily reports about the situation and fully agreed that a political solution must be sought. He was interested that Harold Macmillan thought all parties would serve under the Archbishop but he was worried that the King would continue to veto the idea and do so possibly constitutionally with the advice of his Prime Minister. On Christmas Eve he took the impromptu decision that he would go to Athens, see the position for himself and try to find a way to put an end to the fighting. He decided on this in the middle of a family party round the Christmas tree which President Roosevelt had sent

(64) All three quotations on this page are from the 'Alexander Memoirs 1940-1945', edited John North. Cassell, 1962, pp. 141-2.

him and be there and then phoned Anothony Eden to ask him to go with him.

On Christmas Day Christopher sat down to write to us, he began,

I must apologise for being so long in writing. I got your very welcome letter of Dec 2nd in good time, on Dec 11th; but since then mail has closed down. I have some excuse for not writing because during the days up to the present I have had an awful lot of army to look after whose chaplains either had not arrived or were cut off; and the evenings which get dark very early now, are not much use for writing, as we have had no proper lighting since the troubles started. But from now onwards I shall be more leisured, as the roads south of the city are all freed and various other army chaplains have arrived. Not but what I could have scraped up a letter before, had I really given my mind to it, but still . . . .

Christopher then went on indignantly about 'Dirty Work somewhere'; he had no way of knowing how or the extent ELAS had rigged and been determined to rig the situation; what he thought, and no doubt many of his companions thought too, is most interesting. He wrote,

Well, I have a grisly tale to unfold, could this slithery ribbon but speak with the virtue of tongue, eyes, and heart. And at the risk of censorship and anything else, I must proclaim aloud, and ask you to proclaim aloud, and bear a burning witness, that there has been Dirty Work somewhere. On the part of the Communists, undoubtedly, who deliberately from the beginning exploited every grievance to make anti-British propaganda. But on the part of some capitalists also; I am convinced, or whoever it is who has controlled the wage-paying, price-levels, etc. The question which we have all, soldiers and officers alike, been asking since a week or two after we landed — and the question which should be shouted and echoed till an answer convicts the guilty, is: WHY werent the Greek people fed during the first month that we were here — ? Why did we allow our enormous prestige to dwindle and tarnish, by letting the poor go hungrier than they were under the Germans while bags of food were paraded openly in the streets as 'English Meat', 'English Sugar' at exorbitant prices which only the unpatriotic rich could afford. If there are Germans and Bulgars on the ELAS side, there are also cosmolite Levantines on the other side, who are equally false to the interests of Greece. And why dont we insist that EVERYBODY disarm. I hold no brief at all for ELAS & I absolutely agree with Churchill that the backbone of Greece is the small property-holder who forms the majority and should be left to decide what form of GOVT he wants.

But I hope, I more than hope, that our statesmen are doing all they can . . . to let the moderates on the side of ELAS know that they will get fair play

There for the moment the letter can be left with just an added note that it was on the subject of disarming that EAM walked out of Papandreou's Government.

On this same day, whilst Christopher was writing, the 28th Infantry Brigade of the 4th Division from Italy had fittingly captured the large Brewery near the Acropolis, 'Fix's Brewery' as the British called it, and the Paratroop Company came under the same command to help with the fighting in Omonia Square (called, of course, Ammonia Square by our troops). The Brewery was started by a Herr Fuchs who accompanied Otto to his new kingdom and, remaining in Greece he Hellenized his name to $\Phi\eta\xi$. (65) Field Marshal Alexander arrived in the course of the morning, clad in a sort of Partisan dress and wearing all his medal ribbons. He went up to the roof top of the flats opposite the brewery and crawled across it to get a better view of the ELAS snipers post nearby.

At 3 p.m. — according to Leeper, — Churchill himself puts it at midday — he and Alexander and Macmillan went to the air port, part of the way in an armoured car and the second half of the journey in a 'soft' one, for from that point to the aerodrome the way was clear. They had not, says Reginald Leeper long to wait on the airfield 'and we were thankful'

because it was very cold. When the special plane alighted . . . Mr Churchill in R.A.F. uniform appeared. He sniffed the air and . . . beckoned to us to come up.

The plane was warm and the bar was not out of action.

Here they explained the position to him and Macmillan and Leeper outlined the suggestion they had made to the Field Marshal of calling a conference of both sides with Archbishop Damaskinos in the chair. Mr Churchill warmly agreed and told Reginald Leeper to get hold of the Archibishop and Papandreou at once and bring them to the Ajax, which was lying just outside the harbour and was where Churchill and Eden were to stay. There was no delay though the Archbishop was in bed, that being the only warm place he had. Churchill and Eden were driven to their quarters but not before the Prime Minister had noted that Kalamachi Airfield was guarded by 2000 British airmen 'all well-armed and active'.

The Archbishop on going on board the Ajax had to run the gauntlet of the crew's Christmas night fancy dress party. They, not knowing of any visitors, thought him one of themselves and danced gleefully round the tall figure in his episcopal hat. Once this embarrassing incident was explained away the meeting went very well, Mr Churchill instantly appreciating the great quality of the Archbishop. The Conference was fixed for the following day, to take place at the Greek Foreign Office.

(65) See Osbert Lancaster: 'Classical Landscape', p. 74.

Major Tom Harrison the Brigade Major of the 28th Infantry Brigade arranged the next morning, Boxing Day for an armoured truck to take Mr Churchill to the inaugural meeting. The steel-sided truck looked, said Reginald Leeper, like a grey Black Maria. Churchill records that before he got in he said to his private secretary, Jock Colville

Where is your pistol? and when he said he had not got one I scolded him for I certainly had my own. In a few minutes while we were crowding into our steel box, he said 'I have got a Tommy gun.' 'Where did you get it from' I asked. 'I borrowed it from the driver' he replied. 'What is *he* going to do?' I asked 'He will be busy driving,' was the reply.

What Churchill may have forgotten or just did not think worth writing down, was that after driving about a quarter of a mile through Athens with small-arms fire rattling off the sides of the 'box' those in front heard a great thumping from behind and a cry of 'let me out'. Winston insisted on going in front and drove through Athens with his pistol cocked ready to fire back at any who fired at him. Nor did he mention it in the telegram, which, since he felt penitent about having left her on Christmas Eve, he sent Mrs Churchill; he said instead

H.M.S. is very comfortable and one can get a good view of the fighting in North Piraeus at quite short range . . . I went into the Embassy . . . and I addressed all the plucky women on the Embassy staff who have been in continued danger and discomfort for so many weeks . . . Mrs Leeper is an inspiration to them

.   .   .

The conference was intensely dramatic . . . Thanks were proposed with many compliments to us for coming, by the Greek Government and supported by ELAS representative, who added reference to Great Britain 'our Great Ally' – all this with guns firing at each other not so far away.

After some consideration I shook ELAS delegate's hand, and it was clear from their response that they were gratified. . . . We have now left them together, as it was a Greek show. It may break up at any moment.

And so it probably would have done under any one else but Archbishop Damaskinos was a very great man; a great leader, a champion of the oppressed, fearless whether he was facing the Germans or condemning the atrocities of his own people. He was deeply spiritual and all who knew him honoured him.

Though in this case it was hardly relevant the Greeks have a great respect for their priests. They have looked to them for leadership on many occasions and it is they who have kept the national spirit alive.

Padre Lees was made aware of this respect whilst with the prisoners and hostages whom ELAS had taken. When the looting of watches, and of such things as the British had with them, occurred, he had only to say *'Ego Papas'* and it stopped. And there was a Greek hostage with his party who borrowed his surplice, and did not wish to give it up again, — even when needed for its proper use, — so that the planes overhead which might be thinking of bombing him would take him for a priest and aim at someone else. (66)

Churchill and Eden flew home on the 29th and spent the whole evening and until 4.30 a.m. the next morning, with the Greek King. No one, it is acknowledged, save Churchill, could have persuaded him to name the Archbishop as Regent. Churchill did and so enabled peace to be restored in a very few days.

Indeed 'our statesmen' had done all they could — Christopher ended this letter he had begun that Christmas Day with this paragraph,

All this Greek business must seem very flea-bitish and annoying to you in England, when there are so many more important things happening on the Western Front. But as they fill a much larger part of my mind I could not keep them out of this letter.

Seeing the terrible misery of the people, and also the death of some of my friends at close quarters, has had the obvious effect on me, as, apart from the Blitz this is my first experience of war. The danger part was quite a relief by comparison.

The apologia was not necessary. It was the way Churchill saw it too;

When three million men were fighting on either side on the Western Front, and vast American forces were deployed against Japan in the Pacific, the spasms of Greece may seem petty, but nevertheless they stood at the nerve-centre of power, law, and freedom in the Western World. (67)

Winston had done his best; it was not his fault if Greece in the future would be ruled not by democracy but by military oligarchy.

.   .   .

On 11 January 1945 the Truce was signed and shortly after that Christopher paid a visit to the troops in Salonika. He wrote to us after he had returned to Athens, on 27 January,

The place is certainly looking a good deal healthier and we seem to have got very well out of the affair on the whole. Our prisoners are due back today, and great entertainment schemes are being laid on; perhaps I may see Billy over here in his professional capacity.

I envied very much Patrick's description of the yule-log and the

(66) Lees, op. cit.
(67) Op. cit., p. 283.

cellar; unlike him I have always been a confirmed Christmas orgier; but he, too, I suspect in the face of five firmly festive infants, will sooner or later, like Scrooge, have to alter his outlook and make a virtue of necessity.

I was most excited to get a letter from David Cochrane about the Danestone Trust, (68) and was so inflated with pride, that I showed it to all my companions, with the result, I fear, that I shall have to stand drinks all round for some time to come. The Greek wines are of a very mixed quality. The Macedonian struck me as very poor but the Cretan was just the opposite: it was superlative and made me think of Keat's 'Beaker full of the warm south, Full of the true, the blushful Hippocrene.' The wine of Samos is good too, but very sweet and not sparkling like the Cretan. The Athenian wine is peculiar to Attica, it is called 'Retsina' because they line the inside of the barrel with pine-resin to give its distinctive flavour: the ordinary poor Athenian drinks nothing else, and once you get used to it it is very palatable and comparatively inocuous.

Salonika is rather a grim place though on the rare occasions when the sun was shining, one got most tantalising glimpses of the distance — Olympus on one side, and the Holy Mountain (Mt Athos) on the other. Since I came here I have been doing quite a strenuous conversion course from Ancient to Modern Greek, and now know enough to make conversation with peasants, artisans, etc., quite possible and interesting. Thanks largely to Churchill the British now enjoy, south of Olympus, an almost terrifying prestige. I must say I think that all things considered, he is the greatest statesman that has been born into the world for a long, long time. (69)

After this it was nearly five weeks till we heard from Christopher again. During the intervening time he had seen Billy 'in his professional capacity'; Billy had got a job as producer in a company called 'Stars in Battledress' which was made up of actors and actresses temporarily released from the Forces, which came to Athens for three weeks to entertain the troops. Billy produced Terence Rattigan's 'While the Sun Shines', which Christopher greatly enjoyed. He wrote about this and said as well that he himself had very little work to do —

the only problems being those presented by people who want to get married to Greek girls or vice versa.

He wrote too,

I paid a visit to Eleusis the other day — this being the right time of the year for the performance of the Mysteries — travelling along the Sacred Way past Salamis. The actual grove and temple etc., of Demeter are spoilt by complete neglect and by noisy surroundings,

(68) The Danestone Trust, so called after Christopher's grandfather's house, near Aberdeen; it was the Trust in which 'Black Jock' had tied up his daughters' money (see p. 4). The legacy about which the Crombie family lawyer David Cochrane had written came from Fanny's share.
(69) 27 January 1945, from Athens to Madeleine.

but the scenery and sea-scapes on the way were wonderful. I find myself very hampered by not remembering anything of my Greek History. (70)

He had written this on 1 March and then no letter came until one he posted on 24 April which contained a most intriguing description of another visit to Salonika.

I had to pay a visit to Salonika this month, and thought it would be fun to go there by automobile, as the roads, though bad had just been declared open. So set off in a Dodge with one companion. It certainly was fun, at least in retrospect. The high spots were — Delphi and the Castalian Gorge — the Pass near Thermopylae — and the valley between Olympus and the Pierian mountains where we were 4000 feet above sea-level with patches of snow by the roadside. We loitered on the way up, spending three nights in little villages. Then, after finishing what had to be done in Salonika, came rushing back in a hurry, as my companion (the C. of E. Chaplain) had to be back to meet the Archbishop of York. Then occurred a clear case of more Hurry less Speed. We switched onto the wrong road from Larissa, the one to Volos instead of Lamia, and did not realise the mistake until 40 miles of shocking road had been covered. Rather than face return by two bumpy sides of a triangle, we tried to cut across by a rough track to Pharsala. About a kilometre from a respectable side-road a muddy stream presented itself. The rear port wheel just failed to clear by an inch or two, we had no spade, and the nearest village was in the hills three miles away. Mules and donkeys failed to get us clear because their traces kept breaking. It being now evening, we tossed up and my companion set off on the fifteen mile walk to Pharsala. I remained with the car being regaled by passing shepherds with bread and wine and detailed and contradictory descriptions of where we OUGHT to have crossed. The following afternoon I was glad to see a great recovery waggon with cranes etc. looming up on the horizon but imagine the abrupt change in my emotions when I saw it bowl slap into the thickest part of another stream. The crew, a feckless pair, (though I say it myself) had come out without their necessary hauling kit. Another twenty-four hours were then spent watching the changing light on the hills where the Argonauts hewed their timber, till at one o'clock a third automobile arrived and pulled out the second which then pulled out us. At the precise moment when we quitted the ditch with a loud 'sluck', the Archbishop of York was sitting down to lunch with all the senior officers of the R.A.F. suddenly gone religious and commenting in shocked undertones on the absence of the requisite chaplain.

Your countryside must be looking very lovely now. There is a complete absence of song birds here, and in general of fresh greenery. (71)

Christopher left Greece on his birthday, 30 May at the behest, he said of conscience though with great reluctance,

(70) 1 March 1945, from Athens to Madeleine.
(71) 24 April 1945, from Athens to Madeleine.

for there really was no work left to do. But *what* an interesting time it was there. (72)

He went to Foggia about which he had harsh things to say. He had lost most of his possessions getting there; his kit was stolen, his typewriter smashed. His only clothes now were Khaki drill,

> 4 August 1945
> So I dont know what I will come back to England in. Trivial but annoying was the loss of a collection of bedroom slippers which marked the stages in my Phoenician-like trail of wanderings.
> Foggia is the dustbowl of S.Italy and rivals the coast towns of Sierra Leone and Liberia for squalor. A Norman Duke, Manfred, founded it in reparation for some crime or other, and then hastily abandoned it giving rise to the Italian proverb: Fuggi da Foggia — Flee from Foggia. It was 109 deg. in the shade, (such shade as exists) yesterday with a furnace wind making merry sport with the garbage in the side streets. But suddenly, in winter, the wind will cut to the bone and the fine grey dust that now chokes everything will become glutinous and impenetrable mud. History to compensate for nature's cruelty bequeathed it one advantage namely insignificance. But now that has been ruthlessly torn away by five years of trampling troops and screeching armaments. But one real advantage it still has, bequeathed not by history but by history's Buffoon, poor upside-down Mussolini; formerly Foggia must have been Hell indeed, 25 years ago, when it was surrounded by marshes and water was sold in the streets, but now the marsh is a wide golden plain dotted with thousands of ex-fascist farms which can feed half Italy, and a mighty acqueduct, a real masterpiece, brings cold clear water from the Apennines to every house in Foggia.

And Christopher ended this letter with glad news,

> A good thing is that Fr Martin D'Arcy has just been elected our Provincial, i.e. Boss.

He wrote again on 25 August to say that he would have to remain in Foggia for another month or more.

> There wont be anybody to take my place here till the end of September. It leaves me with an absolutely ideal opportunity for sight-seeing in October-November, for my worthy Principal Chaplain is so relieved at my agreeing to stay over my time without undue protest, that he is prepared to give me an air-movement permit almost any where I want. But, alas, I have no more desire to sight-see than to eat cold pork fat. I think it would be unendurable to the point of tears to visit Assisi, or Fiesole, or Venice or the Tyrol, and find them as they are, pestered and plastered with Naafis and Notices and Military Police and Venereal Treatment Centres and Compulsory Educational Tours. (Music Appreciation for the following at 17.30 hours .... Disciplinary action will be taken

(72) 14 July 1945, from Foggia to Madeleine.

against those failing to attend — ran a notice in our Orders yesterday; and no one seemed to see anything odd about it.)

Christopher came home by way of Rome — 'the most Naafied of the lot', and reached England towards the end of November. He spent most of his leave with us at West Wick, and since he was allowed some petrol for it — it had of course been strictly rationed and used only for the most necessary journeys ever since we had been in Wiltshire — we were able with this aid to explore the unknown 'towns and places of Wessex' together. Then of course came demobilisation:

4 January 1946, Hednesford, Staffs.
I am in the last and worst of R.A.F. Transit Camps, sleeping 20 in a chilly hut, elbowing for food etc. In point of fact it is not a bad place, and the harassed officials do their best. But after my month of bliss in Wiltshire, it came as rather a horrid revulsion: and all sorts of small things, scraps of conversation etc, aroused quite unexpected antipathy in me.
If all goes well I will be back in London tomorrow evening. They havent charged me for my lost equipment which is nice of them.

In London he put his gratuity through the letter-box of Mrs Douglas Woodruff's (73) Office for the Relief of Refugees.

'Thursday's Bairn' had gone far and now this particular odyssey was over.

(73) Mrs Woodruff has run the C.W.L. office for refugees since its inception, having worked in Italy during the war — she is now also vice-chairman of the Standing Conference of British Organisations for Aid to Refugees, and vice-chairman of B.C.A.R. and she was on the Oxfam Council.

PART THREE

PEACETIME ENGLAND

1
ST BEUNO'S

Christopher had spent the months after his return temporarily attached to the staff of the big Jesuit church in London known as Farm Street. He was waiting to do the delayed last lap of his Jesuit training. This period, known as the Tertianship, was proposed by St Ignatius for the members of the Society so that 'at the very end of their training, when they have given great care and diligence to schooling the mind (in the course of their studies) they should give even greater care to schooling the heart.' (1)

Hopkins had longed intensely for this opportunity to rid himself of the scars made by the disappointments and failures of the three years which had passed since his ordination. He went to do it at Manresa in 'the still rural solitude of Roehampton.' Writing from there to his friend Canon Dixon, he said:

It lasts ten months. We see no newspapers nor read any but spiritual books. In Lent we go out and give retreats and so on; beyond that *in eremo sumus* . . . my mind is more at peace than it has ever been. (2)

At the end of the time he was 'emotionally and intellectually flooded with light' and with 'his own special insight into the mind and heart of God' (3) The Tertianship begins with the Long, or Thirty Day retreat, which is also made in the Noviceship — 'St Ignatius's *Spiritual Exercises* is the handbook used for those engaged in this energetic activity.' (4) For Christopher it was a time of catharsis followed by a new welling up of religious thought. He had come to the Tertianship after seven years of useful work and needed time, too, to get rid of scars — scars which had been made by his

(1) 'The Training of a Jesuit, The Tertianship' by Fr John Coventry, S.J.
(2) 'Letters of G.M.H.' edited Abbott, O.U.P. 1935, p. 69, letter of 11-12 October 1881.
(3) 'Sermons and Devotional Writings of G.M.H.' edited Devlin, Introduction, p. 107.
(4) 'New Translation Spiritual Exercise' by Fr Thomas Corbishley, S.J., Burns & Oates, 1963.

close experience of the violence and hatred and the myriad miseries of war and civil war. It was in September that he went, not to Roehampton, but to St Beuno's, at St Asaph in North Wales — this was where Hopkins had done his Theology, and there he would read Scotus from the same books which Hopkins had used. That same month he began the all-important Long Retreat; as soon as it ended he started to write his long poem. He wrote in a letter of 9 February:

I have now written 654 lines of my narrative poem, and I am still somewhat short of the half-way mark. Do you think there is a man alive in England today who could make the same boast? Fortunately I should surmise not.

It is a poem on a different plane from the light Elizabethan songs or the pieces heavy with Hopkins imitation, which he had written up to 1941. He called it 'Of Seven Cities' and he planned it as 'a modern Odyssey of Man', in seven cantos, of which the 654 lines make up the first three. The first Canto, The City of the Sphinx had for its theme, man in the servile state; the second, The City of the Songhai, the valley of captivity; and the third, the City of Kurana, brought the hope of the Ephiphany. (5)

In these three cantos, amidst the tales which were the vehicle of his purpose, he ranged backwards and forwards amongst the memories of his experiences and lifted, once or twice, the veil which normally he kept drawn over his own spiritual intuition.

First he purged himself of his minor bogies. Now, with his tongue in his cheek, he translated into verse

> Back on trailing footsteps to the Adjutant . . . Where is the
> Movements Book, please?
>
> 'Hail Sphinx and Goddess', said I 'give me please
> Facilities to explore the mysteries
> As per my movement order herewith signed'.
> I waited. Sand gritted. And wind whined.
> A strange a sphingial shudder hit the air,
> Dinted it cringing, glinted in her stare'.
>
> I am the Ant-heap, span of man's extent,
> The room that he's rent for, doom he's meant
> For, origin and term of his ascent.
> Blessed the hearts that hope not and the eyes
> That ask no questions and are told no lies'.
> She stamped my passport, nodded, and I went.

Only the derivation of the name of the second city is hard to find, the first of course coming from Egypt. Songhai seems most probably

(5) For the derivation of the names of these cities see the next page.

to have been taken from the Tribe of Songhoi (or Sonrhay) of which Christopher would probably have heard in his travels when,

covering the whole coast of West Africa and a little more, from 17 deg. West to 32 deg. East

as was noted earlier. (6) The Songhoi formed a distinct state and were the most powerful nation in the Western Sudan from the eighth to the sixteenth century; after that they lost their national independence. (7) Kurana is, of course, the Greek name for Cyrene, the ruined city by which Christopher was greatly attracted and from that source it came naturally to him to use Kyr as lord and Kura as the lord's wife; from the Greek κύριος (lord), κυρία (lady).

These stanzas were the comic relief which he placed before the terrible memories which he was about to impale in verse — memories of planes hurtling from the sky, memories of sudden death on airfields, in the desert, in the street:

> No warning, half-rolled first, scraped second, spun
> With splintering wing-tip in and out between,
> Till tail up-ended, nose bit the ravine
>
> .   .   .
>
> A steel-white fire, the crashing kite — Peter!
> His gloved hands splintered on the choking stick
> The crimson snow-flakes falling fast and thick.

To this horrifying memory of friends and penitents — the men whose confessions he had heard before they flew — from the days of the Battle of Britain to the planes that flew in Greece, he added still

> I tried to bury Peter but he broke,
> Then with tears I'll wash you, blood with salt
>
> .   .   .
>
> He came to pieces in my hands. But, look,
> I loved him, look, I kiss his crumpled disc.
>
> .   .   .

But 'God would have me merry' he had written amongst his spiritual notes at Heythrop and so now the happy memories, things of which he had written in his letters and 'novel' when he was in Africa he turned as well into verse. First, the primitive episode he had described in his letter of 14 June 1944 from Gambut; (8)

> I hunted with the men, great starting buck
> And shy gazelle, and always with fresh zeal

(6) On p. 46.
(7) From the 'Encyclopaedia Britannica'.
(8) See p. 60.

Hailed the ecstatic moment of the kill,
And when we peeled and stuck the quivering meat
To cook in ashes, then with rough humility
they always preferred me the best to eat.

Peace and loveliness were to have their place — the loveliness of Cyrenica, of which the capital, Cyrene, had been called KURANA by the Greeks when they founded the city in the seventh century B.C. (9) He began his Canto, 'The City of Kurana', thus:

A dusty line in the Inane Vast
Between the sky and land, widened at last;
A single tree was standing, hoisted sign
Of order out of chaos . . .

A road and grass and evergreens, the blush
Of vineyards on the rock, and nestling fruit,
And, O, compendious answer to all hopes,
Sheer out of nowhere, pointing down the slopes,
A torrent like a sword in high salute.

Towards the end of this third canto his mind travelled back to homely things, to the beginning of the war, to his first winter in Wales and his welcome at Pen-y-lan:

The Kura, from the kitchen, glided out,
Aloof, but pleased to see me, moved about
Preparing with excuses for its poverty
A welcome that to me seemed wildest luxury.

.   .   .

I loved them much (the Kyr and Kura — i.e. Charlie and Aileen)
And soon discovered how each checked the other
The Kura though so practical had dreams

.   .   .

The Kyr whose own temptation was a wandering star (10)

.   .   .

In youth he had voyaged fearlessly and far.

And with the past Christopher mingled the present in his descriptions

I went within the cave where the spring rose
And watched the beryl waters open and close
A deep diversion in their welling-up
Had shaped the rock floor like a cinquefoil cup.

He had written of St Winifred's Well, as it is called, in a letter in December from St Beuno's,

(9) See p. 59.
(10) Charlie Meade is a well-known mountaineer, a former vice-President of the Alpine Club.

I walked over the other day. It is certainly a most remarkable sight; an enormous quantity of water comes bubbling up from underground beryl-clear and continual. The mediaevals have built a shapely cinquefoil basin with arches to contain it.

Hopkins had also seen the Well with delight. (11) He wrote of it to Robert Bridges, in answer to a letter from him:

Who was St Beuno? Is he dead? Yes, he did that much 1200 years ago. He was St Winifred's uncle and raised her to life when she died in the defence of her chastity and at the same time called out her famous spring which fills me with devotion each time I see it and would fill any one that has eyes with admiration the flow ἀγλαὸν ὕδωρ is so lavish and beautiful.

It is difficult whilst thinking of Christopher's time in the Tertianship not to think of Hopkins's too — the effect on both was somewhat the same. Had Hopkins lived to a ripe old age Christopher could have known him, yet, had he met him would he have understood him any better than in fact he did? It is a great pity that owing to various·difficulties Christopher was prevented from writing more about his life than was relevant to his introductions to Hopkins's *Sermons and Devotional Writing*. (12) Because of their common adherence to Scotus he understood him as perhaps no one else, contemporary or not, has yet done. It was said of Hopkins — and quoted by Christopher, — 'as a theologian his undoubted brilliance was dimmed by a somewhat obstinate love of Scotus Doctrine'. (13) The same 'obstinate love' brought Christopher into disrepute too, at Heythrop of course but probably in Rome too, when he was doing his Theology, for though the trend today is towards Scotism, not only Hopkins, but even Christopher was well ahead of his time in devotion to his doctrine.

In the Long Retreat of his Tertianship, Christopher, like Hopkins drew his inspiration from the Great Sacrifice, (14) on which both, following their mentor, pitched their future thought, with this difference — Hopkins's thought played mostly around the Cross, Christopher's, whose nature was gay, played — right to the last days of his life, in fact then, especially, around the Stable. In his narrative poem there is clear reference to the light which had come to Christopher. For example, in Canto iii,

> I woke next morning on a tide of light
> A wave of thought that from original night

(11) He planned a drama in verse called St Winifred's Well and wrote a little, of what Christopher said might have been a classic today had he not abandoned it.

(12) See p. 101 and supra.

(13) P. xiii of the 'Sermons and Devotional Writings of G.M.H.'

(14) For an explanation of the Great Sacrifice see ibid. pp.107-109.

Welled-up unbroken, so intensely white
As is the first begot of Being Infinite

.   .   .

As looking for the spring I tip-toe trod
A baffling message stirred the woods around
'The Word of God, it is the Word of God.'

Some stanzas earlier in the same Canto lay bare the heart of Christopher's future tenet and teaching

... Feeling (Vision and Desire)
Must from the countryside of sense retire,
And raze the very arx and citadel
Of arch-original and trembling self;

Must drown abandoned in abounding blight
And drop, drop down into perpetual night,
Lose sight for ever of the luminous surge
That tugs the soul towards the infinite verge
Of incommunicably-sealed delight
Whose utter absence is its only urge.

He wrote the same thing to Aileen, ten years later but in prose,

You must withdraw your hands from groping after all the other things you hoped to do and spread them upwards towards God instead, letting them proclaim your emptiness and nothingness — emptiness and nothingness being the pre-requisites for receiving anything of value from Him.

In this hall of mirrors in which we live, we are haunted by innumerable images of what we might have been. But somewhere there is a door that opens to the wide air of Heaven. And if we have the courage to gaze out of it occasionally into the blank unknown, and admit that it (or He) *is* unknown and unknowable, yet Trusted — then we get a little peace — enough to go on with.

The seeds of much more were sown at St Beuno's which would flower later — like Christopher's insistence on personal integration with the Liturgy (15) and the relevance of the doctrine of the Great Sacrifice to possible life on another planet — none of which need detain us now; but there is one more curiously personal matter which must be mentioned. The four further cantos of the narrative poem were never written. The muse which had shot up like the desert plant which year by year puts out leaves and then one year shoots up a flower and dies — died like the desert flower it was. Christopher revised a few stanzas but after 1949 never touched the

(15) To encourage this is one of the reasons for the recent insistence on having the Liturgy in the Vernacular.

poem again, nor after that did he ever seriously write poetry. Years later he gave the reason saying that he had come to realise that writing poetry as it should be written in the twentieth century was incompatible with his Vocation; but there is no getting around the fact that, without his Vocation, there would have been no verse worthy of notice. He turned entirely to prose.

2

BEAUMONT: *'MUNDUS PUERILIS'*

Every Jesuit, Christopher thought, after a decade or more of preparation might reasonably hope for a career in religion which would 'liberate his energies and exploit his talents to the best advantage "for the glory of God" ' (16) In West Africa he had realised that he had great love and ability for mission work among the black people. (17) The last time they were in touch, lunching together in Cairo in 1945, Richard Barnett had received the impression that Christopher was to be sent to 'Darkest Africa' as soon as he was released from the R.A.F. Christopher surely said that that was his hope. And he must, of course have told his Superiors of it when he returned to England. They knew too, of hs desire to write and of his early reputation as a philosopher. Only one of them had glimpsed the depths of his tenderness — towards children of all kinds and towards the Africans — and thought of the toughness which had driven him whilst in the airforce on all sorts of journeys, using his leaves, even, to tramp through the desert, without any other compulsion except the fire that burned so fiercely within to go in search of souls. The others and also his friends and later his advanced pupils saw in him the scholar, the poet, the litterateur; and at that time it was thought impossible to combine the two desires. Fr D'Arcy, 'the Boss' well knew of his great ability as a writer — having taught him he knew of it better than any one else, — and so, at the end of the Tertianship — Christopher took his Final Vows at Candlemas, 2 February 1948, — it was decided that he should go back to teaching at Beaumont and that he should write in his spare time.

That the decision not to send him to the missions was a grave disappointment to Christopher can be judged by an incident which is remembered by Fr Robert Gorman, S.J., who knew Christopher quite well though they were not close friends. Christopher left St Beuno's on 17 July and after giving some Retreats went to the Farm

(16) Introduction to 'Sermons and Devotional Writings of G.M.H.', p. xiii.
(17) See letter p. 149.

Street Church to supply during the August holidays and till the autumn term would begin at Beaumont. Fr Gorman had to catch a train at Victoria station and he had a very heavy bag to carry. Christopher insisted on helping him with it even as far as the platform. It was whilst on the platform that Fr Gorman, making conversation, asked him whether he would like it if he were to be permanently on the staff of the London church. He caught Christopher, it seems, off his guard, for to his surprise, for he was not in any position to give effect to Christopher's desires, he says, 'Fr Devlin took my conversational lead very seriously, and said, with a slight hesitation in his speech — a thing one had noticed before when he was much moved — "I would give anything to go back to Africa". I asked him why and with a distant look and then a smile he said, "I can never forget Africa as I knew it in the war" '. This seems to have been the only time that he showed his feelings; thereafter he appeared to remember only that he had thought of Beaumont with nostalgia when he had been in West Africa, and once he had returned to the School he buried any other desire he had had very deeply, so deeply that in time it became something that he had wanted to do — like going to Oxford — that had not been 'in his stars'. Half-way through the first term back he wrote in a letter to us,

I am completely immersed once more in the 'Mundus Puerilis' It is quite a good life and Beaumont is a very civilised place. (18)

He would have been immensely shocked and saddened had he known when he was there, that Beaumont would have only another twenty years of life. Where there was so much else for the Jesuits to do, as in Rhodesia, he did think that the Society paid too dearly for educating the sons of the upper classes and so he would have sympathised with the other commitments which caused the closing of the school. But of this small school, — there were never more than 270 boys at any one time, which could:

regularly produce an Eleven fit for Lords and an Eight for Henley, 'Vril' — (the school magazine), scholars, priests, officers, boxers, and Queen's Scouts. (19)

he was as proud as he was of the fact that the school entrusted the writing of the history of its first hundred years to one who had on occasion been to his classes and who, he surely rightly thought, wrote superb English. There are those who say it was a waste of Christopher's talents that he was kept as a schoolmaster for so long, but if he contributed anything to any of his pupils, and there is evidence that he did from several of them, his time was not

(18) 7 November, from Beaumont.
(19) 'Beaumont', Peter Levi, S.J., Andre Deutsch, 1961, p. 66.

misspent. His own words in proof of this have already been twice quoted. (20)

As a matter of fact his success as a master had been assured, before his talent was shown, from the first, for it was somehow generally known, that as boy at Stonyhurst he had been publicly beaten (he himself refused to beat any boy). He was a humorous teacher with a biting wit, who was capable of losing his temper without losing his dignity; he would blow up like King Lear in a blistering outburst, or he seemed like Mephistopheles, rising through the floor to his Mephistophelean eyebrows. None of this is remembered by his pupils with rancour but rather with affection and admiration, the outbursts occurring as they did, when boys had failed to turn up when or where they should have done. Though there was also an occasion, specially remembered because it was quite terrifyingly against authority, when Christopher was taking some of the seniors on an outing and had been refused the customary permission for them to smoke.

When he returned to Beaumont in 1947 it was as head of the English Department, though to his own class, the boys taking O Levels, who formed a group round him known as Syntax, he would also teach other subjects such as Religious Doctrine and History. He taught only twenty periods a week, instead of the more usual twenty-five so that he should have time for writing, but in addition he ran the school debating society and was in charge of all stage productions — plays were a great feature of Beaumont life. Extraordinary requests for 'props' came in his letters.

Madeleine, — have you a piece of old silk (or rayon? or nylon?) stockings which you could spare ... the boys who are doing the female parts dont seem to have any sisters.

and

I wonder if you have a FAN of the ordianry open-and-shut kind lying about the house. It is my misfortune to be doing the 'School for Scandal' next week-end; and at the last moment I find great difficulty in hiring or even buying fans — something to do with Japan I gather.

Billy was coming down to Beaumont to help with his play rehearsals but

unfortunately a B.B.C. thing intervened. We are doing 'Loyalties' — not very interesting or attractive but I had to think of something to suit the actors.

This letter ended with the mention of another activity which must have been light entertainment after Greece.

(20) Pp. 37 and 43.

I have been given a badge for attending ten Civil Defence Lectures and/or squirting water.

His industry was prodigious for he would have religious duties, which would take up at least an hour and a half of the day, in addition to his teaching, yet almost as soon as he arrived he began to pour out a stream of articles and reviews; the articles were many of them, of course, studies in some way connected with the two major works which were published in his lifetime, though actually in the first two years at Beaumont he spent more time on a third — on Scotus and Hopkins — which owing to various vicissitudes is yet to come.

Many of his writings were published in 'The Month' and he wrote scores of hasty notes and quasi-illegible post cards to the Editor, Fr Philip Caraman, S.J., as to how he did or did not want them printed. Some were really peremptory — despite which Fr Caraman counted him among his friends,

Here is my Topcliffe article red hot. If you dont want it yet or if you want footnotes, sources etc., put in, you can let me have it back.

Other editors were less accommodating; he wrote to us

In my spare time I am wrestling with an article on Hamlet which I hope to get published in the 'Review of English Studies'.

a little later he wrote us

a ticklish correspondence is going on about my revised Hamlet (21) article. I don't know whether they are going to publish it or not. I think they ought to personally.

But most of his letters to us at this time were written either just before he was coming to stay, and, if so, were about trains or, after he had been, to thank us and tell us what he had left behind

alas, despite great circumspection I have left behind (a) my rosary, (b) my pipe.

or on another occasion,

Our turkeys are in fine and glossy condition. (22) Yesterday morning looking from my window, I saw a pair of ears in the middle of the pond where there is a pediment with a fountain playing. Incredulous I went down to see and found it was what I thought — a fox! It had come for the turkeys, fallen in the pond and, unable to climb out of the steep basin, was shivering to death beneath the

(21) First published Rupert Hart-Davis, 1962, 'Hamlet's Divinity'.
(22) At Beaumont when Fr Clifford was Rector there was a fine farm with geese in the playground, pigs in the orchard, cows everywhere, and turkeys on the lawn. 'Beaumont', p. 63.

fountain. It met its death with great calm and dignity. A .22 bullet in the head, and dropping its head on its paws, but without any further movement, it died.

I think I left the Bird (musician) book behind. Perhaps you could bring it to London sometime. (23)

Christopher needed to know about Bird (musician) — William Byrd — for one of the chapters in his Life of Robert Southwell. It was indeed in a letter planning a visit to West Wick — he used to come for a few days at Christmas, and for his summer holiday, both times, of course, taking over some of the duties of our local priests, — that he first told us of the Life he had decided to write.

Will you collect together your Shakespeare lore, as I am writing a life of Southwell and some interesting connections are occuring.

He wrote this in December 1947 when he had been at Beaumont for a term; but it illustrates something which his training-college students noticed later on, that he assumed others to have a critical faculty equal to his own; his students he would send on fact finding expeditions to libraries and museums which later they suspected were for their benefit rather than his own. He took us with him, the children scurrying to keep up, as he tried to catch the echoes of Southwell's footsteps through the city of London, following his journeys from the Strand to Clerkenwell, to the sites of the Clink and the dreaded Marshalsea and even as far as 'Uxendon' which is called Preston today and is just beyond the point where the Bakerloo and the Metropolitan lines separate. When we walk in the city now many fascinating and sinister characters of Shakespeare's day live for us still.

One letter of thanks in 1949 contained a sonnet — a translation from the French set by one of the newspapers as a Christmas competition; alas that he did not compete.

I tinkered about with the sonnet on the way back, trying to make it a closer rendering, and I'm afraid rather spoilt it, making it neither one thing nor the other. I have typed it so that you can compare it with the prize-winning version when it appears on January 23rd.

> Here fell young Icarus whose daring spring
> Sundered the terrors of the vast inane
> Whose tumbled body torn from either wing
> Leaves all true hearts with envy sore astrain.
>
> O happy spirit whose impetuous fling
> Has bought the future for a moment's pain
> O happy victim whose defeat will bring
> Such centuries of triumph in its train.

(23) 30 August 1948, from Beaumont to Madeleine.

So strange a road found youth no less brave
When power failed him courage mounted higher
As dauntless soared he to the fairest fire,
So dauntless dived he, burning to the wave

The sea for tomb and heaven for desire:
Could fairer destiny find softer grave?

Once he wrote a longer letter; it was about his concern for Aunt Ellie. She alone amidst the older generation of close blood relatives survived. Christopher had been allowed by the Society to give her his legacy from the Danestone Trust — about which he had been so excited to hear when he was in Greece. Writing from Beaumont to Patrick he said

Aunt Ellie who appears to have been undergoing a chapter of accidents, said that illness had prevented her from seeing you, and that she had been going to consult you about willing back to the Jesuits the money which I left her when I took my last vows. I have an awful fear that the money (about 3 or 4 thousand) instead of easing out her old age as it was meant to, may prove a burden and a worry, and that she may end up by making no use of it being so intent on returning as much of it as possible! I wonder, if she does consult you, whether you could impress on her the necessity of spending boldly if the opportunity offers without worrying as to how much she will leave. I *have* told her this myself.

I would like it to be clear that there is no expectation on the part of the Society. I mean, if she leaves nothing, there will be no disappointment, because nobody except me, knows that she ever had any intention of leaving any. Of course, on the other hand money would be very welcome and I would hate to put any obstacles in the way of her leaving it to the Society. Only I do think at the moment the important question is how to spend it rather than how to leave it. (24)

Ellie died, the money unspent, during the spring term of 1949. Christopher had been to see her as often as he could. She was a brave and beautiful woman.

Christopher's admiration for Fr Martindale never ceased; he wrote to him from West Wick in the summer holidays of the next year, 1950, a letter which Fr Martindale kept, for it was found among his papers by his biographer, Fr Philip Caraman thirteen years later; Christopher had said,

Dear Father,
I got hold of 'The Secret of Fatima' (25) just before leaving Beaumont. It was like a detective story, I could not put it down before I had finished it! Somehow or other you managed to convey the extreme probability of Our Lady's intervention in spite of the

(24) Easter Monday (26 March), 1948, from Beaumont to Patrick.
(25) The title is 'The Message of Fatima'.

conventional 'apparition trappings' which with rather suspicious ready-made effect, have enveloped the devotion since then.

I think the effect was achieved (i) by your vigorous presentation of the time-sequence, and your delicate goading of bits of evidence. (ii) by not glossing over any difficulties and at the same time your anticipating the ordinary rationalist and psycho-objections, without going out of your way to attack them. (iii) Perhaps most of all by your sketching of the peasant background, especially the character of the uncle and the little boy. At any rate I concluded the book somewhat disturbed about Lucia's personal contribution to the devotion but quite convinced that a rather terrifying message had been received from Heaven about the need for Purity of Heart.

Yours ever in Xt

Christopher Devlin, S.J.

The next year, 1951, Christopher left Beaumont; he was being sent to Roehampton instead, where it was thought that he would have more time for working on his book. He spent the summer holidays with us, as usual, and then went to Wardour, a Jesuit parish some thirty miles away but still in Wiltshire, to make his own annual retreat, and from there he journeyed back once more to Manresa.

3

ROEHAMPTON

In the quarter of a century which had passed since Christopher first went there, Roehampton had almost completed the change from the rural solitude of Hopkins's time to the urbanised garden suburb of today; the wild gardens and trees, which Christopher, too, had loved, and where he had watched the birds circle and swoop and hawks build their nest, had been cleared away and the land left bare for building sites.

I think there will be so many people in these parts (nineteen 11-storey blocks of flats) that the city of London will be a pool of rest

he wrote us soon after he had returned there. And Manresa had changed too, outside as well as in. Writing to Humphry House who was coming to see him there, Christopher said

I must warn you that a drab institutional front has been slapped on the homely carriage drive entrance and the grounds are a shambles waiting for the L.C.C. to build on.

Miss Daisy Moseley, an American historian doing research on Southwell for the children's book she was writing, went to see Christopher too; she noted that the house had been badly blitzed (and that Christopher was a tall and charming man with a diffident

100

manner). In the raid that had caused the damage, a Junior had been killed, and the Juniorate had been moved to Scotland. But Manresa in 1951 was nevertheless crowded, in addition to the Juniorate, which was only abolished in 1958, it housed the third year Philosophers and Scholastics from Heythrop who were doing their Teachers' Training; for Manresa, by this time had become a Training College, recognised by the Department of Education, and a part of London University. Christopher went there to teach with the title of Professor of Pedagogy and English.

He was bored by pedagogy; perhaps he found it tedious to put into words what to him was so obvious. The kernel of his teaching he gave: 'love your boys', and not a scholastic smiled when he said it knowing that nothing sentimental lay behind the saying; after that there was little else he thought necessary to add and during his lectures he would ask repeatedly, 'What's the time?', and the phrase became a catchword. But as an English tutor he was without parallel and his classes were spell-binding. No doubt a trick of the memory, said John Harriott, but in retrospect one remembers them 'as perpetually charged with amusement and delight, the sun always shining outside'.

John Harriott was one of the three young Jesuits, scholastics whom he taught and who came to know Christopher well, but differently as they are finely different themselves. For John Harriott he was the ideal Jesuit; Henry Wardale knew the Missioner; and Peter Levi as a poet knew him intuitively. Christopher — and so Ignatius instructs his followers — had gone in at all doors — particularly though not exclusively, at theirs — but as is also the rule, he had come out again at his own — and hence the variety of their views.

Despite the tutoring and the lecturing doubtless he had more time to himself during the terms than he had at Beaumont, but the terms were shorter and when they ended Christopher was greatly in demand as a retreat-giver and also as a lecturer. So 'Robert Southwell' was not finished for four years; it had taken in all seven years to write, and after 1953 he had other writing to do as well as it was then that Humphry House proposed to bring out a second and revised edition of his Hopkins Journals, in which he would deal in one volume with everything not primarily religious and with a companion volume of Hopkins's spiritual writings, edited by a Jesuit. And for this he wanted Christopher. The Society and Christopher agreed and so while still writing 'Southwell', he began to edit 'The Sermons and Devotional Writings', — all this without any perceptible diminuition of his usual flow of articles and reviews (and postcards to Fr Caraman). Nevertheless these years at Roehampton were years when he found time for friendship. He came into the centre of London, possibly once a week to go to the British Museum or to the Record Office. 'Will you be in Gray's Inn for lunch and if so can I cadge one on Thursday?' — and happy the Thursday when we were there. His letters to us, as from Beaumont, are only of fragmentary interest though sometimes a piece of news of unsuspected import slipped in,

I find that a new Provincial has been elected, Fr Boyle who used to be my Rector at Beaumont.

Or, ever eager to foster and advance any literary interests I had:

You know that you were mentioning that list of householders at Stratford and also Shak's père's recusancy? I forgot that I have in my notes from the Salisbury Papers, date 1592 a list of Stratfordians who excused themselves from attending church: Mr John Wheeler, Mr John Wheeler, his son, Mr John Shakespeare, Mr Nicholas Barnshurst, Thomas James, alias Giles, William Bainton, Richard Harrington, *William Fluellen*! and *George Bardolph*!! Another list includes a Bates, a Page and a Gower —

Certainly this is interesting 'Shakespeare Lore'. Sometimes, too, he wrote about his articles before they were published.

My Ferdinando (26), a short historical detective story, strictly factual is coming out in Jan — Feb — March. I trimmed it up and down a good deal and think it is quite readable.
On another point, Madeleine, would you say 27 miles in 4 hours was *furious* riding or just fast? In a book I am reviewing a nice lady, Elizabeth Vaux is accused of being mixed up in the Gunpowder Plot, because a man rode madly all day from London to bring her news on November 5th. But the evidence is that he only came from St Albans and his pace would then have been seven miles an hour.
I got a book on Glastonbury out and discovered that Martinseye was a place in Somerset. (27) But the book was rather interesting about old farming implements and customs, and there was a nice entry — 'de pane albo qui vocatur BUNNE' — a good ancestry for the bun.

In one letter he related a touching incident

An ex-pupil of mine whom I used to befriend in adversity many years ago, has just come out of prison (!) and sent me £10 in book-tokens. I am bestowing £5 on the library here, and am to spend the other £5 as I wish — so you must choose a book you want. A visit to Bumpus is certainly indicated.

The ex-pupil had been described by Christopher before,

(26) 'The Earl and the Alchemist', published in 'The Month', January, February and March, 1953.
(27) Christopher was trying to discover the meaning of 'Martinsell' which is the name of the hill on the slope of which West Wick House stands.

The boy was the gentlest creature alive, always nursing some secret amusement. I was reading them an expurgated 'Decline and Fall' once and he became quite ill with laughter at the descriptions of prison life.

His friendship with Humphry House went back in correspondence to Heythrop days when Humphry had first consulted him on Scotus, and it had continued mostly by letter, but now, particularly after 1953 he visited him at his home in Cambridge and came away with happy memories of him and of his wife too. He was immensely saddened by Humphry's tragically early death in 1955.

Miss Moseley had returned to America a firm friend for life and a kind one who did valuable research amongst the Southwell papers in New York and sent him the fruits of it. And then, of course, there were the Meades. Charlie and Aileen were frequently in London and so could be visited easily. But once again Christopher managed a short stay at Pen-y-lan, slipping across to North Wales after he had given a retreat at Stonyhurst. After the visit he wrote from Manresa on the 10 April — it was in 1953 —

Dear Aileen,
It would be difficult without incurring the reproach of pomposity or affection — quite so, quite so: It is really difficult to explain how much I enjoyed my stay and profited by it. What I feel chiefly at the moment is that it was a great renewal. When I first stayed with you, 13 or 14 years ago, it was a tremendous experience for me — barr chaff; it set me up in hope and shortened the distance between earth and heaven. And now, this time, everything seemed to conspire to renew that experience. But I cant explain any more without using words like 'symbol' and so on, so must let it stand at that.

And three weeks later, still wrapped in the delight of the visit, he wrote again,

Dear Aileen,
In the grip of insomnia (and indigestion?) the other night, I was visited with a succession of memories which I had perforce to glance at. As each passed, it suddenly sprouted with bitter suggestions that I had never before suspected; hidden motives of my own, forgotten reactions of others, half-remembered nuances of speech and looks came tumbling into the light with an unmistakeable smell of reality; and I capered before myself in livid guises, cravenly incompetent or squalidly absurd, bestially aggressive or vilely hypocritical. Like Macbeth in the witches cave, a procession of images each one more disastrous than the last.

Believe me or not the only image that remained tranquil and unspoilt was that of Pen-y-lan and its inhabitants. Here, in striking contrast to the others, I beheld myself as (relatively) pleasing and self-controlled, well-intentioned and sincere. The reason for this exception was clearly that, in the others I was seeking to dominate the image, here I was allowing its influence to dominate me. I must admit (for I am faithfully relating things as they occurred to me) it was only Pen-y-lan which produced the soothing effect, not other places where I have met you.

I think this elucidates and confirms the impression I have before received from Pen-y-lan. The place has acquired a character from what you have put into it, in the way of effective effort and passive endurance. And the character of the place is simply this: that it brings out the best in people who visit it — at least with sensitive people. It presents them with an ideal of themselves which they cant help trying to live up to.

I thought it might be useful to set this down in writing while it is fairly clear to me, because it may serve as an expression of gratitude, and also, just possibly, it might be of some comfort to you in moments of discouragement.

Re-reading this, I cant think how I had the impertinence to write it. But it is too late to change it now.

Heavenly weather in London the last few days.

Yours affectionately
Christopher Devlin, S.J.

To Charlie, at about the same date there was a letter on the meaning of certain philosophic terms — questions which had arisen in connection with the book Charlie was just finishing —'High Mountains' (28) And this letter was followed — answering a letter from Charlie, — by one on religion which explains much about Christopher's belief.

Dear Charlie,

Thank you very much indeed for your letter which in a way was rather a relief to me, because I have never understood how any one could be led into the Church *by* anyone else — except of course, by some great author like St Augustine or Dante, or except in special circumstances of dependence. I should think that if ever you did become a catholic, it would be in spite of, rather than because of, existing catholics.

I should think that you might become a catholic if you could see how irrelevant are the external four walls of the Church, how little they have to do with the gateway of the Church which opens immediately on the unseen and how many countless individual ways of approach there are to the gate. But until you did see this — or something like this — I dont see how you could honestly become a catholic.

But how can one speculate on these things? God is so *diverse*. One and Many: keeper of morals, vision of beauty, healer of wounds, answer to questions . . . The great discovery, surely, is that God is all these and many more, and yet One.

All a man can do in pain and uncertainty is what he believes to be right by the best standards available. But both before and after that, it is most important to believe that whatever one does, God will accept in the spirit in which it is offered. This is something that it is within one's power to believe, and one should believe it even if one has to force oneself a little to do so. For not to do so is fatally false

(28) 'High Mountains', Harvill Press, 1954.

humility and puts a slight on God's goodness. It is the unwillingness to believe the best of God that puts up the greatest barrier.

I hope you and Aileen got back safely, and that the house has not suffered in your absence, but I expect your daughters kept it warm.

He wrote a little later to Aileen about the progress of 'Southwell'

I slave away but it's difficult. For example — I was away for Holy Week and Easter, and under the influence of new scenery etc. I wrote a rather good death scene, lucid and tense. But on returning to my books I find that some half dozen details are wrong — not very important historically (e.g. it was a sort of cart and not a ladder at the gallows) but terribly important in a sort of pictorial symbolic way; remove or change them and all the linch-pins fall out of the piece of writing. It's rather an ignominious business really trying to balance accuracy and interest, when neither of them are robust enough to stand by themselves. I must get down to it again.

At the end of 1954 however it was finished and went off to Longmans the publishers. Christopher returned to Manresa, having given a retreat after Christmas, to find a large package. He thought:

'What a pile of proofs and how quick' To my horror it was a battered and besmuttered script returned for innumerable corrections. It had been handed over to some terrible old editor, a retired don, who had filled ten foolscap pages with what he called colloquialisms and slang. Unfortunately — or really fortunately — he had also caught me out in two palpable errors, and occasionally he put in a grudging compliment, so I decided to submit with a good grace.

By the autumn however it was in proof form and given to us to read. Patrick wrote to congratulate him and, in answer Christopher said,

Dear Patrick,
I am extremely grateful for your letter. Having spent such a long time on the book I would be badly discomfited if it had turned out objectively either mediocre or offensive. But regarding you as a very good judge in more fields than one, I find your verdict wholly reassuring, and of course for personal reasons, delightful. Even if no other reassurance is forthcoming, your opinion completely satisfies me that I have not been wasting my time. I hope to rectify the two minor discrepancies you point out. (29)

and so the proofs returned to the printers and Christopher eagerly awaited the publication of his first book.

The four years at Manresa had been a happy time, filled with work and friendship and to one side of his many-talented nature full scope had been given. It looked as though he had indeed settled into the life of writer, teacher and perhaps, exegetist,

(29) From Manresa to Patrick on 7 September 1955.

My books and my academies
My deep divinity.

How long would the other side of his nature have been satisfied
with this life? – the side he also shared with Southwell? Southwell
had joined the new religious Order of the Jesuits because they
mingled the old chivalric devotion to God with learning and a new
spirit of adventure. He had longed to be an apostle in the
Indies. (30) Already this year, Christopher had remarked that
whereas from the age of seven until he was thirty-five his life seemed
to fall into 'chapters' of seven years duration, since then, that is
since 1942, he could divide it into chapters of five years or less, and
this did not displease him. The spirit of adventure was always strong
in him.

When the Manresa chapter abruptly ended, every one was taken
by surprise but to criticise the change as many did, shows, as later
they would find, a misunderstanding of Christopher's character and
of that of the Provincial's also. But the misunderstanding was
inevitable; and Christopher re-acted in exactly the same way as he
had when he had suddenly been drafted into the R.A.F. or, as he
later put it, he tried to resist the will of God with dire consequences
to his peace of mind.

What happened was this; Fr Boyle, newly returned from Rhodesia
where the Jesuit Missions are part of the English Province, went to
Manresa College to make his Visitation there. His mind was full of
these missions under his care. Until he had been chosen Provincial he
had worked for nearly all his life in the schools of the Society; for
nineteen years he had been Beaumont's exceptional headmaster; yet
it appears that always uppermost in his heart lay the zeal, which lies
certainly at some time or another in the hearts of all Ignatius's
followers, the zeal 'to go and tell all nations . . . ' He had come home
determined to send out as many of the finest and most sensitive of
the younger men he could find, men who would usually have been
ear-marked for writing, teaching and lecturing at home. He
appreciated the needs and the promise of the Africans and thought
all kinds of men were needed to bring out the best in them, and not
only the very select band, with special vocations for missionary
work, who hitherto had carried out the task. Time was running short
in which there was

still a chance of building up a decent educated body of Africans
before the gong goes. (31)

(30) 'Life of Robert Southwell', p. 10.
(31) See Christopher's letter to Rupert Hart-Davis, pp. 177-8 below.

Christopher sat next to Fr Boyle at dinner on this day of his Visitation in the late summer or early autumn of 1955 and they talked of the missions and their needs and of little else besides. Fr Boyle is convinced that the thought of sending Christopher to Rhodesia had never crossed his mind; he had had no intention of moving him from Manresa where he was doing excellent work tending the growth of scholastics of a calibre equal to his own and writing two books both of which bore witness to his capacity and to the beauty of his language. His strong recollection is that they were talking in quite general terms of the needs of the Mission when Christopher suddenly offered to go. And indeed Christopher had said, 'Why not send me'? but the remark was involuntary. He was amazed when he realised what he had said, regretted his impulsive words and was surprised when the idea was not dismissed out of hand. Far from doing that Fr Boyle 'with his deep and long conviction of Christopher's altogether outstanding qualities' says that he could 'have jumped at the God-sent opportunity come at last to offer him the sort of challenge that he deserved and that would give his smouldering zeal full scope.' In fact he did not 'jump' at all; instead he told Christopher to take his time in thinking it over and to make his own choice of going or not going. He even warned him that if he made up his mind to go he might fail to get on the Missions proper and might be kept to work among the white Rhodesians in Salisbury, so releasing a younger man to get down to learning the language.

There followed, fortunately as it turned out, a lack of communication between the two which was not Fr Boyle's fault. A Superior of a Jesuit house is in a real sense in a father's place. Father Boyle was not blind to the fact that Christopher had made his mark as a teacher of English at the highest level, or that he had been a first rate schoolmaster with a fresh and original approach which had led to excellent results. He thought nevertheless that he understood rightly the missionary zeal of this particularly dear son and that what Christopher could do in Africa would be of still more value than anything he had yet achieved. He could not know that Christopher bitterly regretted his offer and could not think, and would not ask why, at this stage of his career he could be sent to do what he had been prevented from doing nine or ten years earlier. Christopher had always shunned the limelight, this according to Fr Bernard Bassett, S.J his contemporary, had been part of a deliberate policy which dated from the days when he was a scholastic. Yet true humility demands that a man should know the value of his work — if only to measure of how little worth even the best of anything can be when compared with the infinite — and Christopher knew his own capacities and could not really believe that he had blotted his copy-book; yet, if he had not why should his offer, which would change the whole course of his work, be accepted? He remained silent but took the decision that since it seemed expected of him, he would go. But deep down there were two other reasons which helped him to this decision; one was quite simple, what he had thought once might be for him 'a vocation within a vocation' might still be so. The other was more complex; of all those nearest and dearest to him only Joan Mary was devoted to the catholic faith, by being in England he had already proved that there was nothing he could do about it; by going to Africa he could make an offering to God of the secret sorrow in his heart.

He began to learn Shona, the language he would need, and he gave himself three months in which to finish the editing of Hopkins's spiritual writings. A few days before Christmas this was done; he had put down on paper his insight into Hopkins, man, poet and religious, which had resulted from his early studies and on which his mind had now played, enriching his earlier work, for more than a quarter of a century. And he wrote something more, in explaining Hopkins's he explained his own belief, though it did not always coincide with his subject's. At the end he could say 'in that book I have said all I have to say about my faith'. Then, perforce, he left it for other hands to revise, correct and make ready for the printer. This formidable task — as well as the one of obtaining the Society's approval of the work, devolved on Fr Philip Caraman. On 8 December Christopher had given his fiat to Fr Boyle; on the 19th he wrote to Aileen from Manresa,

I have just finished typing my Hopkins book in a rush, so please excuse my typing with the momentum of it. I had hoped to send my Southwell book for a Christmas present. It should have been out in October, then December was mentioned but now they (Longmans) admit it wont be till March or April: and by that time I shall have gone — ah my dread news has escaped me.
Unless I have been moving about in a dream or a nightmare for the last three months, I have booked a passage for Rhodesia on February 1st, so presumably I shall leave on that date, though it all seems a little unreal, except that I have been learning the Shona language for the last three months as well as struggling with Hopkins.
What can I say now? Nothing except the usual things, the intensity of which you will have to take for granted: that if I dont see you and Charlie again, you will always remain in my mind and heart as very special people, and I can still and always will remember in the vividest detail all the times that you have been so kind to me. I have often reproached myself that I have not tried here in London to get to know better your daughters whom I like so terribly much. I always promised myself that I would when I had finished my two books and had more liberty to move around as I expected to have.

But now I am off to another hemisphere for I dont know how long — 5 to 10 years is the usual time before I leave.

I will be out of London from tomorrow off and on till 12th January seeing brothers and sisters and people, then back for the rest of the time so that I know you will let me know if that coincides with any visit of yours.

After Christmas the hope that Christopher privately nourished that 'the unexpected would happen' and that 1956 would not find him leaving the country, faded, and then indeed he did move about 'in a dream or nightmare'. His misery was no less hard to watch because it was dumb. When two weeks only remained he began to buy the clothes he would need, for which the Society had given him the money. He never ventured to shop alone. His trunk at Farm Street, half-full of his papers, should have been on board his ship by 29 January. On the 29th he still had not finished his packing nor made any arrangement for getting it to the Docks.

On Sunday, the 30th, he offered Mass at the High Altar and preached at Farm Street, this was a great honour accorded him by the Community there. For some obscure reason none of us went and he was hurt. On the 31st we had a farewell dinner at our flat in Gray's Inn Square to which Fr D'Arcy, Fr Brodrick and Fr Caraman came; Fr Brodrick (32) was a good friend, too, and warmly respected by both Christopher and Patrick. Billy could not come, and, alas, Aileen was ill, but Charlie came with one of their daughters, Coney; none of our sons could get home from school but Clare and Virginia, our daughters were there. A picture fell down during dinner. This had also happened in the 1880s when the Jesuit Provincial, Fr Edward Purbrick had dined with his friend Archbishop Benson at Lambeth Palace (33) — (many years before the ecumenical movement) — but the significance of this fact, if any, was not on either occasion apparent. Ours was a good gathering and it broke up late despite the thoughts of the early start to be made next morning.

Clare and Virginia came with me in the car, and we fetched Christopher from Farm Street at 7.30 in the morning. It was 1 February and the coldest day recorded for many years. Fr Richard Clarke, who always saw off departing missionaries, helping them with any last minute problems, had been going to Bishopsgate Station with Christopher, but seeing the family nature of the occasion tactfully and silently withdrew.

Christopher had said nothing at all to Fr Boyle, the instrument of

(32) Fr James Brodrick, S.J., distinguished author of many books on the Jesuits.
(33) 'The English Jesuits', Fr Bernard Bassett, S.J., 1967, Burns & Oates, p. 407.

Providence and to the end Fr Boyle thought that 'his going was the result of his own generosity and zeal. If these had not been so outstanding, I do not think one could have faced the protests of those who with very good reason thought he should have remained in this country to continue his work on Hopkins and Southwell to which he was eminently suited.' But Christopher knew of few protests, he only knew the time had really come, and that he was going.

Dropping Virginia at her school and Clare at Waterloo, for hers was at Salisbury, we drove in silence through the city. We said good-bye without even a handshake and as though we would meet on the morrow.

I left Christopher at the station gazing at a timetable of no possible significance for him.

PART FOUR

JOURNEY TO RHODESIA

1
THE WAY THERE

The bitterly cold weather continued echoing without Christopher's frozen feelings within, though of the icy chill he may, like King Lear, have reflected,

> it will not give me leave to ponder
> On things would hurt me more.

For three nights it was so cold on the ship he had boarded that he slept in his clothes and longed for a hot water bottle — a thing he never used. He had a tiny cabin to himself on the M.V. Bloemfontein, a ship which had been commissioned by Field Marshall Smuts shortly before he died to carry British immigrants to the Union; now she carried passengers as well who wanted like Christopher to make the long journey round the coast of Africa, or to land at the ports on the way to the Cape, or up the East Coast, and the immigrants were mostly Dutch or German. At Rotterdam, the first port at which she called, the ship was held up for a day waiting for a hundred Germans, whose train had been delayed by ice and snow; from there Christopher posted, on 3 February, a letter to Patrick. It was warm at heart,

I just seize this opportunity to thank you so much for your noble and most successful efforts at the dinner party on Tuesday evening. The three Jesuits were all delighted and much impressed.

I can't tell you how grateful I am to you and Madeleine for making my 'last' days so pleasant; but fortunately between us there is no need for any effusion in that respect.

We have been here since early yesterday morning and leave this evening. I strolled around the town quite a bit and found the Dutch very pleasant — and bought a stock of light cigars very cheap.

I hope you are not going to have a terrible winter at the last moment.

And from then on we received a gay almost day to day account of the voyage — once more 'God would have me merry', and he was able to treat the story with a light touch; it was of course intended for the whole family though usually addressed 'to Madeleine'.

Midday Monday 6 Feb. 1956. Lat. 37.50. Long 11.50 (approx) (between Azores and Lisbon)
At last we fast are fleeting for the South across the broad Atlantic. We had a ghastly time messing about Rotterdam, the ship an icy morgue.

The sea is marvellous at present, a bit rough but still blue and very bracing.

The ship is more or less what I expected — certainly not worse, considering there are nearly 700 passengers all one class. A preliminary survey of them offers no temptation to disturb my mantle of solitude; and as soon as my cabin becomes habitable (it is even still too cold to do anything but sleep in — which I do excellently) — I will start writing.

Cold though it has been I am still pervaded interiorly by the warm glow of your kindness to me — at all times, but especially this last week or so.

About a third of the passengers are Dutch or German and will be getting off at Walvis Bay. Another third will be dislodged at Capetown; but a lot of trippers will get on there to go up the East Coast.

I like my pen very much. I feel the whole shopping campaign was really very successful and do so thank you again for it.

Tuesday, 7 Feb. 10.30 a.m.
We have run into a bit of a storm on the way to Las Palmas. It is the pitching of the ship which makes my writing so bad.

I must go on deck now, for though I am (I protest) a good sailor, I dont like staying below too long!

11. a.m. Shrove Tuesday. 14.2.56. Gulf of Guinea (sailing towards Lobitos)
It was nice to get your letter at Las Palmas. We arrived (after an awful storm which laid many people low) at 1 o'clock on the night or morning rather of Wed. 8th and left again at 8. a.m. So it was hardly worth going ashore, though I did go for a walk on the quay in the early morning. It looked a most enchanting place in the morning mist and dawn light.

The weather was absolutely lovely just after Las Palmas. Now we are still on the Equator Zone and it is of course sultrily hot. But I am most fortunate in that my cabin has a port-hole of its own on the *port* side. i.e. facing east. So, as we are going South.S.East, I only get the sun for a little in the early morning, and a breeze is always available.

To counteract this blessing, I have sustained two terrible losses. I have lost my spectacles, — inexplicably, and broken my type-writer — irreparably. (That reminds me I wonder whether you have recovered either of your umbrellas?) I lost the spectacles last Saturday and was just congratulating myself I could still type quite easily without them, when the spring of the old machine bust, earlier than I had expected. Despite obliging enquiries and attention both losses seem irreparable. But I have got used to the losses now, and reflect how many other things I might have lost.

A poor lady Rawlings (wife of an Admiral) going to Las Palmas lost her bag with her passport, money etc, and was even lucky to be allowed to disembark at all at Las Palmas.

The ship's crew are without exception extremely nice; but I still find the passengers on the whole rather ghastly.

I am at a table of 8 all going to Beira, but we maintain quite tolerable *modus vivendi* with each other.

Tuesday. 5.30. p.m.
A notice was put up about my spectacles this afternoon, and, lo! within two hours they were handed in at the bureau. Great rejoicing on my part.

Ash Wednesday. 4.30. p.m.
I saw my first Albatross today. It has been flying alongside the ship for several hours, but very far out. There hasnt been much else to see except, just after Las Palmas, a school of whales and some marvellous dolphins sporting in the spray. We did not go near enough the coast to see my old haunts, except Dakar in the distance.

Thursday. About 5. a.m.
We are due at Lobito about 7 a.m. It is getting hotter as we get nearer land, so I have got up to finish this letter. It looks as if I shall see the first sight of the African coastline at the same time as dawn breaks — most romantic.

I had an idea that being south of the Equator made some difference; but the sun seems to rise in the *South*-east just as usual. the stars are marvellous and it is fascinating to watch their changes of position.

6. a.m.
Dawn over Lobito! Very wild and rocky. I must go to get ready for Mass.

7.30. a.m.
Lobito turns out to be very pretty. There are two tongues of land inside the mountainous jaws of the Bay. One of these is the docks, warehouses etc. On the other are 2 miles of beautifully coloured houses and gardens, each house a shop separated by trees from its neighbour. On the rocky shores — the teeth of the jaws — are the native huts. On the hill tops I can see a factory, a barracks and a monastery. The whole gives an impression of immense leisure without stagnation.

I must go ashore (when the gangway is finally lowered) to post this, wearing my despised panama hat which I feel is eminently suited to this place. It is parlous hot. The Army and Navy beach suit is already clinging limply to me.

10. a.m. Sat. 18th Feb. '56. (Between Lobito and Walvis Bay)
Weather changed completely after Lobito, and is now cold and stormy — because of trade-winds I am told; but after Walvis Bay it will be hot again.

10. p.m.

We are anchored 2 miles off W.Bay — near enough; it smells horribly. We are not allowed ashore (no loss), a launch comes to take off 100 Germans tomorrow morning; I cannot but feel they will be no loss either, though I personally feel kindly towards them. The 100 Dutch seem to be going on to Capetown It is apparently Strydom's policy to people the Union with non-English nordics. Outraged English passengers say that the swastika has been scrawled on certain places on the ship. I will send a letter on proper paper (1) from Capetown describing our fellow passengers etc. I am getting involved . . . . .

10.30 a.m. 20 February

We got away from Walvis Bay and have been ploughing away like mad through a cold and rocking sea. So we expect to arrive in Capetown at 9. am. only one day late, tomorrow.

I have actually friends at Capetown — 2 Jesuit Professors at the University at Rondebosch. I wrote to them by air from Lobito.

10. a.m. 21 February

We have arrived at Capetown, but they are being slow with the mail — so many people getting off.

Same day; Feast of Blessed Robert Southwell

Passengers are divided roughly into

A. Those who misbehave (barge and throw orange peel about etc.)

B. Those who are thoroughly enjoying themselves orderlily à la Butlin.

C. Those whom only reduced circumstances have driven to condescend, etc.

The ship really caters for Class B. and does what it can for A and C. My table mostly consists of what I would call Class B. There are 12 persons at it, but I am only in communication with 8 of them. We have one waiter to each side plus 2 at a further table, i.e. one waiter to ten persons. Ours is a very courteous Greek. Meals take an awful time, but he is very good and efficient. I have no complaints at all about the food. The *menus* are incredibly pretentious but the food is plain and well cooked.

Mr and Mrs H. are a young married couple emigrating. R.A.F. maintenance type. Very correct and excruciatingly dull. Mr H. was in the finals of the deck-tennis. Mrs H. is jadedly pretty but sensible.

Miss M. E. — (a catholic) is pert and gormless but amusing. She would be a misbehaver but is kept in order by the H's. She was at the convent school in Newcastle when Joan Mary was at the training college there, but does not remember her there. (She is going out to marry.)

Mrs ? a gorgeous creature of uncertain age, with a terrific cockney accent and piled up yellow hair, a sort of superior barmaid. She is going out for a holiday to stay with her son, who is unmarried because (she told me) he has never met any one to equal Mum. Unfortunately she decamped after the first few days to a more

(1) Most of these letters were written on thin grey-blue air-letters.

distinguished table — 'unfortunately' because I was meditating decamping myself, but could not follow such an example; it gave such offence.

Mrs D. an indomitable old granny who has sold her cottage in Oxfordsheer to join her married daughter. She eats on very slowly but doggedly, and her mind wanders a little, age 77.

Mr C. A cheery Welsh business man, much travelled. He soaks everything (except the ice-cream) in Worcester sauce. Not much to say, but the Worcester sauce provides a perennial joke.

Miss B. like Miss E. is from the North (Durham) and is also going to Nyasaland to be married; but she is a cut above Mary. She is very winsome and is liked by all. Mr C. says, 'He's a lucky man who's going to marry Margaret. A most considerate girl.'

Mr A. incredibly lugubrious with an alarming squint. Poor man he is going to Rhodesia as a cure for T.B. He has been ill most of the time, and only now, under the kindly influence of Miss B., is beginning to utter a few words out of the side of his mouth.

Mrs F. an ancient Rhodesian lady, very like a horse.

Mr ? a young man about whom I know nothing except he is a buffer between the croaking rallies of Mrs F. and Mrs G.

Mrs G. — another ancient Rhodesian dame, more like a buffalo than a horse, but very well preserved. I took her for 60 but she said that she and (the late) Mr G. were married 1902. This is her 14th voyage. Her husband owned a mine. She is amusing and quite informative when I can get her to concentrate.

21 February, Rondesbosch

I got letters before going ashore — yours and a lovely one from Clare (please thank her very much) also from my friends at Rondesbosch, who very kindly met me at the Quay and have taken me a lovely drive around the Bay. It is wonderful being able to walk and talk properly after three weeks severe limitation in both. I must say this place is incredibly lovely, though there is something about it not wholly sympathetic.

5.30 p.m. 22 February

We are rounding the coast of Africa from west to east, and there is a magnificent roll on the ship as we enter the Indian Ocean. The coastline keeps disappearing and reappearing as promontory succeeds promontory growing in outline from a smudgy cloud to a rocky fortress. I cant help wishing the Portuguese had settled permanently in these parts; they would have made less of a mess in their buildings of such magnificent settings.

Nevertheless Capetown was a most pleasant interlude. I was introduced to some charming catholic families including a young Jewish couple, converts, who are departing for Salisbury shortly, like Abraham into a strange country; so I will see them again.

By the way, could you look up 'Southwell' in Shakespeare Henry Sixth Pt 2. I always meant to long ago — to see if the name came in any blank verse that might give a clue to the pronunciation of it: I mean 'South-well' or 'Suthle'? I dont suppose it does but it just re occurred to me.

News from the Beira table

115

Old Mrs D., who is rather a dear, does not really wander in mind; she just hangs on grimly to the last remark she either heard or thought herself. Mr H. is a chartered secretary, whatever that may be. Mr B. is still cheerful but worried about the delay in schedule.

3.0. p.m. 23 February
Just arriving at Port Elizabeth

25 February p.m. and 26 February a.m. Between East London and Durban.

I have just had 2 nights ashore, quite an excitement. I got off at Port Elizabeth (where I posted my last letter) on Thursday morning, 23rd, and visited a sick Jesuit, an old acquaintance, at the Blue Nuns hospital at the top of the hill. The Blue Nuns refused to let me go back to the ship, so I spent the night there meaning to reembark next day. But on Friday morning a car arrived from Grahamstown, 80 miles away and bore me off there, promising to drive me to catch the boat at East London on the following day. Grahamstown is a pretty little place in the hills, completely in the wilds, consisting of almost nothing except a University and 5 schools — 3 boys and 2 for girls. The Jesuits have a school there, St Aidan's founded in 1876. So I stayed there from teatime yesterday till luncheon today (saw a cricket match against St Andrews) and then was driven the 130 miles from Grahamston — which the car did in under 2½ hours, as 55 is the average on these roads, beautifully smooth and usually utterly deserted. I got on board a good hour before we sailed but actually some time after passengers had been told to be aboard; so my prestige has gone up considerably at the Beira table where there had been much speculation and trepidation at my absence from so many meals — including 2 breakfasts.

Then on returning to my cabin this evening I found not only your letter of the 16th addressed here but also yours and Virginia's of the 18th addressed Durban (and Durbin) which I suppose the ship's office had kindly sent here as we shant be in Durban till Sunday evening.

Durban. 26 February 1956 To Clare

Many thanks for your letter, so much better written than this is going to be. Alas, there are no cats (4-legged ones, I mean) on board ship and there seem to be very few of them at all in this part of the world. There is, however, a variety of snake, large and black, which is *said* to be only slightly poisonous to humans and is further *said* to make a pleasant domestic pet which keeps down rats and mice with great efficiency. This was averred by the keeper in the Snake-pit at Port Elizabeth, who put it inside his shirt. But perhaps the idea does not appeal to you.

I had 2 days and nights away from my fellow-passengers and discovered on my return that I had broken the law and might have got the ship heavily fined. So at least the Purser said who delivered me a mild and apologetic lecture ('By the way, Padre, — Er — ') on the subject; but it has given me a reputation for daring and mystery among my neighbours at our table. This table is a perfect setting for an Agatha Christie murder story. For the *mise-en-scene, dramatis personae* etc. you must consult my letter to Mother from Capetown.

116

The scene of the crime is fixed for tomorrow when we are going on a sight-seeing tour accompanied by Mrs I. (a magnetic blonde of uncertain age). The Tour is through Zululand and the Valley of the Thousand Hills. Here, apart from 'quaint touches of Native life' there is a 'curvaceous highway' whose 'rocky magnificence is a never-ending source of wonder to visitors'. The instrument of the crime is Mrs D's stick, a long ebony one with a heavy silver handle (which she bought at an auction). I am prepared to be suspect No 1, but I have not fixed on either the murderer or the victim. And what eludes me completely is the *Motive*, though I feel Mrs I's past might supply one. Perhaps you could run your eye through the list of characters in my other letter and get a Poirot-like intuition as to the root of the mystery.

Will you thank Virginia very much for her letter. I have it in mind to write to her.

2

AFRICAN JOURNAL:
1956 SALISBURY

Salisbury

A lot of nice people met me at the station last night.

So Christopher ended the first letter which he wrote home on reaching Salisbury. The 'nice people' were his fellow-Jesuit missionaries and he responded at once to their greeting, and their warmth helped him to forget that he had not wanted to come. He stayed there only six days and each day made him more determined to get away from the town to the 'unevangelised' space beyond. This re-action was inevitable to one of his nature and of course he had a very real fear, and a sound basis for it, that he would be used as a curate at the Cathedral and thus would minister chiefly to the needs of the White Rhodesians. Nevertheless when that danger was past it took a long while and a time of groping before he was enlightened to the urgent need for special work in the town. The story will be unfolded through his letters which may fairly be called his African Journal, and other writings. The preface lies in an article which he was asked to write on the day after his arrival, by the catholic paper, 'The Shield', on his impressions of the country and the capital city. Acknowledging that only a lunatic or a fool would attempt it, he wrote an article of 1200 words!

I came up from Beira by night in a steam-drawn carriage whose non-conditioned air was thick with smuts and midges. But in the early morning as I tore down the wire-netting, a clean sweet mountain-wind came blowing through. Hill after hill, fantastically shaped, each different from the other, stood out against a lovely crystal glow. Dawn over Rhodesia: we were entering the high gateway of Umtali. Here indeed was the place and the moment for inspiration.

But as morning faded into the light of common day and the marvellous boulder formations grew less frequent, an impression of flatness spread over the mind as well as over the landscape. Not an unpleasant flatness: simply a sober acceptance that facts were more important than fancies. It may have been the joyous sight of friends to greet me on arrival, but my first clear impression of Salisbury was that the people were of much more importance than the place.

It seems worth adding his impression of the town. He said his eye

travelled harmoniously down a wide street of gracious porticoed, two-storeyed shops and offices and then blinked with shock at a great biscuit-tin of a sky-scraper that pushed its way up regardless of its neighbours. On the other hand there was what seemed to me one lovely tall building — I think it was called Tanganyika House — which soared above its neighbours yet did not disfigure them; it also blended perfectly with the surrounding trees and avenues.

And then, when he reached the last paragraph he revealed — whether it had come to him when he went through the 'high gateway' or more prosaically in the streets of Salisbury — his sense of the country's inherent tragedy. He shot a barb, seeing clearly the evil that lurked;

In the last four hours of my first twenty-four I visited two schools — the African Location at Harari, and I saw something of the educational work that was being done there — and St George's; (2) I stood spell-bound at the splendour of this great College, dedicated to the protector of the defenceless, Here, from these two visits, was one vast and portentous impression — the impression of two peoples in one country.

His first letter home was written from Salisbury and dated 6 March.

I think my last letter to you was from Durban. Durban, after a day of terrible rain, became very hot, but turned out to be cool compared with Lorenzo Marx, and then Lorenzo M. was a bower of bliss compared with Beira. (Here it is lovely and cool.) In spite of the heat I was thrilled (as at Lobito) with the Portuguese modern architecture. The Cathedral at Lorenzo M., and even more the Jesuit church at Beira (about 1950) were a joy to see — a sort of carefree piling up of cubes, with a lot of steel tracery, all completely natural and very airy.

(2) St George's was the Beaumont or Stonyhurst of Rhodesia. It took Black Rhodesians after 1962. Since 1964 when the then Jesuit Superior, Fr Corrigan, decided to found it, there has also been St Ignatius's at Salisbury. It is multi-racial and under its first headmaster, Fr Desmond Ford, S.J., it has come to have, as was intended, all the distinction and educational and social advantages of St George's.

I wish I could have got some proper pictures, especially of the latter, but it was Sunday when we arrived at Beira — 3 days late. The journey by train sorted itself out eventually and I quite enjoyed it.

I am to be in Salisbury for this week and then 6 months on a mission station in the wilds — more or less — to get the language and feel of the country. Sounds a very good programme, and will mean getting about a good deal. (3)

On 13 March, with this programme in mind, he set off for St Paul's Mission at Musami, and this, he wrote, was to be his permanent address until about August.

3

MUSAMI

From the moment he reached Musami Christopher was entranced. His mind raced back to 1942 and the Africa he had known then 'and could not forget'. He wrote to Aileen ecstatically,

I am here in something like the Africa I hardly dared to expect. It is quite cut off. I am only supposed to be here to learn the language. But I hope to do a great many other things as a means to that end. I don't know what I am supposed to do after that — lecture, write etc. I mean to get a little mission for my own if I can.

In this last sentence Christopher stated his great desire, a desire which occurs over and over again in his writing; it was a nostalgic longing for the work of the pioneer missionary who had carried the Gospel into remote places; it was later that he noted, 'the boundaries of the earth were contracting fast', (4) which was making other missionary methods at least equally desirable. That he was well aware of the future, is shown as the letter goes on:

Of course around this more or less idyllic present there broods increasingly and encroachingly both the Past and the Future, both for myself and things in general — Apartheid, Mau-mauism etc.,

So I live in a state of suspendedly animated happiness in which every detail seems special and larger than life.

He is referring when the sentence begins, it need hardly be said, not primarily to whether he could make good in the new career to which he had been switched but to the 'great divide' as he later called it, on either side of which Black and White Rhodesians were sensitive of each other (as they were till 1964), and wondering what could be done about these things in general, and what, in particular, he could do about them himself.

(3) Letter to Madeleine.
(4) In 'A Shona Eclogue', 'The Month', March 1959, p. 150.

Meanwhile there was this idyllic Present and there was Musami. The work done there was in full accord with his ideas; the missionaries who worked there — a remarkable band of men, embodied his high ideals of what Jesuit missionaries should be. He saw them, and rightly, formed in the mould of Francis Xavier, missionary saint who had been sent by his great friend, Ignatius of Loyola, on the same task to India just over 400 years before and whose ideals have been those, surely, of all missionaries ever since.

On 15 March, two days after he had arrived Christopher described the Mission in its remote setting, and his fellows there, in a letter home,

This is a fine healthy place although it is only 50 miles from Salisbury, it is quite in the wilds as the main road is 15 miles away and there are only bumpy tracks all around. The country consists of field and forest between 2 running rivers and a range of these rocky hills, like enormous cairns that the South Africans call Kopjes (coppies). This mission is just at the foot of one of these, which I havent yet managed to climb; it is a collection of vast boulders spiralling up to a peak with pleasant glades and bowers in the crevices and hollows. The mission is much bigger than I had envisaged. It is a school with 600 boys and girls and it controls 20 smaller out-schools, about 3000 pupils in all. The buildings are a mixture of old and new, the church and cloistered houses in the middle, with kraals around the fringe but all only one storey high. There is a large convent with a few white nuns and many African sisters who look after the girls; a hospital; buildings for the men teachers; dormitories, classrooms, workshops, with gardens in between; a magnificent stadium, blasted out of the rocks, for football; a mill; a generating plant; and married quarters — as some of the 'boys' and 'girls' are well grown . . There are three white priests: the superior is a vigorous young man who has installed electricity and plays about with dynamite; then there is a marvellous old French Canadian aged 84, tougher than Alan Quartermain would have been at that age, who disappears periodically into the wilderness to visit out-schools for days on end and returns as benignly imperturbable as he went; and then there is a very respectable priest of 70 odd, who sets the tone of the place. There is also an African priest and a scholastic, whom I taught at Roehampton and who is thoroughly enjoying himself, (5) and a lay brother who looks after the multitude of trucks, etc. Other inhabitants are a baboon and a monkey who have boxes in separate trees but insist on sharing the same one, and a couple of gigantic dogs, called lion-dogs (though I think their real name is ridgebacks) who are quite absurdly benevolent — fortunately, because a friendly push from their nose is enough to send a grown man staggering.

The place is a curious mixture of noise and silence — noise because the 600 Africans are always chattering or singing hymns, ancient or modern, sacred or profane, but these noises are clear-cut against a background of absolute quiet; at night this complete

(5) Henry Wardale.

quietness prevails and I sleep profoundly. Human relations are extremely pleasant and informal, and we have a drink every evening at sunset. I only teach an hour a day — the senior boys — 'Macbeth'! Would that Timothy were here to give me some bright ideas how to explain it; so far their only reaction has been appreciative disapproval of Lady Macbeth whom they find amusing. I suppose they found the witches small beer after their own variety. But this is only my second day. Future reactions may be more interesting like the Zulus with 'Hamlet'. When I get a bit more of the language I hope to make some interesting journeys to the out-schools, as driving here presents no problems except the bumps. But apart from that there are plenty of places to explore and things to see, including some rock-paintings hitherto unknown except to the mission; the Scholastic is going to take some photos of them and I will send you some.

Both sunrises and sunsets are superb, the skies are entrancing and there is a wonderful variety of colour in the land. It still rains a bit, mostly at night, but in a week or two it will be winter, i.e. very bright hot days with cold nights, even frosty in June, and will last till August, the end of my stay.

The weekly mail has just reached Musami — Your letter of 8 March and two screaming letters from T and M dated 19th Feb. Please thank them very much. M. says 'I tried to pass into a billiard table yesterday but failed.' What can that mean? (6)

The next day, 16 March he wrote letters to both Clare and Virginia To Clare he said,

Across a river is a weird and high hill on top of which lives a witch (what cacophony!) Very Rider Haggardish. There are two real rivers with rapids and waterfalls and crocodiles. Wild animals in order of frequency are (1) baboons. (2) snakes. (3) crocodiles, and (4) *a* leopard — but the last I think is almost mythical. Tame animals include no cats, I fear. (Kitsi is the native word for them because they are only imported when present) but two gigantic dogs which lollop about knocking people over in a friendly absent-minded sort of way; they have the most noble heads and beautiful eyes. The birds I have not yet had time to study. The swallows obtrude themselves; just like English swallows except a bit frailer and they wear a red cap instead of a red bib — perhaps it slips down when migrating. Their African name is nyenga-nyenga (or woo me, woo me). Then there is a blackbird which has a burst of song in the morning like our blackbird but cannot keep it up — in compensation it has a red and orange breast and stomach, but further afield there are a much more exciting set of birds that I havent yet tabulated — with trailing tails and flaming colours. The colours here in general are a good study. There are all kinds of green from the pale green of the mealie crops to the dark green of the forests. The earth has all shades from light brown to deep red. The hills are grey, blue and purple. The flowers, I understand will be terrific but only a few are out as yet. The human colours, however, — shawls, shirts, head

(6) 15 March 1956, from Musami to Madeleine. T & M stand for Timothy and Matthew who had written from their prep school.

121

bands etc. — rival the flowers. When the evening light pours through the wide windows of our spacious white church, packed with men and women, boys and girls, it is a beautiful sight; the sounds they make are sometimes almost as beautiful.

To Virginia he added a description of the farm

The crops are mostly (1) mealies (i.e. maize). (2) a sort of vegetable barley (zwiyo — a whistling red) which is used both for porridge and for beer. (3) and monkey nuts.

They plough and plant with the first rains in October; the nut harvest is on at present, and the mealie harvest will be any time now. They practically live on mealies. Here there is an electrically worked mill which changes the husky ears into soft flour. There are also cattle and pigs.

For pets there are a very amusing pair — a baboon and a monkey. There used to be a couple of small buck, called 'klip-springer' by the Boers, a sort of gazelle, very pretty; but unfortunately they died before I came. It is hoped to get some more soon.

I have just climbed a marvellous mountain. The climb was one of those nice ones that are very exciting without being really dangerous as long as you had rubber-soled shoes. But in one place I did get stuck for a bit, and, to my horror, a pair of enormous crows or ravens began to hover over my head uttering awful gloating squawks. I found out afterwards I was near their nest, but at the time I quite thought they were waiting to pick my bones.

A week later Christopher wrote to describe the visit of a cousin — and her husband — to the Mission. She was the daughter of his mother's eldest brother, James, and was always called Kitten, no one ever remembered her baptismal name. She was married to Admiral Sir Peveril William-Pawlett who was at this time Governor of Southern Rhodesia.

'Terrible rains have descended to close the wet season' Yesterday Peveril and Kitten were due to arrive for a state visit. It poured torrentially from 3.a.m. to 11.a.m. an hour after they were due. Then suddenly they arrived catching everybody unawares. It was very noble of them to brave the floods. They behaved very nicely and simply. Fortunately the rain stopped for the hour of their visit; but it began again later and today, a mist hides all the mountains. It is depressing but cannot last more than a week, by all precedents,

I have learnt to drive again pretty quickly, perforce, for last Sunday I was called out to do a baptism at a place about six miles away; it was under the mountain on the other side of the plain — the one that the witch lives on top of; it is called Rock of the Goats but whether there is any connection between the goats and the witch, I dont know.

Talking of witches; Macbeth makes slow progress, there is a hard crust induced by education — for example in the Correspondence Course, which the boys would be taking if I were not here, it says 'it is a good thing to read the play but if you cannot do so, learn the following summary . . . . ' (7)

(7) 22 March, from Musami to Madeleine.

122

23 March

Your letter of the 14th has just arrived with its terrific news. That Clare should also be thinking of it fills the cup to overflowing. (8) If the impulse to take the step has come, I dont think you ought to wait too long before beginning instructions; and for those it is best to go to a comparative outsider. That sounds rather chilly but I think it is the test. Affection prepares the way; the heart seals the act and makes it personal; but the act of Faith itself is essentially of the mind, detached and judicial.

26 March 1956

We have *two* posts a week in and out, one by truck to the main road on Fri-Sat; and the other (less reliable) by bicycle on Mon-Tuesday. There are two Evelyn Waugh characters: the bus owner and driver who goes about in rags but is worth £30,000 and has an income of £5000; and a terribly nice Italian store keeper (with a French wife) called Mr Biretta. The rains are beginning to slack off now.

Would you thank Clare for her letter. Tell her it would be no good saying 'Allah' to the witch but it might work if she says 'Dombozenbudzi' 3 or 9 times; that being the name of the mountain the witch lives on top of.

29 March, Maundy Thursday.

The old priest of 84 is called Daddy Daignault; he has a lovely French accent, but he never stays here longer than he can help; Musami means to him what Salisbury means to the other priests — bureaucracy — to be avoided; he went off into the wilds in his landrover a week ago and is now cut off by the floods, to his great satisfaction no doubt. The less old priest of 74, who was in charge of the mission here in 1930, is very crusty and correct, but witty, and comes out every now and again with unexpectedly outrageous remarks: this evening it was said that the sisters who look after the fields and gardens wanted some fertilizer; he said, 'why should the sisters want fertilizer, when we have a perfectly good baboon?' He made his studies in Rome in the same house that I did. I taught the scholastic at Manresa 2 or 3 years ago; he is a fine young man. The Superior (9) — the Dynamiter — who is aged about 40, is an extraordinary character, quite indescribable in a sentence. I get on very well with him; he taught at Beaumont in between my periods. We are having the new Holy Week services conducted with great verve. In English schools boys volunteer to take it in turns to watch before the Blessed Sacrament, 2 by 2, from Thursday p.m. to Friday a.m. But here there is no need for volunteers; crowds of boys and girls will be there all night singing to their hearts content. On this day the Blessed Sacrament is removed from the High Altar and lodged in a makeshift Altar in the body of the church: so the effect is that of a new Incarnation.

The Mission is in a district reserved for natives (where the soil is light and sandy, not the rich red soil of the plains) The Chief of the tribe is called Magwende. He has just flown to Capetown to take part (expenses paid) in a MRA meeting. He is an object of suspicion to

(8) Conversion to Catholicism.
(9) Fr Davis.

123

the Government, but is a very good friend to the Mission; he genuinely has the interests of his people at heart. The 4 great chiefs of this part of the country, N.E. of Salisbury, all have the same House-name or title which is handed down from father to son or uncle to nephew etc. They can trace their lineage back to a period which is documented by Portuguese writings – in being 16th century. Portuguese Jesuits came here first in 1561 – then there was a gap in the 18th century; the English Jesuits returned here about 1870, the first white men except for the famous F.C. Selous who is the original of Alan Quartermain.

Easter with all its ceremonies held up the 'journal' for ten days but on 9 April his pen begins again to flow in happy description. On that day, as well as writing home, he wrote to Fr Philip Caraman, who was of course struggling with Christopher's Hopkins typescript; but the letter was not about literary affairs but spoke of Fr John Caraman, S.J., who was also on the Missions in Rhodesia.

Am so looking forward to meeting your brother. I came here after a few days and have been mercifully cut off from Salisbury ever since. This is a most marvellous place. There are a lot of granite hills to remind me of Scotland. The small community, both old and young (from Henry Wardale, aged 25, to Daddy Daignault aged 84) is most attractive, and the African, tho' maddening, is very much worth working for.

His other letter of the same date was in answer to several letters from the family,

Many thanks for your letter of Easter Sunday and a joint one from Timothy and Matthew and enclosure from Gil and Dominick. The TM one was very sedate – though with an undercurrent of reproach. 'The last news I got of you' says Matthew 'that you have bust your tipe-writer' and Timothy hopes that I got the poems which he did in Prep.
     It is hard to think of books for spiritual reading – I'm afraid I read very few – though anything by Knox or St Teresa of Avila are two disparate names that spring to mind. But I think you will find it best and more interesting to explore for yourself. I am still trying to take in the joyfulness and magnitude of your conversion.
     I am propped up at the moment having stubbed my toe crossing the river yesterday. But it is wonderful having the Sisters here. They just put on some anti-phlogistine, and it will be all right by tomorrow.
     I like my companions here, young and old, more and more every day.

11th-12th April
You asked if I would like a paper – well, Fr Whiteside (74) has adjured me to get some weekly magazine, either the *Tablet* or *Punch*, he doesnt mind which. So I would be very grateful for one of them – both if you could spare. He has spent all his life in lonely

missions, and is short of reading but does a lot of it. The other old man, Daddy Daignault returned from his journeys to be received with jeers which he bore with equanimity, eating the while an enormous meal and remarking that one had to be careful what one took at night. Apropos of I forget what, he told a story of the old days, about a certain Father Crispin (accent on the 'pin') who turned a witch off the mission land. Forthwith the mission was surrounded by Jackals (accent on the 'als') in broad daylight (accent on 'light'). A Brother died that night (Pressed, Fr D. admitted that he had been ill already.) The other Brother fell ill; and a frantic message came from Fr Cris-pin asking to be delivered from the Jack-als. These facts are vouched for by Fr Cris-pin who did many strange things (says Fr D.) but he never told a lie.

When I was saying Mass for the girls this morning a snake — 2 ft — fell plop from the roof onto the sanctuary floor. All the girls in front swept towards the door with a weird thin screaming, much more frightening than the snake. But the altar-boys stood firm, and the snake vanished peacefully under a statue of the Sacred Heart. So what with one thing and another life is never monotonous here.

I have still got innumerable places round here to visit. It was a fascinating country across the river where I went to one of the nearer out-schools. (10)

On 13 April Christopher added a note to say that he had received a copy of his 'Robert Southwell', now at last published, and then on the 14th he wrote his nephew Timothy,

Many thanks to you and Matthew for your 2 letters. Please tell M. I will be writing him. I have drawn a map over the page of where I am. It is a bit out of proportion, because the Mission is nearer actually to the River on the East than to the River on the West. There are no bridges over the Rivers (except on the Main Road) but at some places there are stepping stones of great rocks. There are crocodiles in it but I have not seen one yet. I crossed it the other day to get to one of those places marked with a cross. The places marked are the little schools and missions dependent on the big central mission.

Some of the hills are made of enormous rocks the size of houses, perched precariously one on top of the other. I have seen eagles there and eagle-owls and lots of ravens and some quite big baboons.

The black boys I am teaching Macbeth were very impressed by a part I have always thought rather silly — namely the moving wood of Birnam. But they thought it a fine touch.

And now into 'the idyllic present' there encroached a mutter from the Past — It received short shrift. The Hopkins typescript had run into serious difficulties. 'Without any attempt to understand the subtleties of Duns Scotus' from whom Christopher had shown that Hopkins had drawn his views, one of the Jesuit censors had condemned those views as heterodox and dismissed them because they were not Thomist. It was the old difficulty once more. Now the

(10) April 9 to 13, from Musami to Madeleine.

125

book was to go before a third censor but meanwhile Fr Philip Caraman wrote Christopher to warn him of the alterations which might be asked of him. His letter drew this reply:

23 April 1956, Musami.
Dear Philip, though your letter was very welcome, I found the contents somewhat alarming. The idea of making 'very fundamental changes' in the G.M.H. Introduction is almost laughable in my present circumstances. And even if I had the means and the capacity, I might well not have the will to do so. I have worked to the limits of my capacity — and, no doubt, well beyond them. Let those who make the objections make the corrections. They are obviously in the best position to do so.

Fr D'Arcy's criticisms are another matter — those I can manage.
But I can give you absolutely no guarantee that I can make 'the very fundamental changes' that you speak of. One thing I assure you that I cannot do, and would not even if I could, and that is to re-write any part of the Introduction from a Thomist point of view.

And he ended with the passage mentioned before (11)

I am and always will be a conscientious Scotist. Intellectually, the Faith is meaningless to me without it.

And so April ended, and it would be another two months before the matter was happily resolved the third censor not asking for any 'fundamental changes'. And May began with a visit to Salisbury.

2 May
I am in Salisbury at the moment about to give a Retreat; but somebody intercepted your letter of 25 April on its way to Musami — for which many thanks.

About my address. I think it would be best to leave it as it is for the present; there seems to be a possibility that I may stay there for a year or two.

The Retreat is to the ladies of Salisbury and was dumped on me by the Archbishop the day after I arrived, so I could not escape it. (12)

Salisbury *is* a dump and no mistake. I must say I have been immensely cheered by the possibility that I will not be residing there when the language period is over.

Someone has lent me Trevor Huddlestone's 'Naught for your Comfort'. I see in today's paper it was attacked by 'Bomber' Harris who is quoted as saying that there are precedents in British History for dealing with troublesome priests from Thomas à Becket to Archbishop Makarios. Good old R.A.F.! History without tears.

Language makes progress, though very slow — I preached in it last Sunday — 3 minutes — and the Sunday before — 2 minutes!

(11) See p. 30.
(12) Aston Ignatius Chichester, 1st Bishop of Salisbury; raised to Archbishop in 1956.

4 May

This Retreat lasts FOUR days. I shall indeed be glad when it is over, though certainly the poor ladies (10 in number) are more to be commiserated with than I am.

I finished Trevor Huddlestone's book. Very moving but a bit unbalanced. His solution of trying to mobilize world-opinion against South Africa seems to me cock-eyed by every precedent in history from the Spanish Armada down to Sanctions against Italy; you only succeed in consolidating the waverers against you. A speech in London reported in today's papers by a South African Senator seems more to the point. The only hope, surely, is to rally or convert sufficient decent white opinion in South Africa to give a lead to the African population, and to the Indian, too if necessary. All seem agreed that the future from whatever aspect, is very dark and perplexing. I cant tell having only just arrived, but I have the impression that the backwash is beginning to agitate this country — Rhodesia — more and more. Many people hold that the colour bar here (Kalaba the Africans call it — a word which foxed me for a long time,) though not of course so fanatically offensive, is equally rigid, and will soon create the same basic problems.

Many thanks for your letter of 1 May (with interesting enclosures) which managed somehow to be intercepted before my leaving Salisbury — which I am about to do now. The retreat didnt turn out so badly as it progressed because I must say the ladies listened with great attention. Lady Acton who is certainly extremely intelligent, was among them. She is a convert and genuinely holy — but vague. She is a descendant of Lord Burghley, so perhaps she is related to the Meades.

Of Trevor Huddlestone — I think I gave a wrong impression by my criticism of his book. I thought the book was terrific and I am 90% for it. The other 10% was an attempt to put a finger on something which I found not quite right. I think perhaps it is that the Anglican church is quite unused to real persecution; in real persecution it is fatal to break the ranks. The Catholic church in S.A. is resisting with an eye to the remote future. However I dont really know enough about it to pass any judgements. I shall be fully occupied trying to assess the situation in this country. One distressing impression I have is that the longer people have been here and the more 'Rhodesian' they are, the stupider they seem to be about the native question.

For example the business about segregation in the new University. The cry is that the Labour M.P.s who have protested against it are talking hot academic air; a year or two in this country would convince them of the folly of their attitude, etc. Heaven knows I am no favourer of Labour M.P.s but in this instance they do happen to be right, because what people get by a few years in this country is not understanding, but prejudice. The Principal (or whoever he is) who defended segregation was bowing to prejudice, not to reason; the reasons he gave were in fact valueless. He said: (a) the natives eat different food from Europeans and (b) some of them are polygamous, therefore they must obviously have separate quarters. But as to (a) the only Africans who will qualify for the University will be a handful of the most intelligent and sensitive; and the experience of our black priests in the seminaries shows that they have no trouble at all in getting used to European diet and table manners. As to (b) it is most unlikely that any African will turn up with a lot of wives in tow. There must be some other unspoken reason behind the refusal.

I think it turns on what you say in your letter: 'The only way for children to grow up is to be with you.' I think that in this country there is a very deep prejudiced refusal to allow that. For example a new law is coming into force here which forbids *even* one servant to sleep in the same house as his or her employer. *All* must be sent to the 'location' at night, and brought back next morning. And in the locations they quickly lose their self-respect.

I have just returned to Musami tonight. The boys and girls are mostly away on holiday — school reopens on the 16th; but a certain number remain to work for their fees, and cries of 'Morowi, Baba' floated through the darkness from the lighted fires as the truck drove in. On the way from Salisbury I called on an ancient Father Johanny, aged 96, who is said to have all the history of the Mission written out on minute pieces of paper. He is a wonderful little shrivelled old man of exquisite courtesy and clarity of mind. He said, 'So this is the young man who writes about Duns Scotus,' and sent messages to 'le petit Charles' (i.e. Fr Charles Daignault) which I am happy to deliver. Fr Daignault has sustained a severe loss; he had all his vitamins spread out on his table preparatory to a new expedition, when the monkey came in and ate them. Its subsequent ebullience communicated itself for some reason to the baboon who broke loose and came through the church window during Mass yesterday (Sunday). It was captured by the Brother; but not being able to find its collar, he lodged it temporarily in the outside lavatory. This might have been a good idea, except that Fr Whiteside visited there on his way to say Mass and the baboon rushed out on top of him.

Today's excitement, however, was on old woman — at least sixty apparently — who had by some preternatural means conceived an enormous child — perhaps twins. Both the Superior and the Nursing Sister are away at present. The Native sisters were terrified and refused to touch her. So there had been a great to do about getting the nearest European doctor. The ambulance drove away as I arrived. (13)

16 May

Many thanks for the black jersey which came last week. I am actually wearing it at this moment this evening as there has been a sudden unexpected snap of cold and rain. I haven't quite got the hang of the weather out here yet. Vaguely from May to September is said to be said to be winter, but it doesnt really make sense in those terms. That reminds me (1st May to 30 September being the shooting season) that I seem to have become a little more adept with a gun than I was at West Wick. At least after careful scouting I have succeeded in shooting a sort of large guinea fowl or bush turkey; it is the bird which appears as a heaven-sent gift to starving explorers in Rider Haggard or Buchan, I forget which. It was perched on a high rock in the middle of a wood, keeping sentry for five more who were couched between the rocks. Them I missed as the gun is a very

(13) Written in Salisbury and finished and posted from Musami to Madeleine.

ancient thing with only one barrel; but the important thing was that I said I would come back with a guinea fowl and I did. Unfortunately the Sisters only hung it for one day, so it did not taste as 'delicious' as they are supposed to do. We had it tonight and I had to eat a fair portion, so I dont know whether I will sleep very well tonight.

The birds in these little stone hills have suddenly increased in numbers and beauty and variety, but it is terribly hard to get their proper names either in English or African. I am still on the look out for the Bee Eater.

I went to the neighbouring police station (25 miles away over rather rough country) the other day to do a driving test for my licence. The young policeman turned out to be an Old Stonyhurst boy who was evidently determined to pass me. I drove him for seven or eight miles towards the Portuguese frontier, keeping up old-boy chat all going excellently well. Then just as I was about to turn back the truck stopped — the petrolguauge/gauge was defective, and the Brother had omitted to fill up before I left. After an hour or two the situation was becoming a little less friendly. When we eventually got back to the police station, it was long after office hours and the files were all locked up. The young man, with commendable restraint said that I had passed of course, but would have to come back another day to get the licence.

There was much unfeeling merriment on my return. When Fr Daignault got his licence it was done by a gentlemen's agreement that he would never drive in town, at least never on any account on a Saturday.

3 ton lorries are rolling into the Mission bringing back the boys and girls for term which starts tomorrow. But it starts rather in the manner of a continental train; lorries will continue to arrive during the rest of the week. Some of the girls return as they went carrying their possessions on their heads, but others have acquired hats with feathers and gladstone bags. The boys too, range from the very poor to the very rich, but there are no class distinctions — except the one that is coming, between those who have been to school and those who haven't.

Many thanks for all the news of the children in your last May 1-2 letter. I must write to Dominick next on my list — not that I have a list.

I have to go off tomorrow to give a retreat at a coloured school: they have a hard time betwixt and between.

Shot two pigeons this morning, just to prove that the guinea fowl was not a fluke, at the same time found a lark's nest with four eggs — the seasons here are certainly bewildering.

23 May 1956

The retreat was most satisfactory. The boys and girls are all so nice and so pathetic, — not an earthly hope in life except for the odd one that can emigrate to America or England and even then — Most of them speak the most perfect and delicate English, much better than the average colonial, with just a little widening of the 'e' sound: 'brade' for bread. One poor boy of 18 could not keep from smoking and had been threatened with expulsion the next time he was caught. I could only advise him on no account to get caught. At the end of the retreat he came to me and said: 'O Father, I wish I was in Heaven' I said, so do I, too.

25 May
I have no time for more because I have just heard I am moving for four or five months (I hope not more). The Superior of the place I am moving to has just been made Coadjutor Bishop (14) so I have to go there till someone else comes out from England to take his place.
I must frankly admit that I have lost my heart to Musami. But at the same time I rejoice that this will keep me out of Salisbury. It is a good sign for the future. I leave tomorrow. New address: Monte Cassino Mission, Macheke.

4
MONTE CASSINO MISSION

No longer are there to be any references to six months at Musami to learn the language and then the programme of lecturing and writing. The horizon seemed to be widening, the apprenticeship perhaps beginning which could lead to his special desire.
Macheke is south-east of Salisbury but within easy reach, he described it fully in a letter of 22 June but he wrote first from the Mission, there, on his birthday 30 May

Your letter came most opportunely today — the extra days having been spent in the laborious journey from Musami here via Salisbury, though it only takes three hours by car. But I was greatly surprised and rejoiced to get a letter so soon. Most excited about the arrival of the book (15) and so glad your second impressions were not less favourable than your first. I certainly was most impressed by your impressions of it. I always thought it was good but never quite as good as you have thought it. Perhaps it is because I am haunted by the many better books that I think I could have written had I persevered with them. But any way this is better than all the might-have-beens because it has actually come into existence; and it is certainly an honest and industrious piece of work.
I had a very funny letter from Gil and a short one from Dominick also most opportunely today. Gil had a very good little drawing of West Wick on the back; there was an extremely good drawing of a crucifix also; I wonder if that was by Gil too, or by Dominick?
Monte Cassino is further away from Salisbury than Musami, but it is quite near the station of Macheke on the main railway line to Umtali. So there is a post in and out every day. The country is hilly and wildish but not so pretty and mysterious as Musami. Sandstone hills with thick low trees and scrub instead of the great purple granite rocks and caves. Rather like the difference between Sussex and Hampshire, or Aberdeenshire and Lancashire. But there is a very beautiful church built by the Trappists — and a superb African choir which is in great demand for recordings on the African wireless. The

(14) Francis Markall, S.J., succeeded as Archbishop 23 November 1956.
(15) 'Life of Robert Southwell'.

130

Trappists who founded it were a special missionary branch who live an active life. They went to Natal when the Jesuits went to Rhodesia, but there was a good deal of over-lapping until finally by a series of exchanges they formed separate territories. There used to be great Jesuit settlements in Matabeleland (where the people speak Zulu as in Natal) and the Jesuits have all Mashonaland; but we have training establishments in common, as here.

On 4 June Christopher wrote Clare,

I am falling well behind in the exchange of letters and if you were to counter sharply with another one, I should have to retire altogether.

At this place where I have just come, the emphasis is rather on girls, whereas in Musami it was rather on boys. But in their extraordinarily fine choir the boys just provide a steady bass roll, boom-boom. They were told the other day they would have to sing the school song for the African wireless; so they rushed off to prepare one, and came back with one improvised for the occasion: which they were ready to go on singing for hours:

'Mon-te Cass-ino i Missione yedu,
Monte Cassino *chik*oro chedu . . '

(Monte Cassino is our mission, Monte Cassino is our school), with much toe-stepping and hand-clapping and body-waggling, and perfectly lovely harmonizings up and down on the 'yedu' and the 'chedu'. The Mission is in a fertile valley, lonely and well shut in, which has its charms; but I still pine for the purple granite of Musami, and hope and expect to return there about September. But one way in which this place quite surpasses Musami is in the way they do religious services. We had the Corpus Christi procession yesterday, and it quite took my breath away. The place is full of wild flowers and bushleaves of different colours, yellow, red, purple, blue, not much in themselves but when plucked by the bushel and arranged in most intricate patterns, the effect was entrancing; and there were still enough for the little girl first communicants (looking like whipped-cream and chocolate in their dresses) to throw handfuls in the air in all directions. And, oh, the singing. I was celebrant and had to carry the Blessed Sacrament to the different altars where these flowerleaves were arranged on thick carpets of green fern. It was a long way round and the day was gorgeously hot; usually there are two or three priests to take it in turns, but this time there was only me, so it was a bit tiring; but I was borne up easily on waves of never ceasing sound.

I must now finish this letter quickly, as my lamp will be taken away for an hour. There is no electric light; the lamps are extremely efficient, but there are not quite enough to go round, so they are transported from place to place as the greater need demands. It is quite an awe-inspiring sight to see some tall girl come swaying through the darkness balancing this blazing lamp on the top of her head, like the Statue of Liberty; then she curtseys, keeping perfectly straight, and I take the lamp off, trying not to laugh; then she claps her hands softly three times as a sign of reverence and departs.

Soon after Christopher had arrived at the Monte Cassino Mission he had been to visit a Leper Camp and of that visit he also wrote on this day, 4 June,

I went there to see an African Sister, and the frightening thing about them (she was all right that way of course) is not their bodily condition (one has got accustomed to that from horrific pictures) but the mental state they get into of completely blind and burning resentment. I didn't realize that leprosy was still a problem; they are cured fairly regularly, and quickly, but still there are more coming in than go out, and once out there is still the difficulty of being taken back in their villages; we had several ex-lepers living very happily at Musami on plots of land near the hospital, but I imagine they were exceptionally fine characters.

By the way I got a very nice letter from Billy with a most warming appreciation of 'Robert Southwell' (16)

11 June
At present all is obscured by the great cold-wave which has rolled up from S. Africa and smitten us in the form of raw wind and sun-annihilating fog. Everyone says that it has been freak weather this year, but I am beginning to think that it is always a bit unpredictable.

The Community here at Monte Cassino is sadly dull compared with Musami. The Superior, a German, is a nice little man. Then there is another scholastic whom I taught at Roehampton, and it is a great relief to have him. There are 2 Brothers; a Lithuanian for the farm, and a Scotch carpenter — nice but uncommunicative, or at least not intelligibly so. There is also another priest who is now a complete invalid and lives in a hut by himself and collects snakes. He is an ex-Anglican parson but looks completely Mephistophelian, very tall and thin with a little goatee beard and tufted eyebrows curling up at the far ends. He writes articles for 'Nature'. The black boys and girls are terrified of him, but at the same time they cannot help laughing which makes him very angry. He is completely *un*-mephistophelian in character. His two great dreads and horrors are (1) cold, and (2) noise. So he is now having a bad time, because the black girls and boys make a terrible noise singing and stamping — playing games to keep themselves warm. (17)

18 June
I have at last identified a *Bee-eater*, very beautiful. Just missed seeing a *Porcupine* — we have them instead of Badgers. Have you ever seen a *Queen Ant*? They can be 8 inches long, this one was only 5. Absolutely disgusting.

With marvellous unpredictability the weather changed and we have had perfect days of cloudless blue. Now with the new moon it has changed again and there is wind and cloud but sunshine also. The nights keep cool which I think is a very good arrangement.

It was a great thrill to have ocular proof that R.S. is actually before the public; as I had no knowledge of it otherwise — though I

(16) From Monte Cassino Mission to Madeleine.
(17) From Monte Cassino Mission to Madeleine.

132

had a wonderful letter about it from my former Novice-Master, Fr Peers Smith, now at Farm Street. By the way if you ever *should* want to see anybody at Farm St, I think he would be the person. It is all bunk about Farm St being for the aristocracy; a servant girl and a mechanic are the converts I remember most clearly.

I also had a nice letter from Guest, (18) who took pains to assure me that everything was well in hand, and added: 'we shall step up advertising when we have some good quotes in.' I thought Robert Speaight's review was exceedingly generous.

I must tell you the panama hat fell into a leopard's lair but the lair was long disused, anyway the hat was recovered and long may it last. (19)

Then came Christopher's more descriptive letter of Macheke itself which he wrote on 22 June.

You asked me some time ago whether Macheke was a mining town. No blessedly, there are no mines in this area at all. Macheke is only a tiny dump; railway station two stores owned by rival Greeks, a ramshackle 'hotel' and one or two similar shanties. The name is from the river, means 'Divider' in the language; it used to divide the territories of two tribes. Our Mission was very strategically placed, and used to have a lot of schools in either tribe; but now we have them no longer. At the end of the war (1946) the Africans were all cleared out of the valley, and sent to live in other reserves, to make farms for ex-service men — mostly Boers, at least to judge by our immediate neighbours. My boy who does my room and tries to teach me the language, belongs to one of the tribes; so to make conversation in the language, I asked him for its history, and a list of chiefs. So starting ten generations back, he began — very oddly — to gabble and stammer. When he came to the last name, I asked 'And who was *his* son?' He swallowed desperately and said 'I am'! But of course his father now lives in the Reserve of another tribe. The land situation is extremely complicated and it is very difficult to get information; but, by and large, the African seems caught between two mill-stones. The Government wants to clear him out of the towns and keep him back on the Reserves — which ought to be a good idea. But the white farmers determination to keep all the good land makes it impossible for him to maintain a large family on six acres of poor land (the maximum allowed) and at the same time pay school fees and the new poll-tax — minimal those seem to be by white standards. The new tax was imposed to offset the heavy Government expenditure recently on African education; but it is an open secret that that expenditure was a condition strictly imposed by the World Bank in return for the enormous Kariba loan. As far as I can see everything depends on whether the Federal Government is really sincere in its public policy of 'gradual partnership' for the Blacks. Recently at a meeting in this area, Huggins (Malvern) was attacked by the farmers for being too pro-black, and he replied in effect (according to an English farmer who was there): 'Wait till we get Dominion Status, then we can do what we like'. It is to be hoped that this was only a politician's evasion. (19)

(18) John Guest, his editor at Longmans.
(19) From Monte Cassino to Madeleine.

The 'Journal' for July — on 2 July opened with a letter to Rupert Hart-Davis, to whom he had not yet written from Africa,

Africa is wonderful, at least in the wintertime which it is now. I am sitting on a warm brick balcony in the baking sunshine: but the moment the sun goes behind a cloud, or the arches cast a shadow, the cold falls on one like a black and murderous guillotine. We have fires in the evenings; the African wood burns very slowly, smoulders rather, but in compensation there is an unlimited supply of stuff that puts a heart into the fire: jacaranda pods and mealie cobs, etc., by the million, which give off blue flames and a pleasant smell; then, when the wood is penetrated by fire it breaks into lovely red transparent chunks.

We live in a long valley surrounded by wild hills with fantastically-shaped boulders behind which lurks an occasionally leopard or tiger-cat, some small buck and many many baboons which raid the mealie fields and which I have so far signally failed to shoot. In fact the only things I have shot have been a snake, which I discovered afterwards with bitter regret to be harmless, and a large guinea fowl, which I confess was perching, but they are very good to eat; and the only dangerous attack on my person has been by a swarm of bees which are incredibly savage and direct; the wasps on the other hand are dandified and decorative, as harmless as they are useless.

To combat the bees there are beautifully-coloured birds known as bee-eaters, like large kingfishers with swallow tails. But enough of natural history.

By the great mercy of God I am not to be stationed in Salisbury but am definitely assigned to the missions on the native reserves; though at present am marking time till the school year starts. I shall have to teach and mark themes etc.; but teaching black boys and girls is rather different and unfailingly amusing, and it leaves plenty of opportunity for other missionary work. They are so earnest and pathetic and completely unreliable except for the enormous fact that they themselves rely on one completely; but in return they do communally make a terrific contribution to one's welfare not only materially but spiritually, somewhat I suppose as a good audience does to an actor. With the language I make slow but just discernible progress;

I have praught several times, only for 4 or 5 minutes, but earnestly and with many gestures; nobody laughed — at least not at the time.

So glad you got a copy of 'Robert Southwell'. I have had 3 reviews of it so far; a nice warm one from Speaight in 'Time and Tide', a bitter cold one from Elton in 'The Listener', and a neither hot nor cold concoction from Waugh in 'The Spectator'. But in all cases the space allotted has been most generous.

5 July
I have just seen a vision in the dusk of the chapel — a headless cope gliding mysteriously up the aisle — only at the last moment did I see a glimpse of bare feet beneath. Some child transporting it on his or her head.

13 July

I was extremely grateful and absolutely delighted by the TLS review. There is no doubt that justly or unjustly it sets a fairly acceptable standard on a book. I breathed a sigh of relief when I saw I had struck lucky. In fact I think the book is now clear of the narrows.

Lovely sunshine here during the day, and the nights not so cold as expected; there should normally be frost at this time of the year. The native name for the month is 'Fold your legs up' because of the cold at night. I am surprised to find that *all* the native trees here are leaf-shedding, (only foreign importations are evergreen) The leaves should be brown and falling actually now, but there has not been enough frost; then the new leaves come very quickly with the first winter rains. Autumn and Spring together.

14 July

I have to go to Salisbury on Sunday afternoons for the next 8 weeks, starting from tomorrow, to preach a course of sermons. A great bore but it will give me a chance to see the ear specialist and also the dentist. (20)

The Salisbury 'Shield' for June in addition to his article, now three months old, on the city and the country, had carried an announcement that, beginning on 15 July, Fr Christopher Devlin, S.J., would preach a course of sermons in the Cathedral. 'TITLES IMPOSED', wrote Christopher in ink over the notice. The first was to be on 'Did Christ want to found a Church' and the last on 'What are we to think of other churches?' He wrote out the first three sermons in full and then got bored and preached the rest from the barest notes and then ad hoc. He had a very special manner of preaching, sometimes hesitating, sometimes letting the words come in a rush. It was very effective and quite different from any one else. The visits, and he had to spend the night each time at Campion House where the Superior of the Missions lived when he was in Salisbury, were no doubt a trouble to him but they were at least a blessing in disguise for it was important that he should see an ear specialist. Right at the end of June he had written,

I have gone deaf in one ear — but quite deaf. I have had a buzzing for a long time — partly a cold and partly the altitude, it is a common thing at first; then quite suddenly one morning I woke deaf, very odd, in the ear that was on the pillow. A doctor has diagnosed it as a blocked tube; but he couldnt reach it through ear or nose, but thought a specialist could do it through the mouth. So it may be cured. (21)

(20) From Monte Cassino to Madeleine.
(21) To Madeleine posted in Salisbury.

13 July

I am going to a Laryngologist whose name is Ryan. I hope to see him on Monday and will report progress.

16 July

Mr Ryan tickled my ear with a long curving instrument through the mouth (one had firmly to think of something else) and I really think that I can hear better now. But he himself did not appear altogether satisfied, and asked if there was any 'history of deafness in the family' — so I was bound to confess there was. He has given me drops and things to take (upside down) through the nose, and I am going to see him tomorrow before going back. However the other ear is absolutely sound which is a good thing. (21)

The next few letters were scarcely concerned with Africa, though they may fairly be taken as part of the Journal, chronicling, as they did, matters important to him.

Christopher had already known for a month that Clare was thinking of becoming a practising catholic when he wrote her in April and said,

Mother has told me about her decision to become a catholic, and it has filled me with incredible joy. Of course it would be even better if you were to follow her example; though you are already baptized, it would be almost like a new baptism — or a sudden releasing of the old. But I think it is a decision to be made in cold — *very cold* — blood, not in hot. It is terribly hard to know at any time exactly what one wants from 'Life' (!) Baptism Formula begins 'What dost thou ask of the Church of God?' The answer is 'Faith'. And Faith can be the warmest and most intimate thing in life, but also the most remote and chilly — according to one's desires. O Dear, I am stuck (the end of the air-letter) Do you want me to say any more at a later date?

On 20 July he wrote to me,

Please let me know if you possibly can in time the day of your reception and I will say Mass for you that morning whatever day it is. I have taken it for granted for so many weeks now that you were going to be a catholic that the actual ceremony doesnt seem so important — though of course it actually is terrifically.

Scarcely was this letter posted when he heard from Fr Philip Caraman that the Hopkins typescript had passed the censors and, on 23 July, he answered his letter,

Heartiest congratulations on the
solution of the Gerard Manley Hopkins problem. It seems almost too good to be true. I thought the book would have a much rougher passage. Most certainly I give you carte blanche to delete or alter notes. It is the least that I can do. There are some points that worry

me (though the word worry is a bit ironic, since it is you that have to do the worrying). But they are comparatively straightforward difficulties compared to the question of the Censors which you have so triumphantly solved.

I met your brother John by chance for a brief pleasing encounter, but his orbit, enormous though it is, does not include my small resting place.

A TYPEWRITER would be an enormous boon if it were possible to get one out by the outgoing missioners. I did leave a big new one behind with you, perhaps you could substitute a smaller one.

and three days later he wrote home,

I heard from Fr Caraman and he gave me the good news that the Hopkins book has been finally passes by the Jesuit Censors, after a very rough passage, and should soon be ready for the printers

Mr Ryan definitely improved my ear last Monday. But he says there is no doubt the drum is slightly atrophied, so nothing can be done about that. I expect it is the altitude and perhaps also the barbarously beautiful discords of African singing. But he is determined to do all he can — (he does it all free) — and I will go again next Monday.

On 2 August,

I am ever so glad all went off well — your reception and then the First Communion. It is very sweet the way Patrick and the children rallied round to support you.

Thank you very much for your letter with the Times cuttings of the Report. (22) By its restraint and balanced diagnosis it ought to help on, if anything can, a settlement by the latent good sense of the parties themselves.

After this short intrusion of affairs from the continent he had left behind, the letters return once more to Africa; this one of early August goes on,

We are still having the most wonderful winter. By rights it should be windy & cloudy & dusty but in fact there is lovely sunshine with a gentle breeze. I forgot to say that we saw a leopard when driving back from Salisbury last Monday. A terrible red glow came nearer and nearer the headlights till we were just in time to see a grey spotted body jump off the track into the bush. Next night the natives heard it roaring in a nearby hill and next morning a herd-boy came in to say he had seen it. I was called out with the gun, but naturally — and to my great relief — it had vanished. I did not in any case make a very thorough search! They live mostly on baboon and rarely come down to attack the cattle. In fact they do so much good keeping down the baboon that you are fined £15 if you kill one except in self-defence.

I went to a meeting of the Capricorn Society the other night at

(22) Patrick was chairman of the Committee of Inquiry into the Dock Labour Scheme 1955-56.

Marandellas — i.e. the Society for working out in practice the terms of a gradual partnership between whites and blacks in Central Africa. The founder is a catholic, a Colonel Stirling, Unfortunately he couldnt be present. The chairman was a most odious headmaster at whose school the meeting was held; he had put up large 'No smoking' notices — a serious encroachment on liberty in this country, but, as things turned out his odiousness had a very useful side. There were two speakers, an Englishman and an African. The Englishman was a wan pathetic ex-police Colonel (how he could ever have been beats me) who made a personal confession of faith in the Society in the pious expectation that the audience would be on his side. But this was not by any means wholly the case. There was a thick wodge of gentlemen-farmer-yahoos burning to assert themselves. The first question they asked, as soon as speeches were over, was to be allowed to retire for a smoke. This they did in a body and while milder folk were asking mild questions inside, they could be heard raucously shouting outside and fortifying themselves from bottles. Then they clattered back and began a battery of attacks rather than questions. The poor colonel of police was hopeless. The headmaster was venomously effective. But it was really the African speaker who saved the day, ne maintained perfect good humour and common sense. For example after an angry denunciation of some African M.P. (to illustrate what we could expect if Africans were given power) he replied that the whole purpose of the Society was precisely to stop extremism of that sort — on both sides. Then, when an African goaded by these attacks shouted: 'When will the African people be ripe for self-government?' he replied 'There will never be a day when the African *people* is ripe for self-government — but there will be a day when this person is ripe for it, and a day when *that* person, and so on.' It was quite an instructive evening in more than one way.

9 August

I got the Dock Report, itself, today and it seems to be surprisingly interesting and much more human than one would expect a report to be.

I leave Monte Cassino with my luggage on 12 August, as the term ends tomorrow and an extra priest is no longer needed. I will return to Musami shortly after Sept. 2nd when my course of sermons finishes at the Cathedral. In the intervening period I will be supplying at the native church in Salisbury. I have had a very leisurely and enjoyable time here and expect I shall look back upon it with nostalgia in the days to come. All the same it is high time I got down to some hard work.

The whole family was shortly to leave from West Wick on a trip through Europe with Rome as the furthest point. Christopher was very excited by the thought of it. His letter goes on,

You will soon be in the throes of packing and other arrangements, I shall look forward to your stay in Florence and Rome with keen vicarious enjoyment and would be most grateful and thrilled to see a page or two (slip a carbon copy underneath) of the diary you have vowed to keep. Your list of addresses sounds intoxicating.

In Rome it might be rather fun to penetrate the German College, flanked by a protective screen of male children. One of my best friends from Theology days is now Rector, Franz von Tattenbach; and another friend of those days, Vincenzo Isolera was in Rome when I last heard of him and of course there is Fr Bolland at the Jesuit Curia (H.Q.) but I wont write to any of them unless you would like me to. (23)

5
HARARI TOWNSHIP AND MUSAMI

27 August

For the first time since I came to Africa I am frantically busy. I am taking the place of 2 African priests who are away for a fortnight. The Sundays are terrific — 3 Masses in the morning, 2 of them in the open air to accomodate the crowds, hundreds and hundreds of confessions and communions followed by baptisms, marriages etc. I preached in the language on the Gospel 'Be not solicitous' and told them they have more aptitude — and more opportunity — for practising it than Europeans. But what they made of it I do not know.

I am sending this to Fiesole where I hope it will reach you in time. Will you have time to visit Vallambrosa? Probably not there is so much to see in Florence —Savanorola's convent, and Michael Angelo's David (San Miniato) and all the pictures. There is a lovely little monastery in Fiesole itself. — And then Assisi to follow —

By 3 September Christopher had heard not only that Dominick, who had quietly been intending it for some time past, had made his First Communion on 12 August; but he had had a letter from Clare in answer to the one he had written to her in April; he wrote her again, and addressed the letter to the hotel in Rome where he knew she would be staying.

I was terribly glad to hear from you that you had solved your problem by simply affirming that you have been a catholic all the time. You are perfectly right and it is as simple as that. All the complications came from preliminary personal problems, whereas faith is just the acceptance of a fact. But of course, once accepted, it is found to be a highly personal fact, so problems tend to slip into place accordingly.

I hope you are now safely established geographically also in Rome, and that the strain of heat and travel has not proved too wearing. I enjoyed getting your letter with last minute news.

I am just (today) finishing at Harare. My whirl of activities ended with a mass-baptism (mass of people I mean.) in which I was lucky to escape with my life. The worst menace were over-developed children of 2 or 3. One in particular whenever I approached her along the line, pointed at me with a ghastly howl of accusation; and as I have a guilt-complex, this was very unnerving. She ended by

(23) From Monte Cassino to Madeleine.

139

kicking the candle so that wax went over my eyebrows.

But I think I will reserve a further account of the ceremony for a letter to Timothy and Matthew. Meanwhile I am just about to escape back to the comparative peace of Musami, where a few snakes and mad dogs and an occasional leopard are the worst one has to fear.

On 6 September Christopher wrote once more from Musami,

Here I am at Musami again and there you are at Rome, I hope this letter reaches you before you leave. I expect I may hear from you from Switzerland before I send it off.

I am very glad to be back here. Fr Whiteside is as spry as ever but I omitted to tell you that Father Daignault had a heart attack last July. He came back from the hospital with me last Monday and is very glad to be back though not able to do as much work as he wants to. Instead he tells endless stories with large slow gestures in a far-away and very prim voice: the one I have just been listening to was about a French Canadian Father, who could not get up in the morning. Another French Canadian Father, on an important morning, let off three revolver shots in his room. The first F.C.F. turned over at the third shot, said, 'There is no need to knock so loud' and went to sleep again.

Another was about a Trappist monk who was bell-ringer in the community which used to be at Monte Cassino. He was thought to have died but was only in a coma. He was put in a coffin and left in the church overnight, for the funeral next morning; but fortunately the lid was not screwed down. He was awakened by the clock striking twelve; he did not know where he was but only that it was time to ring the bell — so he ran to the belfry and began to swing upon the ropes. The monks came rushing down in great alarm and several fainted right off at the sight.

Another was about a German Jesuit Brother who had been on the Mission for 50 years. When the war broke out the Security Officers came to examine him and one whipper-snapper said, 'Where do your sympathies lie?'. The Brother replied gravely 'That is an ask you should not make.'

Fr D. maintains that his heart is perfectly sound, all that is wrong with him is difficulty in breathing. So every now and again after he pauses in the middle of a long story, Fr W. turns to me and explains — 'Fr D. suffers from shortage of breath.'

7 September
Hooray your marvellous budget from Switzerland has arrived. I am terribly glad that I asked you to make carbon copies of your diary. The driving must be pretty grim, at least the first two days in the rain. But the evenings and the rest days must be lovely. Greatly looking forward to the next installment. (24)

6
ST JAMES'S, GATOOMA

19 September
A minor tragedy occurred as the above address may indicate. On

(24) From Musami to Madeleine.

140

Thursday 13th — unlucky day indeed — after scarcely a week at Musami I was summoned to take the place here of a priest who is down with pneumonia, and I had to pack in half an hour and fly. A violent disruption but the truth is I was never officially established at Musami. The Jesuit Superior wanted me here to start the secondary school in January — which is when the school year starts here: but the Archbishop, (whom I like very much personally) has never given his formal consent to that because he wanted me at the Cathedral in Salisbury. So though he may have to give in eventually, he did not scruple to whisk me off here when the need arose. This Gatooma is about 100 miles *west* of Salisbury; the scenery is very different from the eastern districts where I have been hitherto — it is all flat and scrubby, though well-watered. The climate is a damp heat like West Africa. So, although this place started as a mining town and there still are a number of gold and copper mines, the main industry — apart from farming — is cotton because of the climate.

It is a typical small town (in the process of celebrating its 50th anniversary) rather reminiscent of an old fashioned American Middle-West film, but with a strong admixture of Kentucky racialism. Most of the farmers are Afrikaans. My own parishoners seem to be all either Lancashire (cotton) or German stock: the parish priest now in hospital here, is a German-American: the typewriter is German: it has no semi-colons.

There is an African 'Location' of course, and vast African area 70 miles to the north-west to be visited if one had time and means. But the car like many other things is out of order. The poor priest was getting to the end of his tether when he collapsed. Oh, indeed, my woes are multiple, as from broken glass. Nevertheless the mere fact that it is a parish contains unexpected excitements. But I devoutly hope that fairly soon I will be able to *look back* on it as an interesting experience.

A fortnight then went by and on 4 October Christopher wrote,

I had decided to send a cable today to West Wick, when — yesterday — a three weeks' budget arrived from Musami beginning about Sept. 4th. They had thought I was due back in a fortnight: still it was too bad not to have forwarded earlier. There was a lot of other mail which I simply have not time to read. Indeed I have only had time for one hasty reading of yours: I have not had time to take in all your wonderful stories of the trip — they will provide me with reading for several days to come — but at present my favourite is the 3 boys in the car and the two policemen. (25)

The same day Christopher also wrote Fr Philip Caraman (whose letter to him had been held up, too), and, in the midst of his parish cares he paused for a brief hour; for there was a murmur from the other side of the world which he did not wish to ignore. Professor Trevor Roper had written a long review of 'Robert Southwell' in 'The New Statesman' and Christopher saw it as an attack on the

(25) Both Letters to Madeleine from Gatooma.

Jesuits and an attack which placed his 'own honour in a dubious light'. He wrote a letter to the Editor — (which was published in 'The New Statesman' of 20 October along with an answer to it from Trevor Roper, 'which was unexpectedly placatory'.) (26) and enclosed it in his ·answer to Fr Caraman, to whom he had already expressed his views and who fully shared them.

Your letter only reached me yesterday evening. I submit a letter for the New Statesman; use it or not as you think fit.

It is very good news about the Hopkins book. I will be able to do the proof reading all right, only anything inventive is beyond me. My goodness, I sympathize with Hopkins now, I have such a tearing variety of tasks, parish beetle-drives and ten periods a week of RD (Religious Doctrine) for snotty white kids in Government schools, coupled with sermons in native tongue for the blacks and sick calls into the wilds, topped by forms and forms in 4-plicate and 5-plicate and a clapped-out car that only starts occasionally.

Your brother comes into these parts on the 3rd Sunday (of the month) so I hope to see him then: quite half my blacks speak the language which only he is expert in.

Then life went back to its African groove; on 8 October he wrote home again of parish affairs in Gatooma,

I shall have to tell you about this place bit by bit, because in some ways it is terribly funny.

Last week I saw off the parish priest here for a month's well-deserved holiday in Natal, and things have been a bit easier since then — previously I used to receive an hour's instruction a day where to find an inextricable jumble of things: a back stud or a baptismal register or the key of a drawer where there was a gadget for opening another drawer where there was the key of the cupboard where the altar wine was. He had been ill and finding things too much for him for some time before 10 Sept. when he was finally taken to hospital. I arrived at the house on the 13th to find myself surrounded by a band of hostile looking white women armed with various weapons. Apparently the Parish Priest had a most rigid rule that no one, let alone a woman, was to penetrate into the upper part of the house where he lived. But when he got ill his house-boy (his sole attendant) fled silently and he was left by himself, vomiting, etc. till he managed after a day or two to crawl to the telephone and contact the leading lady of the parish. The C.W.L. (Catholic Womens League) then burst into the house and had him taken to hospital. Then having once violated the sanctuary, they were overcome by the lust for cleaning and set to work on house and sacristy. They were on the third day of operations when I arrived. They thought they were about to be excommunicated and were prepared to resist. But I said that as far as I was concerned they could all have a Papal Medal.

(26) This was not quite the end of the affair for later Trevor Roper published the review in a book of essays without any modification. This time Christopher wrote to him direct and got a very reluctant reply, but one with an apology for where he had been in error.

The African side of my work is complicated by the fact that the majority are immigrants from Nyasaland and speak a different language from that which I have laboriously acquired. But in general things are much easier than they were and the experience is a very useful one.

12 October
This evening — honestly, for the first time — I became aware that, provided nobody called, I had nothing to do for the next three hours. INCREDIBLE! just as I was typing that, someone called.

16 October
Alas, 4 days later. I did have a good deal of time yesterday but it got swallowed up in the oddest employment. Some of the white children to whom I teach RD wanted to do a Christmas play and nothing was to be found in Gatooma, so I said I would write one for them. They seemed a bit dubious but I got an inspiration and banged off a scene of ten pages about the 3 Wise Men coming to Herod. If they accept it I shall have the terrible task of writing two or three more scenes to make a story of it.

The teaching of RD is a severe burden. This morning for example, I had to drive 20 miles along a very dusty road to teach a motley assortment for a whole hour on end, and then back again to take another period here. Unfortunately my assignment here began with a new term and also the hottest time of the year — waiting for the Rains — in November. But in spite of everything I am in royally flourishing health, and find, to my amazement that I am enjoying myself; I cant think why — except that there are times when one is sensible of being able to do a lot of good — especially in the African hospital, but even among the Europeans also.

Your letter of the 9th arrived this morning. Please go on writing when you can even if my answers are few and far between.

What is this about a 'chunk' from me 'on Duns Scotus in a book edited by Ann Fremantle?' Its the first I have heard of it.

I must now race on to give you the second installment of my adventures here. The Parish Priest was a Fine Man but rather a Hitler. From his sick bed he waged a desperate battle to prevent me having his car, which he said was so old (true enough) that only he, a trained mechanic knew how to handle it.

My first big job was on Saturday 15th: a long session of confessions, baptisms, etc. in the Native Township. He said 'Go on the bicycle, that is what I do — sometimes.' (but he *never* did.) Directed by his servant I branched off onto a track through the bush which suddenly turned into a steep decline full of stumps and holes. Halfway down the bicycle chain broke. I went right over the handle bars and staggered into the township — where a good deal of beer-drinking was going on — covered with blood and bicycle oil. The Natives fled at my approach! I remembered I had taken off my Roman collar, so put it on again. Sure enough I became aware that a man in blue overalls — a Shona, not a Nyasa — was standing beside me. A catholic. He took me to his house and started mending the bicycle while he sent out word to summon the 'Sodality of Our Lady' — a group of matriarchs much deferred to. Soon a procession of black mammies arrived bearing basins of hot water, towels, and a piece of sticking plaster, and simply oozing kindness like rich oil. So I met them on their terms, so to speak which was rather satisfactory. When I got back for the European confessions, I got penicillin and more hygenic plaster. But when I appeared in church next morning the Congregation were furious and sent a deputation up to the hospital to protest. At the same time there came a sick call from the wilds — so that clinched it and the Parish Priest gave in though continuing to struggle. The final scene came when I had to drive him round the town, in his pyjamas and copious woollies to get his passport seen to. In the middle of a stream of warnings and commands I stopped the car and said: 'Father you have three choices. You can drive yourself. You can get out from here and walk in your pyjamas. Or you can sit still and keep your bloody mouth shut.' To my surprise he beamed for the first time — broadly waved his hand pontifically and said: 'Go on, go on as you wish.' We got on much better after that. Nevertheless there was marked relief on both sides when he finally departed for his well-earned holiday.

Apparently I shall have to stay on with him for a week or so after he comes back (November 3rd) But the Archbishop who spent a rather harrowingly funny week-end here to open a Fete, (which Father had been preparing for months but which suddenly devolved on me) said that 'it was not at present his intention that I should remain here indefinitely' in answer to a question from me: the ArchB is a wonderful man, but he never gives anything away. I have a feeling that if I see Musami again it will be to collect my luggage. Fortunately, however, I *don't* go by feelings.

20 October

Today, Saturday: A mass Baptism of Africans in the morning. In the afternoon a very special funeral for a leading white parishioner (a very fine man) with all sorts of trimmings and family complications. On top of that: another sick call (this is the bad month) and the usual confessions and all the preparations for my three Masses tomorrow, in different places, sermons, etc. — and a visitor who is coming at any moment now.

The children seem to have taken the play I told you about. I have a faded carbon copy of it for Timothy and Matthew.

22 October

Sunday has come and gone with its strange contrasts: sitting in the midst of a crowd of African miners, like a pedlar, with a box of coloured rosaries and medals; then sitting in the midst of the pious but hard swearing Rhodesian ladies of the CWL. Since you mentioned that *Sume et suscipe* (27) was Fr John's (28) favourite prayer, I have found a new meaning and depth in the petition 'Take my memory', memory being a delicate creature and inclined to pick and chose.

(27) 'Take, Lord into Your possession, my complete freedom of action, my memory, my understanding and my entire will, all that I have, all that I own: it is Your gift to me, I now return it to You. It is all Yours, to be used simply as You wish. Give me Your Love and Your grace; it is all I need.' (from the translation of the 'Spiritual Exercises of St Ignatius' by Thomas Corbishley, S.J.).

(28) Cardinal Heenan.

On Sunday, 28th I do an 150 mile journey — a mere nothing to you, — but for me over these roads — with this car — in this heat — Please say a prayer to St Christopher for its success.

One thing about the people here: there does not appear to be a trace of any anti-catholicism as such. The Parish Priest was terrifically respected by non-catholics. (29)

31 October. The Vigil of All Saints.

I will begin this letter now and get it off tomorrow, All Saints Day. I have two Masses tomorrow a.m. and p.m. but they cancel my morning and afternoon Religious Doctrine Classes at the Government schools so I greatly profit by the exchange.

I think I last wrote on the eve of my 150 mile trip to the Sanyati Reserve. They had been begging for Mass for years and never had it. It turned out to be only 140 miles on the speedometer — but I was nearly seven hours at the wheel, as for most of the way we had to weave between holes and boulders at 10-15 miles an hour.

In a Land Rover it would have been fine. Still, upheld by prayer, the ancient Vauxhall pulled through, trembling in every limb. Only towards the end, over confident, I began to race to get home, because one headlight cannot be made to work — the Parish Priest's entanglement of wires has defeated all the electricians — and went wham over a stone in the gathering gloom and sprang a leak. But got home safely to find the RAINS had begun with terrific fury (so my trip was only just in time.) and my hot water system had collapsed. (It was the Fridge last time, always something). But some kindly soul had left a bottle of brandy on the side-board — so I went warmly to bed.

It was great fun out there. I started after my 7 a.m. Mass here and got there at 11.30, after much wandering and just finished Mass in the open air before 1.o'clock — and then a terrific sale of rosaries and prayer books.

The people said they never believed I would come; nevertheless they had walked and cycled miles and miles to be there and many spent the night on the ground where the Mass was.

There were signs of elephant on the way — big trees freshly torn — but I didn't see any.

The rains are now falling with appalling fury. I must say I prefer the dry heat — but in a week's time I expect I shall know whether I am to stay here or not.

The Parish Priest returns on Saturday.

5 November

Father returned and the house-boy chose that moment to go sick, and has not turned up since. So for the last 2 days the PP has cooked and I have washed up. On the Saturday morning the ArchB turned up for breakfast — an ordeal in itself — and after much humming and hawing and side-tracking said that a Curate was being sent here to do the work (since the PP is really now an invalid) — the 'Parish' incidentally, is 1,500 sq. miles — so that I would have to stay till the curate arrived. At first he said it would be about a month — then as he got into his car he said that it would probably not be till the middle of December. So I thanked him very much for his visit and

(29) Begun on 8 October and finished 26th, from Gatooma to Madeleine.

shut the door of his car; he gave me a rueful look from under his eyebrows and drove off.

Christopher has mentioned Archbishop Chichester (30) several times in his letters. Inevitably he had a great admiration for him and since he thought the Archbishop's retirement affected his own future course it seems right to pause and consider this very fine man and missionary. A man of immense humility, he had worked in Africa, where the Society had sent him from Beaumont in 1929, for over a quarter of a century; and for all that time he had worked with vision and success. But now, in 1956 he felt the world had outrun him and that it was time to hand over to a younger man. He felt disillusioned; he felt that both England and Rhodesia had changed; he was depressed by what he thought of as the dishonesty of the political scene and the inability of politicians to understand the depth of Rhodesia's problems. Just before he handed over to Archbishop Markall, which he did a month after his visit to Gatooma, he had arranged for Christopher to go to the Mission at Mondoro, where Christopher understood he wanted him to remain permanently and where Christopher came to feel that his dream of his 'own' mission might be fulfilled. It is quite clear, though, that when the Archbishop returned to England nothing permanent had in fact been arranged. Eighteen months later Christopher was to see him again; the attraction of Africa had proved too great and Archbishop Chichester returned to the Cathedral staff at Salisbury. But on the sudden death one week-end of Fr Thomas Swift, S.J., chaplain of an orphanage and school for coloured children right out in the country, he offered to replace him. He did not mean for that week-end only for he had packed his bags. He went off to Martindale, to the St Martin Porres School, where he remained happily for over three years and until he went to the Second Vatican Council and died in Rome on the steps of St Peter's on his way to offer Mass. He was 83.

But to return from this digression to the rest of Christopher's letters from Gatooma. He wrote next on November 13th.

I am sorry I didn't send best wishes earlier for your confirmation. The mind is like an untidy desk where an important thing, put in a special place, remains obstinately hidden, whilst unwanted oddments keep helpfully turning up. I am so glad the confirmation was such a wonderful event, not only in its hidden essence but in its external manifestation. Not that the external manifestation is not in a way essential. It is essential that *sometimes* there should be an epiphany, or a transfiguration, or a palm-Sunday — just as the resurrection of the body is an essential doctrine of our faith.

(30) Archbishop Aston Ignatius Chichester, 1879-1962.

An important thing I wanted to say — and forgot — was the death of Fr Daignault. I dont know any definite details, except that it happened on the 28th October (Feast of Christ the King) while I was bumping over the roads to Sanyati. So I think his spirit as well as St Christopher must have aided me.

Nowadays I have much more leisure, since the work is more or less divided. The PP is really rather nice and is obviously making efforts to break some of his 12 year old habits for my benefit. We get on fairly well, and of course he has a lot of interesting experience to be picked up, if you are content to let him follow one track — rather like Fr Weston's 'Memoirs'

20 November
I have eight African marriage complications lined up for solution, though I will only be able to see two of them through. In six cases a good pagan wife who longs to be baptised and a bad catholic husband who is frightened of restricting his liberty, or simply frightened of all the paper work involved. Not that they are really bad, but only in comparison with their wives who rather wring my heart with their patience and purity. I still find it hard not talk Italian to them, they are so like the Italians in their gestures and naturalness.

Last Sunday I had quite an inspiriting experience. My second Mass was to be at a place called Chakari about 30 miles away where the natives had just finished building a church on their own. I went by a slightly longer route through another mine called Golden Valley (Golden for Gain not for Glamour) because I thought it would be easier to find the church that way. 2 miles out of G.V. and 10 from Chakari, on a very bumpy patch, the steering-rod of Fr's car (I mean the shaft that connects the two front wheels) became detached from its ball and socket and I nearly slewed into a tree. I got under the car and tried to tie it up with rope, but it wouldn't do. Just then a solitary cyclist came past. It was an African on his way to my Mass. Somehow when this coincidence happened, I knew I was all right. I asked him whether there was a garage at Golden Valley. He said, no, but that his boss was the mine engineer. I gave him a note to take back to his boss, and in less than no time, it seemed, a station waggon whirled up. The engineer was a splendid ex-navy type; never did the 'Padre' approach seem more welcome. He said he would take me straight to Chakari and then come back and tow the car to his place for temporary repair. You can imagine my prayers of thanksgiving when we drove up and I saw the great crowd waiting from neighbouring mines as well.

Prophecies again! Fr gets a paper and in it crackpot prophets have come into their own! It is called Midnight Cry (reference the 10 Virgins!) It says all is now clear. Russia will invade Palestine. Western Powers will come to aid of Israel Russia will be overthrown. New United Nations will be set up under the presidency of the Pope, this will seem to be all right but will in fact be anti-Christ, and there will have to be another war 'before Saints are raptured' Fr says in previous issues anti-Christ has been Mussolini, Hitler and Stalin. (31)

(31) These November letters are all from Gatooma, to Madeleine.

147

30 November

I leave here in the middle of next month, but with an uncertain future. Being here has been a most useful experience — my first real contact with white Rhodesians. Salisbury is by now amorphously cosmopolitan; but in this tight little town the majority are second or third generation Rhodesian-born, and the minority of newcomers have been absorbed without any notable dilution of the settler spirit. It is a pleasant little town, and there are no class distinctions and very few prejudices — as between whites. But there is an impassable gulf between white and black. There is no positive injustice. The question of smell is treated with the utmost seriousness (it is taken for granted that the offensiveness is purely unilateral) and great care has to be taken in church-building accordingly. As an example of heroic piety I have been solemnly told the story of a catholic lady who used to go to Mass every Sunday in the Native church although, every Sunday, she used to faint before the end of Mass. Whether it was the natives who carried her out after the faint was not related, and I did not like to ask. (32)

4 December

I see that I treated your last letter with scant respect, as it has African genealogies scrawled all over it, since it happened to be in my pocket when I was trying to disentangle them. They are more complicated than Elizabethan ones, for here the grandfather, not the father, is head of the family — I mean no family is considered a unit till it has three generations living — and within the unit fathers are interchangeable (in name, not in fact of course) all along the second line; so they are quite aggrieved if for purposes of the record you ask whether so-and-so is *really* the father of so-and-so. Spelling also is as peculiar as the Elizabethan, but it has the advantage of following two fixed rules: one, that L and R are interchanged always, and the other that you always put a vowel sound between two consonant sounds. Armed with these rules will you please translate the following two boys names: ALIKANJERE and FAIRYKISS

Hardly a fair question since when it reaches you you will probably be struggling with exams. I hope your play went off well. My own play, I'm afraid has run upon the rocks. I didnt think I would be staying to produce it, so just handed it over to them: and they chose their own parts with the inevitable jealousies and resignations. Also the Parish Priest does not really approve of his house being used for rehearsals. I leave here next week; perhaps some kindly soul will take over, but it is a bit late now.

I shall be sorry to leave the African church to which I have become much attached. A thing that never fails to amuse me is the presence of the babies swathed around their mothers' backs when they come to the Sacraments. There is one precocious little boy in particular who cocks a knowing eye over his mother's shoulder when she goes to confession and sometimes answers loudly and confidently when the priest asks her a question. He is however in some disgrace because when she came up to Communion he stretched out his hand and cried in a loud voice 'I want a bissikweet too.' I am sure that that is the sort of story that is told about saints in their infancy — as about St Thomas Aquinas who seized an illuminated

(32) To Patrick.

prayer so tightly in his fist that no one could dislodge it, and then finally popped it into his mouth and ate it up, 'a sign' says the hagiographer, 'of his future etc, etc.' but it might just as well have been a sign that he was going to be a great persecutor. So I have prophecied that this little boy will certainly be a priest and a great preacher because he already out-talks the priest in church. (33)

11 December

Well this is my last day here, and I have just paid heart-rending farewells to my beloved Africans, who have showered the most peculiar gifts upon me, including an envelope, which must have an awful lot of money in it, but I cannot bring myself to open it for fear of destroying the inscription. I have discovered that they have never known my name and have referred to me as 'Father Good Samaritano'. Very shaming. I have done so little for them — never inconvenienced myself, except superficially — and they have given me so much. Tonight I have to face a sundowner given by the white members of the parish. I wish I could think that the gulf between black and white is the least bit less than when I came here; but there is not a grain of evidence to that effect.

Douglas Woodruff (34) had a nice little article in the Christmas number of the 'Southern Cross' on the Three Wise Men, lamenting that their names were so rarely taken in Baptism. So, if you see him tell him that my next three boys in a row — if the parents agree — will be Caspar, Melchior and Balthasar. By a coincidence I was called away in the middle of this letter to do what will surely be my last baptism here, and by another coincidence it brought my total up to exactly 90 in the 90 days I have been here.

The rains are terrible. Fortunately some kind soul is giving me a lift to Salisbury tomorrow. I am giving a retreat near Salisbury and then will have to make my own belatedly. (35)

20 December

I have just heard that my destination for the next six months (or so) of next year is a Mission called Mondoro, about 100 miles south of Salisbury. I am going to take the place of a missioner who is going on leave to Europe. It sounds interesting work and a great relief that I am not being posted to Salisbury; it looked a near thing at one time. My retreat ends here, at St George's College on the 25th, and the Superior (36) is then very kindly sending me to Musami for a fortnight's holiday before I go to Mondoro. One of the things that saved me from the Cathedral in Salisbury is that a new man is unexpectedly coming out from England to function there — none other than my old Rector at Beaumont, Fr Clifford.

The pouring rains have brought in a most ghastly invasion of winged insects; although the windows are tight shut, they come crawling in under the door. (35)

(33) To Clare from Gatooma.
(34) The distinguished writer, editor of 'The Tablet' 1936-67.
(35) From St George's, Salisbury to Madeleine.
(36) The Jesuit Superior was Fr Enright.

F. B.C.D. 149

7

MONDORO 1957

Christopher's second year in Africa, 1957, opened with two interesting letters written from Musami. That of 4 January reported that he was having a very pleasant holiday there, with excursions for work at week-ends. He was not needed at Mondoro till the 15th and even after that, he wrote it would be better to keep the Musami address till he was definitely settled elsewhere,

what with the Superior being ill and one archbishop succeeding another, directions from above are in a very fluid state.

The next letter, one written on 14 January, included a quotation from a pleasing letter he had had from Conyers Read, the American historian, who had read 'Robert Southwell' in the American edition.

He made 2 historical objections – but only on his personal authority, I couldnt help noting, not on evidence. Then he said, 'But my final word would be one of high praise for an admirable presentation of one of the most admirable and lovable figures in the whole history of Roman Catholicism in England – "a spirit without spot." '

and then Christopher went on in the next paragraph to something very revealing,

I am on the verge of leaving here for Mondoro where I shall be for 6 months. Then I will return here – or so I am told – as to a more or less permanent station. I say 'more or less' because that is all I can say. My attraction to this place remains constant. I have been doing some of Fr Daignault's work since I have been here, in his jeep, and have been living in his room. I have also inherited his breviary, since I was sorely in need of a new one.

His desire to work in solitude remained unchanged.

And so on 15 January he went to Mondoro and excellent was the work he did there.

Letters this year, as in the succeeding ones, would come at less frequent intervals but still there would always be enough to make the Journal more or less continuous. His first one from Mondoro was written on 4 February 1957.

There has hardly been any rain since I came to Mondoro, for which I am most thankful, though the people are crying out for it again. This is a still greener country than anything I have seen in S.R. so far; a poor country but surprisingly healthy, with apparently very few of the more noxious type of insect.

Saturday night, since the hut was a bit smelly I slept out in the Land Rover — the mattress just fits into it nicely — and had a very good night, in spite of the stories of witches floating around. In the early morning I saw the outline of a black cat on the hut roof; it looked just as though it was licking itself; then suddenly it shot out two dark scimitar wings and swooped away; it was a very large long-eared owl, I suppose.

Sunday morning there were confessions non-stop from 7-11, then Mass with 200 communions, then babtisms and interviews. There is never a fixed hour for Mass — the people expect to make a day of it.

A thing that I have come to look forward to is that, when I lift the chalice, I see the reflection of all the people as in an amphitheatre in their many coloured garments, surrounded by the trees.

But looking after the schools here needs patience and attention to detail. I wish that I knew something about building, I feel I ought to have the knowledge by hereditary right. But in fact I havent.

16 February

Apart from our own truck which goes into Salisbury irregularly, there is only a native bus which lumbers in at week-ends when rains and roads permit. They are not roads really, only pathways of a somewhat moveable nature. The Mission itself is set on a spur of ground and so is called *Gomo*. (the Hill), and all around for a 30 mile radius is bush and forest and grassy plain; it is pretty now that it is still fresh and green from the rains; it used to be great hunting country but now nearly all is cattle and sheep and goats, with cowbells which add a pleasing touch. The soil is so light and sandy that it is continually getting washed away to form innumerable abortive river-beds. About 30 miles away to the west, some hills mark the end of the Native Reserve and there the mining country begins.

I cant quite fathom the politics here, but parties seem roughly the same as in the Union. On the one hand, now in power, is an uneasy alliance between the big-money interests and the progressive representatives of the Colonial Office; an example of this alliance seems to have been that the condition of the great Kariba Loan from the World Bank was the admission of Africans into the new university. On the other hand is the Dominion Party composed of farmers and other 'settlers' (a surprising number of them Afrikaners of recent import), who would gladly break with the Colonial Office and break up the Native Education Department, if they got into power, as I suppose they might well do; (the position of the churches is of course neutral; in fact as far as we are concerned, one sees the same sort of division between those who work wholly for the blacks, and those who work wholly for the whites; those who work for both, as at Gatooma for example, have to cultivate a dual personality or sit astraddle of the great divide.) Meanwhile the Native Education Department presses madly on to get things so far rolling down the slope that it will be impossible to stop them. Though Africans are theoretically admitted to the University, yet in practice there are hardly any native schools that can qualify them for it. So all schools have to be up-graded beginning from the bottom. Which reduces the matter to my own small sphere of power, where I have temporary charge of ten scattered village schools situated in a clearing of the forest or the fold of a plain. Important are the local politics because the sum for building extra classrooms has to be half paid by the local elders who are mad on having schools, but for their own purposes. I see it is now February 19th. Heaven knows when this letter will reach you.

20 February
At present I am grappling with a new scale of teachers wages, just published but to be retrospective from July. So they must all get back pay, (I have exactly 50 teachers) but with deductions for any absences. But are the deductions to be made in proportion to the new scale or the old? Hum, Hum.

When I go out to inspect my schools I will be camping out for several days on end. And am looking forward to that and am making careful preparations. The German Father, whose place I am taking here, left me a very neat and comfortable portable bed. If you see Billy will you tell him that owing to the sand here I can do the old desert trick of boiling with petrol on a sack in a tin. On second thoughts — perhaps not tactful to talk about cooking with petrol in view of shortage at home. But I save a lot of time by camping out and not coming back here.

The next letter, chronologically, contains nothing in particular about Africa, it is an expression of his faith, the faith, his mainspring. It was written to Charlie Meade and was an answer to a query from him.

1 March
Our knowledge of God is *personal* in one sense and *not* personal in another. He is not personal at all in the slightly sentimental or egotistic sense that we often give to the word. (e.g. 'He is a great personal friend of mine' or 'personally, I approve of that') but personal in the objective sense that I am the object of God's knowledge and am sure that I am, vaguely but with all my consciousness and being. The comparison with a dog breaks down hopelessly in that God's knowledge of me is the actual cause of my consciousness and being; but there is a good image of comparison in the way a dog responds with all its being — from ears to tail — to the sound of its own name in its master's voice. And certainly a good dog is a model of anxiety to do God's will, though often puzzled as to what that will is. The human difficulty is to reconcile God's *im*personal survey of the universe with a personal interest in the speck that is me. But it is absolutely certain that if we pray to do God's will, that prayer is heard and in the knowledge that it is heard, the two extremes of bigness and littleness meet. St Augustine was able to express it in his great cry: *'Tu superior summo meo: tu intende intime meo'*. (Higher than my highest thought can reach, yet nearer to me than I am to myself).

Only snippets from the rest of his letters in March are of general interest but in April there began a series of stories of the Africans

152

whom he served in remote places and to whom he brought or in whom he strengthened the Faith. There had been a couple of such stories before written from Gatooma, but these were nothing to the spate which would now come from his pen at intervals for about eighteen months. The descriptions are entertaining, never patronising, filled with understanding and they reveal the natural terms on which he met the people. They begin on 9 April but before that, in a letter of 7 March, he wrote of a story told him by the German Father whom he was replacing and who had not been back to his own country since he had left it in 1938. Christopher was being shown the country in which his work would lie for the next 6 months; they were picnicking in the bush at the time and the Father described to Christopher how the two Jews in front of him had come to the last customs barrier of Hitlerite Germany.

One turned to the other and said 'Thank God we are out of that hell'. Immediately a hand fell on his shoulder and he was hauled back. Did you ever hear anything so heart-rending? This Father's family are just across the Eastern Zone and we do not yet know whether he has been able to visit them.

On 23 March Christopher noted that

the rains have departed but leaving the country in quite a different shape.

and on the 29th he wrote of his interest in the case of Dr Bodkin Adams, which Patrick was trying at the Old Bailey in London. The Doctor, had been accused of giving his patients over-doses of drugs and of so causing death. He was found not guilty. Christopher wrote,

Many thanks for all the cuttings of the Adams' Case. At my present stage (29.March) acquittal looks certain. The Defence has made it seem that far from striving to kill, he strove artificially to keep alive, galvanizing the poor old body with this stuff.

The letter of 9 April began in the following way,

It is a grief to me that I have never time to take notes of the different birds, I see. There are no adequate bird-books in this country. I have just seen a flock of wild parrots for the first time here; green, grey and yellow, no bigger than a thrush, with an unmistakable nose in miniature.

and then he plunged into the African stories,

I had a terribly funny baptism today but I have only time to give the first installment of it. Returning from my rounds I received an urgent message:
    'The mother of Chipangura is very ill and desires baptism.'

'Who is Chip. and where does he live?'

'He lives at Maveto'

'Where is Maveto?'

They told me it was the first household after the turn to Rukuma, so that sounded all right. But the first household had to be reached down a terrible path from the main track. A man emerged, not a christian, polite but uninterested.

'Chipangura does not live here.'

'Is this not Maveto?'

'Yes, this is not Maveto'. Maveto was the next household towards the east. So back to the track and down another frightful path, till stopped by an impassable hole. Two women emerged from the 7 foot maize, 'Hail, Hail, Baba' and bursting with eagerness to help. This was indeed Maveto but the mother of Chipangura did not live here. She lived at Kunze which was the next household towards the east. Loading on the two women to make sure, I at last reached the place and was ushered into a hut. Here sat a woman with *the* most enormous feminine parts I have ever seen in real life. At once a number of men women and children, seeming to spring from nowhere, began to enter the hut silently and squat down. After a long series of 'hails' all round, I said 'I am informed that the mother of Chipangura desires to be baptised.' Alas, I had spoken out of turn. After the preliminary hails you must wait to be asked 'Did you sleep well?' To which you must reply, 'I slept well if you slept well.' 'We slept well.' – without these exchanges no business at all can be conducted on a friendly footing. While all the conceivable relatives and connections of Chipangura were assembling, the women I had brought launched into an endlessly repetitive story of how they had met me and come hither in the motorcar, while I covertly observed the enormous woman in the middle, wondering of what disease she was supposed to be dying. At last the story ended and I said 'Very true' – a remark which was well received – and a hush fell upon the assembly. (to be continued)

11 April

I think I had got myself involved in relating one of those endless African incidents – at the point where 'an expectant hush fell upon the assembly': – All eyes were turned to the door, which made a diameter of bright light across the circle of interior semi-darkness. What entered through it was a chair – The Chair, I should say, carried by two small boys like acolytes, upon which I was installed, having hitherto been sitting on the mud-shelf that runs round the hut. The Chair was followed by the great Chipangura himself, which meant a fresh wave of greetings and explanations all round. Then once again all eyes were turned to the door This time, half led half carried by two girls, came a very aged crone shaking terribly in every limb. She was deposited in front of me, and I suddenly realised that *this* was the Mother of Chipangura – not the steatopygous dame in the middle – she was the wife of Chipangura. So at once I asked the old crone if she wanted to be baptized. She shook her head in quite violent and decided refusal. I asked the people: 'Did she not then ask to be baptized?' 'No, No,' they cried in unison (meaning Yes, Yes) – 'She has asked continually, but she is ill.' Meanwhile a table

154

had been brought. So after some fruitless questioning I set out my pieces. The elder of the two women I had brought in the car was appointed Godmother; and I began the baptism. When I had said the last words, the crone let out a long, low, but quite blood-curdling howl. Somewhat shaken, I said, 'That is the evel spirit going forth from her'. They all nodded. They believed what I said. They believed it better than I did. For it was with feelings of slight surprise as well as intense relief that I noticed, as I proceeded with the Confirmation (which we are allowed to do in these cases), that the old lady had relaxed and was looking much more human. When it was all over, I shook her slightly and said: 'Well now your a believer: you can go to heaven. Are you glad?' She spoke for the first time and said, 'I am glad beyond measure', and began to cry quietly. So the edification all round was tremendous. The story goes on and on and on after this, and finally ends with another baptism. But I am too exhausted in retrospect to continue it. Perhaps in another installment . . . . '

By the way I hope you got the first installment safely. When I went to post it early last Friday morning, the great postbag was already locked up. So it was entrusted to a 'native bearer' who said he knew a way of inserting it through an aperture in the postbag. I couldnt help wondering whether he knew a way also of reversing the process — but, as a matter of fact, in general, I have found the people here to be surprisingly honest.

Well, as I had become a spasmodic wireless fan for the duration of the trial, I returned in time to hear the news of the acquittal on Tuesday night. And now await with great interest the cuttings of the summing-up. What an extraordinary process it has been. Thank you very very much indeed for the great bundle of cuttings. The last one with the picture of Dominick drifting down in tow, was price-less. (37)

I also heard on the wireless that sunshine had changed to sleet in England, but that long bright spells were expected in the west, so I hope you will be there for Easter. No, we only had one bad flood here, the week-end of March 10-13. I got caught by it, but got through just in time. The four wheel drive is a marvellous invention. (38)

The installments of African stories here for a brief time stopped and did not begin again until June but meanwhile the Journal continued with matters of varying interest. On 12 April Christopher wrote that the Mission was being besieged by bees —

incredibly ferocious. They camp in trees round the hill and make desperate attacks to find lodgements in our chimneys from which they are repelled by chemicals. I think we are winning the battle.

After this came, on 22 April, a description of Holy Week and Easter

Holy Week and Easter have come and gone, — together with the paying of wages, chasing up of registers and a medley of money for school books, holy pictures, candles, soap, rosaries, sugar etc., and

(37) The reference is again to the Adams case.
(38) Letters from 7 March, all from Mondoro to Madeleine.

there appears to be a conflict of evidence as to whether the present writer is on his head or his heels. The Easter Vigil is certainly a most beautiful service, but NOT for outside on a cold night. All big services have to be outside here, as there is no church as yet; and the weather suddenly became 'exceptionally' (it is always exceptional) cold for this time of the year. The poor people went grey as ashes. But life goes on unabated; a crescendo of baptisms up to Holy Saturday is now succeeded by a diminuendo of marriages for the rest of the week.

Somebody promised to send me the Aberdeen paper with an article (39) 'Local Boy Makes Good' — with a subsidiary eulogy of Billy and a non-committal reference to a *third* brother' which I thought might be rather amusing; so I enclose a belated review of Southwell — from the paper for which Uncle Theodore used to write, edited in Bangalore. (40)

On 1 May Christopher asked for a full account of the party to be given by Longmans to launch Fr Philip Caraman's book 'Priest of the Plague', he wrote

I went to one once but fled early. Evelyn Waugh holding court with a check coat and large cigar, someone else seeing how many people he could cut, and a host of strange ladies in nightmare hats, probably fish from the waist downwards, who seemed to have risen up just for this one occasion before sinking back into the depths of improbability.

I paid a brief visit to Salisbury last week for some shopping. It was my first visit since Christmas time; I never go there without a flutter of apprehension lest I be caught and detained. As I was walking down the street, a figure with a waxed moustache stood before me, laid a hand on my chest and said twice in a peculiar voice: 'I never forget a face . . I never forget a face' I said: 'I do, frequently, — Ha — Ha —, Ho — Ho', teetering to escape. He tightened his grip, deepened his voice and said: 'Sad memories . . sad memories'. Fortunately a swirl of passers-by tore us apart and I fled like a cat. Only when I was well away did I get a very vague recollection of an R.A.F. group that I was once with, several of whom, I afterwards heard went to gaol.

On 8 May, Christopher wrote to Timothy,

Thank you very much indeed for your wonderful long letter. I laughed like a hen at all your adventures at the Tower with the Bishop, especially at the awful moment on the underground after he had left you. It was very good of him to do all that when he is so busy.

Winter, which has just finished for you, has just begun for us. But all it means is that there is no more rain (a good thing for travelling) but winds instead, and very cold at nights, though the sun generally stays pretty hot through the day. Sometimes, today for example, a thick cold mist envelops everything — for we are five thousand feet above sea-level — until late in the morning; but at any moment the

(39) About the Adams case.
(40) 'The Aryan Path', a Theosophist newspaper.

sun may break through the clouds and then it will be as if a roaring fire had been lit in heaven and everyone will get warm suddenly.

Do you remember I drew you a map of the place I was at this time last year — it was called Musami? This region, where I am now, is not so attractive but the work is more interesting. It is divided into Highlands and Lowlands. The Highlands are a semi-circle of hills about ten miles to the south. Unfortunately my Kingdom lies across the river to the north. However the one who looks after the South is getting very old and may collapse soon, and then I will annex his Kingdom and rule over all. I travel around seeing that all the village schools are kept up properly (for which I get a salary paid by the Government) but my real work is to use the schools as centres for saying Mass, and being parish priest for the people who live around. My Kingdom is at present about 400 square miles in extent and comprises about 4000 subjects.

I travel about in a Land Rover. I think it has a longer wheel-base than the one at West Wick. The back is just long enough to fit in my camp bed comfortably, and the canvas flaps on the sides make quite a good tent for sleeping. I usually face the back of the car to the east at night (unless there is a terrible wind blowing from there) so as to see the beginning of sunrise when I wake up in the morning. For a cooking fire I used to fill a square tin with sand, pour ½ a pint of petrol over it, throw on a lighted match, and you have a fire that lasts about an hour. But I found that only the sand in the grazing areas of my Kingdom was dry and fine enough for this; also the fire got very dirty. So now I have a very efficient little primus stove which is really more satisfactory. I have also got a lovely little axe for making a wood fire if necessary; it is also very useful for cutting down bushes if you have to make a new road for the car. I have to carry most of my food and water; from the people I get gifts of rice, and eggs and mealie-cobs which are very good if toasted a bit and eaten with salt and butter. My subjects are reckoned to be pretty low in the scale of Africans, and are ill-spoken of by white people. But I find they have a great capacity for salvation. Their sentiments are not to be trusted but their instincts are sound.

27 May
I am most grateful to hear that the bird book by Roberts is coming. The other book has some good pictures and much useful information; but its woman author is of a stupidity almost delirious: some wonderful non-sequiturs; ' "What about leopards" I asked my hostess. "Oh they still come about. Just lately D. shot at one which was sunning itself in the grass over there. He sprang into the forest. All we found afterwards was a foot and a claw" People who live close to animals are not afraid of them.'

And this of a visit to Dakar:
'It seems strange to our English ears to hear natives talking French, for in all French possessions French is the medium of instruction, as English is in America.'

You ask where I will be on my birthday. The 30th is of course Ascension Day. I shall be at a place called Rukuma where I expect hundreds to Mass. On the following day I shall be at a place called Nyasambo, then in a place called Guvamombe on the Saturday, ending up on the Sunday at a place called Gavaza; here I shall be uninterruptedly busy from 7 till between 2 and 3, when I shall have a meal and return leisurely and not ungratefully to the Mission. At present 4 days is about my limit for staying out.

Returned from a minor excursion to find a great basketful of correspondence: Clare, Dom, T and M and yourself, all aimed to arrive 'rufely' (M) for 30th. Very glad they were earlier for I heard on my travels that one of the 2 buses had turned over and was out of action and now the one that arrived today has 'lost a part' and will have to retire. The large letter bag for me attracted the usual question from my confrères, so there is a drink of brandy tonight, as I will be away after that: this in answer to a remark of T's 'I dont know what birthday cake your pupils will set you out with.' Please thank them all most warmly, including Gil for impertinent letter received last week.

On 3 June Christopher returned to his African stories:

Got back last night from my birthday tour and found your airmail of May 25th. I had a very pleasant tour, the weather being in complete contrast to last week's when there was the last of the rains and the first of the frosts combined, whereas this time there was the warmth of summer and the freshness of winter combined. My first stop was Rukuma; it is on the far slope of the long escarpment that forms the north side of the valley of the river that is the south boundary of my domain (all my domain lies north of the Mission.) Rukuma is pleasantly situated and quite well built, but it is not one of the schools that I secretly like; but they are very anxious to be advanced to a higher standard and are rather obsequious in consequence; but it is a good centre for the southern part of my domain. I had two Masses there; then the Whitsuntide baptism of the boys and girls who were judged ready. The only funny thing was the marriage, a stalwart little pagan Matabele girl called Sevelina and her rather feckless young man called Maximilian, who 'got married' by native law last year. The people here have a great eagerness for all the Sacraments except marriage of which they are extremely shy. In this case it was the pagan girl who started painfully to learn the catechism determined to be married properly and persuaded her christian husband to sign all the dreaded documents. She had first approached me last January, when I first arrived, but it took a long time to get things fixed and we were only just in time I think for the baby. In fact this is the first of a trickle that will develop into a flood of marriages to be rectified. So I was in some perplexity as to how public or private it ought to be; to condone the transgressions or to celebrate the good example of repentance. They came early, looking very miserable in the morning cold. I asked the young woman some questions preparatory to baptizing her. The young man groaned and threw up his hands in pious horror whenever she made a mistake in the catechism answers. So I asked him sharply if he had brought a ring with him. Of course he hadn't. So I sent him off and he returned eventually with something which I am pretty sure was borrowed from the curtain rod of a wealthier neighbour. In answer to my strictures however he protested that he did understand the

158

solemnity of the occasion. Although the marriage was performed swiftly and quietly, word went round and they were led about with all the customary wild screamings and dances. I thought they would have died with shame and was much relieved that the baby was not born there and then in the excitement, but they seemed well pleased. Let us hope 'angels in heaven' were, too!

At 2.30 I escaped from Rukuma and made my way slowly over broken ground to Nyatsambo, stopping in a solitary place on the way to cook a meal and say my Office. Nyatsambo is the opposite of Rukuma, a crazy tumbled-down school overrun by goats and parents who have no respect for the sanctity of the classroom. Typical of its craziness is that two secretary-birds — who are supposed to be the shyest and wariest of birds — haunt the place like enormous tame pigeons; the children shout and throw things at them, but they only shift a little and come careening back again, about twice the size of herons. Nyatsambo will never be advanced to a higher standard because they will never fulfil all the paper-requirements: yet, ironically the teaching is of an amazingly high standard. (I have just verified this from the records here which show that they have the highest number of entries to the high standards at the Central School.) As you may imagine a number of funny things happened, of too fragmentary a nature to be recorded. One impression that remains is of a shoal of the tiniest children pouring out of their hovel of a classroom into the sun headed by their squat little mistress who was teaching them English. 'This is the ground. This is the sun,' they shouted with irrepressible enthusiasm. 'We are pointing at the ground, we are pointing at the sun' — they collapsed for one moment of rest, then up and on and on again — 'We are jumping on the ground' — 'We are jumping on the ground' — as if this land which only produces thorns and weeds in this area, had for them a secret source of energy. I am always rather anxious lest the Mass and other religious functions interrupt the regulation timetable. On my first visit to Nyatsambo I drove the parents away; not now I realise that the school goes on with its own unquenchable vitality whatever the interruptions. This time among other things there was the baptism of a deaf mute whom I had put off on an earlier occasion, not quite knowing how to satisfy canonical requirements in the case of one who could neither speak nor be spoken to; but this time the fact that he made the journey on his own initiative spoke louder than words. And really it was very nice afterwards to see him beaming and goggling all round while everybody crowded round and shook his hand and clapped him on the back. He chose the name (spelt it out on paper) 'Alphonse' — quite unknown in these parts. I wonder why. No one could tell me.

From Nyatsambo on Friday afternoon, I proceeded by a circuitous route to Govamombe. Govamombe is a good school, as correct as Rukuma, but with much of the vitality of Nyatsambo. I have to attend all the classes from 8 to 1 o'clock to fulfil the requirements of an 'inspection' — then in the afternoon the baptism of those who passed the previous day — 30 in all, but as always a number of aged and newborn locals crashed in on the function, making a total of 40. The star performer was an aged crone (aged by African standards, about 70) who had been a girl during the Matabele War which she described with great vigour and incoherence. She was deaf but insisted on understanding all the bits of the ceremony which I spoke in the native language. A fine tall crone with a long staff. 'What's he saying? What's he saying?' she kept bombarding the less aged crone who was her Godmother. Once, after I had passed her and gone back to the middle of the semi-circle, she came tottering forward brandishing her staff to declare that she did indeed renounce the devil. It is a great advantage about ceremonies here (except of course those where the priest actually takes the part of Our Lord, as in Mass and Confession) that you can burst out laughing without impairing the dignity of the ceremony. Also, which is very fortunate for me, one can burst into violent rages without causing more than a very temporary disconcert. Not that I do not resolve continually to avoid such rages, if only for the selfish reason that they leave one with a headache — just as one must always drive gently and soberly, never with a joie de vivre, to avoid the sudden spine-splintering bump in an unseen hole.

6 and 7 June
From Guvamombe to Gavaza which is the big centre for the northern and more thickly populated part of my domain, where I go every second Sunday of the month: it is a large clearing of the forest and is supposed to be bewitched, a story that crops up periodically on the occurrence of any disaster there, major or minor. Certainly the flickering lights from surrounding homesteads make strange effects among the trees, and there is an enormous owl there — the one I thought was a cat on my first night there — if you remember — and various other appendages including an epileptic. But in the daytime, especially on Sundays, it is a scene of great animation. I was glad however this time that my previous assignments that week had lessened the number of confessions, so I was able to return to the Mission in good time.

Several days have elapsed since I began this letter, during which I was out again Tuesday — Wednesday and have received *and* deciphered your letter written on the Feast of St Mary Magdalen dei Pazzi. You must forgive me if I thought of another connection also: the Italian family of the Pazzi is a famous one, but the word is also the plural of the Italian adjective for 'crazy' or 'crackers' It used to be a sort of Seminary joke in Rome to wish people a happy feast on this day. (41)

The next letter, that of 17 June, was mainly descriptive,

It was very kind of you to write for my birthday, not only because I never write for yours, but also because I think I owe you a letter in any case, if not two. The address you put (42) on — 'St Michael's Mount' — was rather brilliant, for in fact this place is situated *supra montem* amid the surrounding plain; the native name for it is the Gomo — (plural makomo) meaning a hill or hill-fortress. The prayer after Mass: 'O God our refuge and our strength' goes rather nicely into 'Yave, gomo redu ne simba redu'. Apart from that there are no proper hills in my domain, though one or two quite handsome escarpments. But the real charm of the countryside lies in the limpid

(41) 27 May-7 June onwards to Madeleine.
(42) To Clare; from Mondoro.

non-glaring brilliance of the sun. Under its kindly eye the multi-tudinous and useless thornbushes discover that their purpose in life after all is just to have a glass of dew on every thorn for the morning sun to shine through – and incidentally to supply minor poets with a rhyme for morn, other than dawn. The actual sun-rises are rather disappointing – too quick. But the moon rises are protracted and terrific, carefully staged entrances when at the full. Night has fallen and all the principle stars are waiting patiently in their places but still no sign of Moddom. Another ten minutes passes. A few late-comers slip unobtrusively to their stations; one or two juniors tumble over ignominiously, turn into shooting stars and disappear from the scene. The tension is just about to become tedious when some wisps of cloud around a certain place are turned into silken runners and go speeding this way and that, clearing a cloudless dome on the horizon. Then – suddenly – at last – behind a black gate of treeš on the cleared skyline is seen portentously a dark bright crimson heart of fire. Can this be Milady? O, dear me, no. This is just a scarlet band advancing with an almost audible thrum and fanfare. It seems to part in the middle giving place to a golden light, pure but shapeless. Can this be she, or at least her coach? But it is seen to be not like a coach but a pavilion building itself in the sky; a gold-brocaded *piano nobile*, a light blue silken upper storey, and dove-grey floating pinnacles. The eye is so taken with the spectacle, so sorry to see it begin to fade, that the long-awaited moment comes unexpectedly after all. In a sudden flash one sees her soaring; high, high above the trees; riding on the sky: completely unattached. You might think it would be an anti-climax after all that preparation, but the dazzling steely brilliance of the thing puts that out of the question; it also reminds me after the threat of so much nature-worship, that the moon is a thing not a person; but it cant help being a symbol; a spinning silver coin symbolizing, all worldly dazzle, which may fall heads for God, or tails for the devil. My goodness, it has suddenly occurred to me – though I'm sure it must have been remarked before – the reason why men value gold first, then silver, then diamonds: because they are earthly counterparts of the Sun, the Moon and the Stars that once they used to worship.

6 July
Dear me, a great deal of time seems to have elapsed since I last wrote. Our mid-week bus is till out of action and I have had two breakdowns in succession, a broken fan-belt on Thursday and a puncture on Friday with complications: the spare wheel had lost air and my pump kept coming to pieces.
A little while previously the Inspector had been here from Salisbury, a somewhat loutish man who turned down the application

of two of my more abject schools for a higher standard (standard 3) The chief cause of his rage, I think, was that he got stuck on the way, and had to walk and was not well received by the inhabitants – with which I sympathize, but intend nevertheless to take the matter to higher quarters.

13 July
Here is some news of some of your old friends. The Mother of

Chipangara is still sitting happily in the sun (nobody seems to die around here – I have only had one so far). Chipangara himself has been under instruction and came to be baptized the other day. His wife – the vast woman – is still a pagan, but that may be because she feels she cannot walk to the neighbouring school for instruction. The young man who married the Matabele girl has become most officious in doing good. (He is, however, an awful ass; when I expressed some concern that his wife had not had her baby yet, he said 'ah well, that's her affair. I can do nothing for her there'.) He brought me however to another inaccessible village where a very old man was said to be dying. Indeed he *was* old, his name was 'Chamiyenka' which means the Rain-Maker; he had actually fought against the Matabele (with charms not with weapons) and no one living can remember him except as an old man. I gave him quick baptism and extreme unction, but he did not die, so I came back the other day to give him the rest when he was a little better. When I had finished I said 'You are now a friend of God', and it was seen that he was making an effort to speak. Everybody gathered round to hear the edifying words. He said 'Give the Father a hen.' So it was done according to his command. Unfortunately I was only at the beginning of my rounds, and his daughter, herself an aged crone, indignantly refused to take it back. So I had to travel around saddled with the poor hen. However it survived peacably enough till I got back to the Convent. The Matabele girl and her sister-in-law also gave me two rather beautifully woven mats. I am going to have a Nuptial Mass for her as she is now ready for Communion and have given her husband a proper ring for her. I travel around now with an assortment of brightly coloured rings. They only cost 6d each, but are very popular, and are an inducement to people to put their marriage right.

We are having a mild heat-wave here too, considering it is supposed to be mid-winter.

23 July

I am in Salisbury now, most incongruously having been handed up to give a lecture to a literary society! but I am going back to Mondoro tomorrow morning where I am now thoroughly involved with baptism classes and marriage cases, not to mention a village that is rioting and a teacher that is going mad, not homicidal I hope, but he has a glare like an Evelyn Waugh character.

1 August

Thank you very much indeed for the wonderful account of the Enthronement. (43) Father John does indeed recall the Golden Age of Bishops. He does make one believe that it is an order divinely instituted by Our Lord quite apart from the priesthood.

Chamimika, the Rain-Maker, has passed away. So with any luck, so to speak – he should now be in Heaven. His hen was eaten yesterday in honour of St Ignatius. (44) The rioting village has been temporarily pacified. The mad teacher has yet to be encountered, but I have found a substitute for him if he is sacked, which is a useful thing.

(43) Enthronement of the Archbishop of Liverpool; now Cardinal Heenan.
(44) 31 July, the feast day of St Ignatius Loyola.

8 August

I still have not confronted the mad teacher. The trouble is that I keep mixing him up with another teacher who is like him but who is not mad. Both he and the rioting villagers are respectively from the two abject schools condemned by the Inspector. The villagers 'rioted' (they only surrounded the car and howled a bit) because I refused to baptize them in large numbers — one had got baptism on false pretences, poor wretch. But the better element has now asserted itself and all is well.

There was a scene, unsurpassed by any in the Aberdeen Cathedral in the old days, when I hurled a shilling through the window of the hut that serves as a church. (A shilling is the gift given for baptism) As however it was not the coin in question, it was recovered by a frugal-minded embassy and presented to me before leaving. How keep a straight face?!

Sevelina, the Matabele girl, has safely delivered a baby boy.

After giving this news and new story, Christopher had only one more month at Mondoro; there is one more extract from a letter that is worth giving and then the one in which he wrote of his sadness at leaving.

12 August

Have just discovered your letters of 2nd and 6th in a corner of the Boss's office — Alarming but he gets overworked on a Sunday.

The Archbishop of C. as reported in our Rhodesian Herald has just denounced catholicism in favour of catholicity, feel like writing to all believers in Monotheism, Methodism, optimism and patriotism to change their allegiance to Monotheity, Methodity, optimity, and patriotity.

27 August

Alas — another change of address to report though this time a familiar one. I will be there by September 10th —St Paul's, Musami.

I had got so fixed in the work here that I had forgotten (and indeed had been led to forget) that I was only on loan so to speak. Musami, of course, will have its compensations (though its character has changed in the past year), but I did feel so strongly that I was doing God's work here, it is hard to think of God's will overriding God's work. The poor villagers who 'rioted' said, 'If you dont baptise us we will never get another chance.' But of course that is nonsense, for God has care of everything however small and devious.

Sevelina's baby was baptised Christopher. They turned up for the baptism with an elder boy, aged two, whose existence had hitherto, been undisclosed! So I baptised him Patrick!! There has been a great crop of fine baby boys recently — one in defiance of a CURSE, which is a great triumph.

In this letter Christopher enclosed a light-hearted one to Timothy advising him — and Matthew — about hut-construction. It is, he said,

extremely difficult to make any dwelling which will:

163

(a) Keep the rain out in a heavy shower
(b) Let the smoke out if you have a fire.

After all, think of the ages of experience and misfortune people had to go through before they came to such inventions as: Tent, Wigwam, Hut, Log-cabin — , which I suppose is the best of all.

The Natives here never learnt to keep out rain and let out smoke at the same time. So they always — even still — have 2 huts; one with the roof loosely thatched to let out smoke: for eating and cooking in; the other tightly thatched for sleeping in.

In his last letter from Mondoro, written on 5 September, Christopher wrote of the return of the priest whose place he had been taking; since he had been a 'Nazi Victim' he had been allowed into the Eastern Zone without trouble, it was materially desolate compared with the Western but he had yet found the Faith 'flourishing wonderfully'.

It is clear that at Mondoro Christopher had found the kind of work *he* wanted. The missionary work in the wilds, 'which gave his smouldering zeal full scope' and, for better measure, there was attached to it the overseeing of the raising of school standards which he knew to be urgently needed. Without good education, Africans, like any other people could rarely take a responsible part in government. It had looked to him at one time as though he would stay there permanently (45) and he enlarged on this in a letter he wrote home from Musami on 16 September.

Musami is certainly a nicer place than Mondoro, but the work at Mondoro was more interesting; and I am a bit worried about leaving it for several reasons. Amongst them the Jesuit Superior (46) before he went away intimated that I was to stay there and the Archbishop (47) was much annoyed at my being moved but did nothing to oppose it. There are other factors which I may mention in a later letter.

But the main thing is that my initial repugnance at returning has been quite washed out by the kindness with which I have been received. It is a great thing to be at a place where you are made to feel that you are wanted.

and then, turning in thought to his eldest nephew, Gilpatrick, who was about to do his military service, he wrote,

I owe him a letter from long ago, but I have lost the one of his to which I was going to make some pretty smart replies. He had asked me for some advice before going into the Army, but all I could think of was:

(45) Christopher wrote this in a letter to his American correspondent, Miss Moseley, in a letter of 17 September 1957.
(46) Fr Enright.
(47) Archbishop Markall; bishops do not normally interfere with the arrangements of Religious Orders.

'when spending money, spend it well;
when sloping arms, make it tell'

— which is what our Sgt-Major used to say.

8
MUSAMI 1957

The work to which Christopher had returned at Musami consisted of teaching in the first and new Jesuit secondary school for Africans in the Archdiocese of Salisbury; coupled with this was the much more congenial task of going out into the wilds at week-ends and in the holidays. The work was not the same as Fr Daignault's had been. Christopher had, indeed the grand old Priest's breviary but someone else had been given his work, when Christopher was sent to Mondoro, and also the Landrover he had used, which was really a necessity if you wanted to penetrate far into the bush. Musami, too, had changed. He wrote,

the world is intruding more upon the place and it gets much bigger and there is a threat of a main arterial road being driven through.

Of course what had happened, and was bound to happen with modern development, was that the work which began in remote places was later crystallised in big educational centres. Christopher was not really suited to work in one of these, but, all the same he was not wasted there, whatever he may, when bored, have thought.

There is nothing of much interest in the letters he wrote at this time until one of 5 October when he gave a lovely picture of some of the 'boys and girls'

We are gasping like fish in thunderous heat. Pessimists say it may go on like this till December. But all my experience is that the weather never continues the same for more than a month.
    Prophetically as I wrote those words (it was October 4th, then) there came a torrential downpour. With the first rains a madness sweeps over the people. A party of girls who were celebrating the feast of St Francis by a picnic at the river, two miles away, danced all the way back, soaking wet, hop — skip — and jump — carrying branches of trees and uttering a wild chant at every third step. The boys all rushed out bellowing in sympathy, while a mob of tiny children scurried before and after, turning somersaults in excitement. The baboon and the monkey of course joined in.

But, alas, the rain was only a temporary relief after all. When Christopher next wrote, which was over a month later, on 10 November, a Sunday when he had been out in the bush there still had been no more. He wrote,

I am at the moment slightly prostrate from the sun. I set my altar up in the shade before confessions, but misjudged the sun which came racing up behind the tree; so half-way through Mass all the people were happily in the shade but I was caught from behind. I think this is one of the two times in the year when the sun is directly overhead at noon and one stands in ones own shadow. However I have had this affliction several times before and have found that it departs quickly after a couple of aspirin, (helped by brandy) and a night's rest.

The usual remedy worked, he added on the 11th, but the rains still held off.

On 21 November Christopher wrote to Fr Caraman to let him know that the proofs of the Hopkins book had arrived. He said,

We are having a terrible month with the rains holding off and people are getting desperate. I have had 5 cases of madness and suicide in the last three weeks. One of them you would have been interested in; a youth who hanged himself in a hut but was cut down in time. He complained of a raging fire within him and drinks SIX large pots — a gallon or more each — a day and three by night. Shades of Francis Wodehouse! I have heard his confession and given some spiritual counsel so we will see if that brings any relief.

The like tale of Francis Wodehouse had been told in William Weston's Autobiography, written in the late sixteenth century, which had recently been edited by Philip Caraman. (48) Father Weston — he was a most interesting priest who had been on the English Mission in penal times but had ended his days in Rome — had written,

He emptied to the dregs so many mugs one on top of the other that he put down 8 gallons in all . . . It was like pouring water into a raging furnace; all the liquor was immediately taken into his stomach and absorbed. Yet in spite of this the secret fire was not extinguished.

He had had, it seems a guilty conscience and the notes at the end of this edition say the tale 'is interesting as an example of the way the super ego can produce severe bodily symptoms'. Elizabethan and Jacobean England were never far from Christopher's thought — not even amongst alien people and in the wilds and still gasping for the rains.

On 25 November there is an interesting letter to Aileen Meade in which he described the classroom in which he sat as he was writing;

I am at present presiding over a test & have just seen 2 boys cribbing but neither have in any case the faintest hope of passing. On one side of the room are 22 boys ranging from tall balding professional
(48) Published Longmans 1955.

individuals who might be 20-30 to tiny little earnest monkeys who look as if they were ten. On the other side are 11 dusky maidens perched uneasily on large bottoms. They are all doing a Latin exam. Occasionally there is an earth-shaking roar outside and a buffalo tries to put its head in, but finding the door too narrow for its horns moves grumbling on. An even more terrifying crash from above is only the tame baboon cavorting over the roof. Outside the main window is a fair view down to the valley and the hills beyond; but, alas, it is being blocked by a great new building going up for the next stage in the education of those who pass.

In the same month Christopher wrote to Joan Mary to thank her for some dictionaries and grammars which she had been able to send him; they were, he said, just what was needed and he had sent them to Mondoro, 'which is a very poor mission compared with Musami.' Then he added,

Well, the world does seem to be in a strange state: with a dog whirling round and round a thousand miles above us: like Claudio's idea of the after-life in 'Measure for Measure':

> 'To be imprisoned in the viewless winds
> And blown with restless violence round about
> The pendant world.' (49)

Not till 13 December could Christopher write home that,

The rains have come at last *six* weeks late after the false start. After a few months we shall be getting very sick of them; but at present it is very nice to see the new grass springing up, and all the people ploughing and hoeing madly. There are always fine intervals, too, and I hope we get one of these for Christmas.

He continued:

A crisis has occurred here; — while the baboon gets milder and more benevolent, the monkey gets wilder and naughtier, and has now begun to invade the church. So, after great efforts, it was caught and transported by motor car to a forest far away across the river. All sober citizens rejoiced. But after 4 days, how no one knows, it was discovered back on the mission utterly exhausted and mewing piteously, thoroughly repentant like the Jackdaw of Rheims. But now after 3 more days it is wilder and wickeder than ever. And now no one at all can catch it.

I have just finished the 'Tichborne Claimant'. I really do recommend it to Patrick. Perhaps you could give it to him in a birthday-cum-Christmas present from me? It is maddening because of the loose ends, but most intriguing and Douglas Woodruff does leave you with the awful feeling that he *was* Sir Roger after all.

On 21 December, Feast of St Thomas, the Apostle, Christopher wrote,

(49) The Russians had put a dog in orbit in November 1957.

167

I am saying my Christmas Midnight Mass at a village called Rota which is a centre for a good many catholics. It is across the Shavanoe River (which is still quite shallow owing to lack of rain) and away up a winding track among the hills — a pleasant place, rather Swiss-looking, grey rocky hills sticking up out of green shut-in plains. I ought to go after that to another village 6 miles away; but it means crossing another river, with very steep banks by a weir, and the car I use is very old with rather shaky brakes and steering. So I have prudently sent word that they must come to Rota and I will say Mass there again in the morning. It is all made very easy with these new fasting regulations. (50)

and on 3 January, 1958 he wrote again to describe this time in the bush.

I had a very successful Christmas. There was a lot of rain before and afterwards, which has brought out the crops beautifully but the actual day was fine and dry and the night was cloudless with a full moon. So I had a very good crowd for my Masses.
The climate here fits in well with at least one of the Christmas Prophecies — Isaiah's 'Drop down dew, ye heavens, from above, and let the clouds rain the just: let the earth be opened and bud forth a saviour. . ' (51)
I am going tomorrow to supply for the priest at Maradellas, a small town like Gatooma but more 'fashionable'; but it's not worth bothering about any change of address. Then the term and school year begin on January 20th. Not greatly looking forward to that.

9
MUSAMI 1958

Christopher had now been back at Musami for three months and he was disgruntled; teaching at what was a low level was not only drudgery for him but he thought it a waste of his time taking up, as it did, the hours which he would like to have spent in the bush.
Early in January he wrote a letter in which he broke the silence of two years before and he wrote of the time when his involuntarily spoken words — 'why not send me?' — had been taken at their face value. He still asked what he had been sent to do — but that was a different question from why he had been sent. It may well be wondered since he was so unhappy when taken from his work at home, how soon he realised what he could achieve in Africa, or whether he knew that this would be his finest work. The answer must be that he knew. The habit of Particular Examen which begins in earnest in the Novitiate, accompanies a Jesuit in some degree

(50) The hours of fasting had been shortened to three; before that the fast before a mass — and there are always three to be said at Christmas — had been from Midnight.
(51) Isaiah Chapter 48, verse 8. (Introit of the Mass for Wednesday in Ember Week, and also Saturday Masses of Our Lady, in Advent.)

throughout his life and naturally is not only concerned with failure. Christopher in the first days in Rhodesia must have come face to face with the fact that his misery, anyway once the first shock of change was over, was unnecessary. Quite early on he had written,

it is a new life and promises to be a rich one. I find myself greatly drawn towards the people, their needs and problems. (52)

and when, he wrote on 18 June 1956, the first year that he was there in Rhodesia,

all we can *count* on is being subject to God's general providence with a special intention for us sometimes hermetically sealed within it (53)

it is impossible to believe that he did not know well enough of the 'special intention' for himself. In November that year he wrote that he thought that there might have been an 'overhead connection' between his going and what had followed which could prove that his decision to go had been right. 'I never dreamt' he had written 'that there would be such an immediate eruption of visible blessings' (53)

But now in this letter of 4 January 1958, written one day after that in which he had described his Christmas celebrations, he went very fully into what had been and what was in his mind; he began;

Now I must say something about (though I cannot answer) a question which you are often asking me: how long am I likely to be in this country, at least before getting a holiday. I cant answer it as I am still not sure about something which I could not get an answer to when I was first sent out here, viz: A. Was I being sent out for some special post 'suited to my talents'. B. Was I being sent out just as an ordinary foot-soldier?

As mentioned earlier, he never asked Fr Boyle; had he done so he would have received the answer.

The latter seemed unlikely because of my advanced age and the fact that I had just qualified after long labour as a writer and was not aware of having done anything disgraceful which would call for transportation. On the other hand through the Provincial's talk of 'great opportunities' etc., I seemed to see no bigger than a man's hand, the prospect of 3rd or 4th curate in the Salisbury Cathedral.

Across these human calculations came the fact that during the war I had found a strong attraction in working for the blacks even to the point of feeling that it might be for me 'a vocation within a vocation', so to speak. This was the thread I decided to follow, and so started learning the language in England, not merely in response to a 'feeling', but also (though I didnt mean it as crudely as I put it

(52) To Miss Daisy Moseley, March 1956.
(53) To Madeleine.

169

now) as a prudential insurance against being a curate in Salisbury. The feeling that I was after all destined to work for the blacks was greatly strengthened (a) by your conversion and then the 4 childrens' and (b) more logically, by being enabled during my first year to overcome a series of obstacles and become more or less a 'proper missionary'. However, that as you see, puts me in category B.

I think I would be there in any case. There was some talk when I first came out of getting experience for writing, travelling about, etc., — but no means of travel. And then the shortage of men. You cant say 'O no, I am a special person. . ' 'Who says so?' There was never really any practical choice except parish-work for the whites or mission-work for the blacks.

Perhaps it is hind-sight that makes this argument so extraordinary; for many, possibly, the complete separation of the two categories was valid, but for Christopher and others too, it was not, and he was mistaken in thinking as he did. However the letter goes on to the question of leave. For Category (A), he said, a holiday at home in pursuance of a special job was not out of the question but for those in category (B) it might happen after 10-20 years — or never, and the letter went on,

Unless of course one quits altogether. (54) What makes me write that last line is that, owing to a peculiar tangle in high quarters here, I am faced all this coming year with a burden of teaching (teaching of course at a very low level — and at a very low salary, incidentally much less than half what my former pupils at Manresa are getting) such that it will virtually deprive me of the direct priestly work among the Africans which has hitherto been my subjective mainstay and my objective raison d'etre; for a bright African could do better the job I am at present down to do. I cannot escape the knowledge that I am being wasted, not merely as a quite gifted priest, but (what is much more important) as a priest at all.

It was not conceit that made Christopher write those last lines but a sure knowledge of the tools he had been given to use; but all the same he was not always right about the way in which he should use them. His complaint about the salary, which of course was paid by the Government, was rather tragic and the reason it was so low will later be explained, for the moment is it necessary to say that it was not for himself that he minded? — he wanted the money for the Mission and to spend on his work. He ended the letter — since he knew how much his family wanted to see him,

I am afraid (for your sake) that I must follow the thread I have followed up to now — it is not the first time it has got tangled — aided by the mundane knowledge that life is full of changes and

(54) He meant the mission-field, not the Society, though his letter of March makes it clear he had no intention even of 'quitting' that.

surprises and unexpected solutions.

I hope this doesn't make bitter reading for you, but I think you will agree that the part about 'unexpected solutions' is something to be very much believed in.

In Christopher's next letter, that of 17 January, he referred to 'tangles mounting up on all sides of which my own is only one very small example'. They were due to illness and would soon be resolved. His letters of February contain little of interest but one written on 21 March shows that by then he was quite calm. He wrote,

It *is* true that I am 'wedded to Africa' — that is the best phrase to express it. What I do think however (quite cold-bloodedly), is that after a time I will get a more interesting job which will make return visits to England more feasible. I am able to say that in quite a detached manner because I am not counting on it, being perfectly happy in my present state. Africa is a very tranquillizing place. The teaching gets much easier with practice, and my missionary week-ends are always a mild excitement. The heavy part of the rains are over and gone, and the weather is pellucid and pleasant (55)

Christopher was most successful as a teacher at a high level and when his pupils were en rapport with him; his lasting success at Musami was certainly not his teaching but came from the fact that the boys and girls accepted him as part of their family. Later this will be shown from the letters he received from them. It was of paramount importance. For Africans the Church was so to speak, a new Tribe. Christopher made them welcome and he felt a burning dissatisfaction towards those who did not extend this welcome across 'the great divide' feeling that they came near to driving the black peoples away from the family of the Faith.

On 31 March Christopher wrote of his Holy week plans once more

I shall be conducting my Holy-week services, solo, with much irregular pomp at Rota. Unfortunately the new church (to hold 500) collapsed in the rains before they could get the rafters on.

and then on Easter Tuesday, 8 April.

My Holy-Week was well attended, and I was kept busy day and night. Needless to say there were various adventures with the Pascal Candle. And endless processions by torchlight.

I am ashamed to say I didnt do The Washing of Feet. It wasnt so much cowardice on my part as genuine perplexity. If you had just sloshed a bit of water it would have seemed rather a mockery; on the other hand if you washed properly, well it would take a time. (56)

(55) All the letters this year so far, except the ones quoted as to Lady Aileen Meade, and to Fr Philip Caraman, S.J., were to Madeleine.
(56) To Clare.

Just over a fortnight later Christopher wrote again this time both about education and politics,

24 April

At least this weary term has dragged its fourteen-weeks length to a stopping place. What made it aggravating was that instead of having a peaceful Easter Week before the exams, two vile Inspectors chose that time to turn up early on Easter Tuesday morning, and go through their shabby bag of tricks: announcing they were going off for the day, then doubling back and appearing in the classroom suddenly, and so on — just like Pursuivants! They stayed till Friday, rising late, sleeping in the afternoon and eating largely. One of them said it was time the Missions realised they must feel the crack of the whip . . . . but I think it may be the Inspectors who will feel the 'crack of the whip' if the Dominion Party gets in this General Election of 5 June

Our politics have suddenly assumed an intelligible shape with the 'Tale of Mr Todd'. Mr Todd, the Prime Minister, a Protestant Missionary, was suddenly thrown out by a revolt in his Cabinet, but seemed to have most of the Party (The United Party — in power till the other day) on his side; at least they refused by an enormous majority to accept his chief opponent in his place. Instead a man called Whitehead was summoned all the way back from America to be Prime Minister and was supplied with a fairly safe seat for a bye-election — only to be thrown out by the resurgent Dominion Party (aparteid and soda) who feel that this split has given them their chance. The Todd affair is now simplified by everybody — rightly or wrongly — in the crudest terms: that Todd took African Emancipation seriously whereas his opponents took it as a matter of window-dressing. Hence, for example when Todd brought in his measure for giving the vote to Africans who had reached a certain standard of education, the Native Education Department at once began to reverse their grandiose policy and Inspectors rushed about trying to stop schools, cut down grants etc. ('the crack of the whip').

Though all the details are true, this general picture is unfair. Of course I am sure the real reason is lack of funds; but to the Africans, who think money is unlimited, it seems all part of the conspiracy against Todd, and Todd has lent colour to this by leaving the party with his supporters. So I think the Dominion Party is sure to get in. If so, it will almost certainly make a great mess of things. The one thing that will rouse the passive resistance of our apathetic Africans is to have their thirst for education first excited and then thwarted.

It was not until 8 May that Christopher wrote again specifically about the mission and then it was in a letter to Timothy; this letter was prefaced by a slightly nostalgic paragraph,

8th May, Feast of the Apparition of St Michael the Archangel (in a high cave on Monte Gargano — where I have been and got a shiver as of a strange and mighty presence; it is a mountain promontory on the point that would be the spur if Italy is regarded as a long riding-boot, and is practically an Adriatic island, being surrounded by sea on three sides and being cut off by marshes from the mainland on the 4th; very steep on the north side where the cave is, but sloping down through woods and orchards to very pleasant beaches on the south, it is also the abode of Padre Pio, much frequented by Italian pilgrims but relatively free, I think, from tourists of other races, to be included in any itinerary if you ever found yourself in those parts; it is reached from the mainland (which is a very dull plain) by a single sort of causeway through the marshes and up the mountain, it was here that I saw a fine sight which I have seen in the bush here also: an eagle swooping up from the wheels of the car with a great snake struggling in its talons; in a promontory on the Greek side facing Ithaka (Odysseus's isle) an eagle at quite a height dropped a *tortoise* with a terrific crack on the rock beside me, and I was reminded that this caused the death of some wise man (Solon I think) as recorded by the early Roman poet Ennius who used the odd form of speech 'cere-fregit-brum' for 'fregit cerebrum'. (57) Another memorable portent of the same nature happened to your father and me on the top of Lochnagar when a peregrine falcon hurtled through a very thick mist and dropped a grouse at our feet, in 1942.

My dear Timotheos, I think when I last wrote to you, it must have been nearly a year ago, I outlined my plans for establishing a kingdom for myself; but those plans were frustrated as I was only in that district on a temporary basis. I have now moved back to Musami and think I drew a sort of map of it for you about 2 years ago. The trouble about establishing a kingdom here is that I have to go to too many places too widely separated, with stretches of heretic-land in between. However there is one corner where I go more frequently than elsewhere, and here I am carving out a realm for myself whence all hereticks must flee. It is pretty inaccessible with good natural frontiers. When the people have finished building the new church (which fell down during the rains) I will get them to build me a little round house, whither I may retire in my old age. The only terror is now a bridge has been built over the main river, and the purpose of this originally was for a great main road to be driven through here from Salisbury to the Portuguese frontier and the coast. But mercifully, so I hear, it has now been decided that the obstacles would be too great and the main road must go elsewhere. If so, that is excellent, for we are left with this bridge which is a very fine one, built last year but no road, only rough tracks on either side, good enough for my car but not for town traffic; so the bridge remains, like a lovely white elephant, but a godsend to the natives who used to be isolated when the river was in flood. Now they can get over at this time to sell their early crops to the stores.

It is harvest time now, the best time of the year, a sort of mixture between spring and autumn; the rains are only just over so the earth is still green and fresh, and at the same time there is the nip in the air of approaching winter. Winter is June and July. In winter most days are lovely and sunny, though the shadows where no sun is cut like knives, and the nights are frosty cold; but sometimes the sun doesnt appear and then the day is terribly dank and chill and the night quite stuffy by comparison because of the blanket of cloud.

(57) Christopher of course was remembering from his school days. It was not Solon but Aeschylus and the 'odd form of speech' was: 'cere-comminuit-brum' (Fr T. Corbishley).

173

Ten days later Christopher wrote to Clare who was learning Italian at a convent in Rome; she had written asking for spiritual advice and the answer shows the direct matter of fact manner of his teaching. Anyone who has struggled with prayer will realise — as the scholastics to whom he taught English at Manresa realised — that Christopher always assumed others to have as much knowledge and experience as he had himself and that all others needed from him was to be shown how to apply that knowledge — Many books made up of letters of spiritual direction have been published through the centuries; many of Christopher's friends, particularly those who knew of his success as a retreat-giver without having been to one of his retreats, expected him to add to their number. But this, just like the work of the Catholic Evidence Guild in his boyhood, was not his way. He lived his life in union with God; such was his example and those who sought his teaching had usually to pick up from that such crumbs as they could. The letter to Clare is almost certainly unique; he began it lightly enough,

So many thanks for your letter of 5th and the other of 7th May. I did not realise that you were going to flit with such extreme rapidity to Les Oiseaux Convent, or as I would prefer to say to Gli Ucelli or possibly Ucellini. I have been trying madly to remember the street where you live, Via di Villa Patrizi; I once went to tea with the inmates of the Patrizzi Palace who were cousins of Fr Bernard Basset, S.J.; but even if the Palazzo is in the same place as the Via, I cannot recall but keep mixing it up with the Barberini. So you see it would ill become me to offer any advice where to go and what to see, much less to try to compete with Mère Marie Yvonne (enchanting name): '. . . you will see a little green door, push it open.' There was a don at Oxford who used to intersperse his lectures on Roman history with such remarks as, 'It's — er — where the bus stops, you know.'

I think it has to be taken for granted that not much help of the kind you are looking for can be had in Confession.

Confession is mainly a divine arrangement for the lifting of sins; and where it is a question not so much of particular sins but of a general dis-ease, then Confession can only provide a general remedy. What you are thinking of would seem to be called 'Spiritual Direction'. A devout person, (generally a woman!) has a 'director' (a priest experienced in spiritual things) to whom he or she goes outside confession to say what is happening in her soul (e.g. what inspiration to good she has had and what difficulties and desolations in the way) and to receive advice, e.g. what difficulties should be made light of and which taken seriously, or what kind of prayer it would be best to practise at this time. Admirable as such a practice can be and has been, you can see how it lends itself to a certain amount of affectation and old lace. I think it is rather a thing of the past now, perhaps gone out with the entry of psychoanalysis. The modern equivalent of its very necessary function is provided, I think, by those sodalities or professional guilds (e.g. Catholic nurses) or

Youth Groups who have a chaplain (actually called a 'spiritual director' sometimes) attached to them. But that is not of much use to you.

The best thing really is if you can get over the initial obstacles to make a 'Retreat'. In a retreat you do see more clearly what is going on in your soul and feel more impelled to talk about it; and the priest giving the retreat is generally well equipped to give advice and also has this great advantage that you will be seeing him this once and probably not again, so there is more chance for the Holy Spirit to work unimpeded.

What the priest says may amount to no more than the 'dont worry' of the Confessional. But in the light of a Retreat it comes like the comfort of Our Lord to the Apostles, 'Peace be with you. Do not fear. It is I.' What I think I am trying to say is that God's way of helping us is often not by any illumination or clear direction in the mind, (I mean not by any actual message) but just by the presence of Christ which brings with it its own special kind of illumination and clarity. Christ is always present, but sometimes the mists lift from our mind and senses and we know it with a great certainty that Christ is there and with him all good things, all answers, way, truth, life.

However it is not necessary to make a retreat to have such a gift from God. Perhaps in one of the Roman churches, big or little, if you can elude your companion for a few minutes, you may find that peace which is the prerequisite and the promise of his coming. If so ask at once and insistently that you may know His will for you and do it; for that is a prayer that never goes unheard.

Alas, our term is beginning again, and I must hie away to drudgery.

'The prayer that never goes unheard' — the core of Christopher's teaching — he had said the same thing in his letter of 1 March to Charlie Meade. And as always he insisted that anything to do with the Faith 'is essentially of the mind, detached, judicial'. For him the idea of a 'director' was, for the common run at least, too personal. Possibly no better advice could have been given to given to his eighteen-year-old niece who had no thought of choosing, as her aunts had done, the life of a nun.

From the end of this month till the end of the year the Past kept impinging on the Present and threatening change in Christopher's immediate Future; shadows dancing in his sunlight. At first there was nothing really new. On 15 June he wrote to Fr Philip Caraman,

I have now received the imposed pages of the text of Hopkins, and the notes from O.U.P. and I really am more grateful than I can say for the immense care which has obviously gone to the checking of details and correction of my mistakes. I do hope the book will be a success, certainly not for my own sake, but to justify all the labour that has gone into it.

I wonder if you would send me for review 'A Shona Epic', (the first of its kind) which has just come out; by H. W. Chitepo (O.U.P.)

I could make it a peg for an article on the nature of the people if you like.

Then on 3 July his mind turned again to his time with the R.A.F. — as it had in his letter of May to Timothy — for it was when he had taken a party of airmen to see Padre Pio (and had himself been much impressed by him) that he had gone to Monte Gargano. Now Patrick was to go to Palestine; Christopher had been there, of course when he went from West Africa via Cairo on his way to his new posting with the Force waiting at Aleppo. He wrote,

Jerusalem is all but a blur to me— just a few vivid pictures, e.g. of the Via Dolorosa and of an African soldier kneeling motionless in a room, the Praetorium I think, while an Arab swept busily all round him with a broom and between his knees.

I remember jumping off a bus and climbing Mount Tabor reaching the top just at sunset and spending the night with the two Franciscans on top: a wonderful modern church there, Italian, modelled on an ancient Syrian one I had visited near Aleppo. Also of course the Lake of Galilee and the terrific pull up and up to Mount Hermon — Just have a look at the Lake of Galilee, without visiting any special place.

On 14 July Christopher wrote home with Africa uppermost in his mind, until the very end —

I had forgotten that I would be overwhelmed this week-end with the great St Paul's holiday. The actual holiday is the public one (Rhodes and Founders) which lasts from Saturday to Tuesday inc. But here we keep it as the delayed Feast of St Paul — and the still more delayed Corpus Christi procession, not to mention still more delayed Easter Duties for those who come from afar. All the 22 out-schools turn up in force, along with their parents and many others and most of them camp here from Saturday till Monday, so the smoke of a thousand fires goes up all around us. There are sports and singing and competitions of all kinds and a great display of goods and much buying and selling — and many confessions. It is in fact (except that we have no fireworks — not yet any way) just like a gigantic Italian 'Festa' in honour of a patron saint.

But just as he was ending the letter the posts arrived. In red ink he scribbled an addition,

I will write next post about Rupert's proposal which has taken me quite by surprise.

Rupert Hart-Davis, Humphry House's literary executor, had sent a letter to say that it was time for House's work to be carried on and for the definitive biography of Gerard Manley Hopkins to be written. Every one concerned, he wrote, wanted House's work to be used by a sensitive and intelligent writer and all of them from his widow, Madeline House, to the O.U.P. agreed that Christopher was the ideal person to do it. Rupert added,

I realise that if this suggestion had been made before you left for Africa you would surely have jumped at it, but I suspect now you are feeling differently and may have come to feel that there is an important job for you to do in Africa . . . I can't think that to come home for, say, a year and write this book would necessarily destroy the fruits of all your efforts. . . . you must know that you are ideally qualified to write it . . . I honestly think that it is your duty to Literature and to the Society, to take on this job if the Society approves . . .

The letter came as a bombshell. Christopher was taken completely by surprise. Fr Philip Caraman acted for the Province in all matters relating to Hopkins. The Archbishop of Salisbury's consent would have to be obtained if Christopher was to write the book; he was at this time on a visit to England, so, on 18 July Christopher wrote to Fr Caraman asking him to approach Archbishop Markall to know his view. He wrote,

My position, very briefly, is that I would love to spend a year in England on writing a one-volume life of G.M.H. — but only on condition that they dont say — 'All right, but if you go home, you stay at home.' I mean I am definitely committed to Africa. So it's up to the Provincial and Archbishop Markall and that's why, if Markall is to be approached, it would be better to do it while he is in England. (58)

At the same time he answered Rupert Hart-Davis's letter.

18 July
Thank you very much for your letter. It was delightful to be remembered that way and I wish I could answer yes at once. But, as you know very well, we are at the disposal of our superiors in these matters. However as our own inclinations are taken into account, perhaps I had better say just what I feel about your proposal even though the decision does not rest with me.
I feel a considerable load of gratitude to you and to those who judge me fit to write this life — that is the first thing.
Secondly, I do feel, as you suggest — that there is an important job for me to do in Africa. There is still a chance of building up a decent educated body of Africans before the gong goes, so to speak: and for that task all the sensitivity and intelligence one can command are desperately needed. I am committed now, and having put my hand to the plough, etc.
At the same time I dont feel that a year in England would necessarily be deserting my post. It might make settling down here again rather hard and it would cause other inconveniences. But on the other hand — apart from all the other considerations which you mention in your letter — the finished work might give me a bit of

(58) To Fr Philip Caraman, S.J., from Musami 18 July 1958.

prestige (which I badly need to penetrate the thornhedge of illiterate inspectors) and even a modicum of cash (which is also badly needed as the Education Dept, having encouraged a policy of expansion have now begun to retract, which leaves us in an awkward position) — enough to pay my fare any way.

But the Jesuit missionaries here have a rather hard tradition about going home on leave. If you go home the tendency is to say, 'All right, if you go home, you stay home.' I couldnt agree to that.

So it comes back to the decision of the respective Superiors in England and Rhodesia.

I have written all this from the purely selfish point of view of my job here. But I know that you will not think that I am unmoved by the points you mention — in particular I am moved by the thought that Humphry would not have minded my taking over his work and would have approved the choice and proposal you have made — though how to use his work in one volume without destroying his particular objective creates a problem in practice.

When he wrote next to us, which was on 25 July he wrote quite briefly about the proposal; we did of course know of it and had indeed written to him about it.

About this peculiar letter from Rupert — I would love to come back for a year but have told Rupert the decision does not rest with me.

Then he went on to describe the celebrations on this his feast day — as he explained in a letter of the same date to Joan Mary, his pupils attached great importance to name days.

I had a very happy day being presented by my pupils with innumerable threepenny bits, sixpences, bottles of pop, etc., which are their customary presents, and serenaded for a long time in piercing harmonies to a refrain 'Stay with us, dear Father, you are our Father do not leave us . . . ' but I infer that this is a customary plea on these occasions, and not that Fr Caraman has been casting his net still further afield.

I was able to secure a great load of corrugated iron roofing, also, for a church being built in one of my villages — 8 ft sheets which, my remembrances of Pythagoras's theorem tell me, will just fit, the width being 14½ ft, if the uprights are cut down to 3 ft — at 3/- a sheet which is just covered by the £5 they managed to subscribe (3 sq by 7½ sq is a little less than 8 sq ft isnt it?) So that is very satisfactory. I have just returned from transporting the load there, having had my lunch by the side of a rocky river called the Nyakambiri, a fork tributary of the Shavanoe.

In England plans were tentatively going ahead. Christopher wrote again on 11 August, to Rupert who had seen Archbishop Markall.

It is incredibly good of you to have taken so much trouble. The Archbishop did evidently see the Provincial that night, for the Provincial (whom I thought to be in Guiana) wrote to me that week-end. The thing has leapt like a bomb from speculation into imminence.

Unless it is going to upset things and people I would very much prefer to come home not immediately but in August 1959, and stay till the end of 1960. I have various reasons for this which concern my position out here.

This request is interesting but what immediately followed was of more interest still.

For nearly thirty years the fact that Christopher had no degree had not mattered. It had not mattered, when he had taught, as he had for four years at Manresa before he left for Africa, at University level; some of his pupils from that time are well-known writers now, and still echo his views along with their own. But the 'illiterate Inspectors' in Africa probably knew nothing of the complexity of Scotus; and if they knew, cared little about the difficulties of understanding Hopkins. Letters after your name were their criterion, and Christopher was poorly paid by them because he had none — save the proud S.J. of his Order. And he minded more and more about the pay for at this time he wanted a landrover, new if possible 'but second-hand would do' — so that he could penetrate further and further into the wilds — in search of souls.

His letter of 11 August, to Rupert continued

Another point is just a side issue which will make you laugh, but I am quite serious about it. I want to get a B.Litt.Oxon. Sounds ludicrous but I simply must get some academic letters after my name to be of any use educationally out here.

I want to be absolutely honest with you, because you have been so very good about this. So I must say that in my heart of hearts — if there is such a place — I don't very much want to come back; it's only a superstition that a sort of spell may be broken. But against that superstition there are such solid reasons, the ones you have mentioned as well as others, that I have no option but to accept subject to my superiors who now seem happily to have accepted also. I feel it is a tremendous honour and will do my best to be worthy of it.

The reason he asked for a year's delay he made clear in a letter to his sister, Joan Mary who was teaching at the Sacred Heart Convent at Woldingham in Surrey; writing to her on 28 August, he said,

What weighed with me most was that I had just begun plans for a church at a strategic point where I go at the week-ends, and if I left this year or early next they would have come to nothing. Apart from that I only feel it a bit odd to go so soon and then have to become acclimatized all over again. But the year's delay and the fact that it is now upon a Province level have taken the matter out of my hands.

The old Archbishop, Chichester, is coming out again, as we prophecied he would. When he was leaving here he was asked if he

179

would ever return and replied, 'I dont know at all — but everyone tells me I will, so perhaps they may be right'.

Christopher's next letter home on 29 September said nothing more about his possible visit to England. He wrote,

My ancient car to which I have become very attached has now been officially given six months more of life. So instead of jealously ekeing out its existence I am inclined now to squander it generously and am branching out into wilder valleys and remoter glens. There are so many wild looking hills across the river that you tend to think the region would be a solitude, as in Scotland. But in fact it is quite densely populated. For every hill you turn the corner of another long and struggling village springs into life. They are mostly people who were turned off richer lands to the south to make room for ex-service Afrikaner immigrants after the war.

The other side of my work — larger but less interesting — the teaching is now drawing to its climax with the public examinations this November. This exam (equal to the old L.C.) is designed as the first step of three (S.C. and H.C.), each of two years meant to lead the survivors to the threshold of the university. But at present there is a gaping void after the first step. The Government having set all this in motion, has now turned right into reverse. The reasons given are financial, but it seems clear they are also political — the fear that the number of Africans entitled to vote would be increased each year till it reached a number which could, if organized, make a difference to an election. So we do not know what will happen next year, or whether this place will have to retrace the steps already taken till it goes back to the level of a village elementary school.

It is a very complicated question with much to be said for and against. But, the psychological root of the problem seems to me to be that 'Partnership' in practice (i.e. admitting certain Africans to responsible posts and being willing to train them fairly tactfully, exploiting their good qualities and putting up with their faults) all this demands a high degree of civilization in the senior partner which you get in some of the traditional English public services, but which simply is not present among the whites of this country and doesnt seem ever likely to be in sufficient strength to be reliable. But I sincerely hope I am wrong in that last gloomy prognostication.

Christopher's feelings are understandable but he was less than fair to the hard core of liberal opinion there was, and still is, in Rhodesia.

The next letter of interest was written on 20 October, it referred to the publication of the review of the Shona Epic which he had asked Fr Caraman to be allowed to do for 'The Month'. He called it A Shona Eclogue.

I have an article in 'The Month' for November or December on a rather lovely poem in Shona which was published this year. It was edited with a translation by the lady who taught me Shona at the African School of studies in 1955. The poem gives a good feeling of the land and its people.

Then before he turned to the Papal Election, the main topic in his next two letters also, he said that Rupert always sent him his autumn book list, kindly offering him free any books he liked. This time Christopher had 'pricked down' five

Everything now of course has been overshadowed by the Pope's death. You will be glad to have had that sight of him at Castel Gandolfo even though only from the balcony; and I think that's all nearly everybody has seen of him in the last year or two. My mind naturally goes back to the gripping February and March 1939 when I was in Rome. I should think there will be much more uncertainty about this election than about the last. But the world reaction to Pius XII does seem very wonderful, doesnt it? It is so strange that what used to be our greatest liability, Papal Supremacy, (the 'sole obstacle' to many High Anglicans) should now stand out as our greatest asset.

27 October
I must say I was very disappointed that the Cardinals didnt elect a pope yesterday, Feast of Christ the King, with the Wind of the Holy Spirit fresh upon them so to speak. It is the first time that the full merciless glare of modern publicity has been directed on all the mediaeval parapharnalia of the conclave (the last one having been so quick) and it is a bit embarrassing.
The more I think about the late Pope, the more wonderful appears to me how he rose above power politics and popular trends, walking on top of them, by sheer intelligent goodness.

7 November
At the very first impact of the Papal election news, I was a bit taken aback and could only think of the unsavoury anti-Pope, Baldassare Cossa, who has been 'John the Twenty-third' until now. John the Twenty-*second* an Avignon Pope, was, I understand, a frail old man of 72 who then proceeded to show tremendous strength and energy, and made everybody sit up until his death *18* years later at the age of 90. But now on second impressions, I feel very well disposed towards our new Holy Father. I really dont know what evidence I have to go on, but I seem to have come to the spontaneous conclusion that he is a tranquil, firm and fatherly old man who will keep the church on an even keel. One thing does strike me for certain is the amazing efficiency of the thing; the machinery is supposed to creak and groan like mediaeval chains, but what other institution or dynasty or even business could lose its absolute head without the faintest knowledge and yet not the faintest worry about who the successor would be? And then in a couple of weeks have a new one without the faintest trouble in the body?

Christopher's letter, this year, for Patrick's birthday was written on the day itself, 25 November; it contained as well as birthday wishes this entertaining passage,

I saw an instance of a Bantu Tribal case in a book the other day

which I thought might amuse you, since I think Madeleine told me that you were preparing with some reluctance a lecture on Law and Morality. It was a judgement of the elders in a family dispute as follows: 'We have powers to make you divide the crops, for this is our law, and will see that this is done. But we have not power to make you behave like an upright man . . .' (58a)
It seems to put the case quite neatly.

He wrote again on 10 December,

I saw the Provincial the other day. Immediate prospects of my doing the book are not good. Whisper it low and do not misunderstand me — I do not very much care. All this Hopkins business rather sets my teeth on edge, and I hoped I had finished with it three years ago. From the way he spoke, however, I should not be surprised if some further move to get me back were not made later on. But in order to do my work properly here I find it best (psychologically) not to take any account of these possibilities beyond mentioning them.

On this note the Journal for 1958 ended. There had been a hitch over the proposed writing of the life; the reasons are irrelevant here — all that has to be said is that the hitch had nothing to do with the English Province, there all concerned, whether in England or Rhodesia, were eager for Christopher to undertake the work — far more eager than he was to do it.

10

MUSAMI 1959

1959 began with a letter written on 3 January — as had 1958, but this one was to Timothy. At first reading it seems of no particular interest; had he not written several like it before and indeed even drawn a map of the country round the Mission at Musami? He had — and indeed in this lies its interest; it was natural for him in writing to this nephew in his early teens to recall his own family games — the domains and kingdoms of his boyhood. When he had drawn the first map on 14 April 1956 these are not mentioned but on 8 May 1957 he writes from Mondoro of his Kingdom in the north, of 400 sq. miles and 4000 subjects; he is hoping to annexe a Kingdom there in the South as well but, alas, his hopes that Mondoro might be 'the little Mission of his own' were dashed. Exactly a year to the day later, 8 May 1958 he wrote of another Kingdom — at Musami where 'I will get them to build me a little round house, whither I may retire in my old age,' — the phrase somehow recalls the time when he was held 'spell-bound in the faery-land of Yeats':

(58a) Patrick used it on March 1959 in the Maccabean Lecture — see Law & Morality O.U.P.

182

And a small cabin build there, of clay and wattles made:
Nine bean-rows will I have there, a hive for the honey-bee
And live alone in the bee-loud glade.

and now this year he wrote,

Dear Timothy, I am afraid it is a long time since I last wrote About 2 years ago I described to you my Kingdom which I was establishing in the place where I then was,

This was, of course, Mondoro:

But I was moved shortly after back to the place where I first was when I came out here (Musami). Here I have carved out for myself a Kingdom which is more permanent, though I cannot give so much time to it as I have to teach most of the time. I am not concerned with the circle just round the Mission, but only with the land between the Rivers — that is mine. I have drawn a brief map of it on the other side of the page. I think I sent you a map of it when I first came out, but now I know it more intimately, the names of all the hills and all the villages. The rivers are cut very deep, so very hard to cross when there is no bridge; in fact the little rivers are harder than the big ones which usually have a drift of flat rock somewhere. There are many more villages tucked away in the valleys than at first appears. The squares I have marked with crosses are new churches in old Mass stations (Rota is my chief one); and the plain crosses are new Mass stations which I have started.

The letter goes on briefly about the distances he travelled and about some of his visits but it is time to pause because suddenly you realise that he has told Timothy something of the success of his apostolate. It is unlikely that he thought of what he was doing, nevertheless here is recorded three new churches (he had mentioned building before but only incidentally) in three old stations — at Rota, where he had placed the large red Missal which the Archbishop of Liverpool had sent him, for as Christopher wrote at the time, the Archbishop had a very soft spot for the African Missions — at Chizanga, where he had said the third of his Christmas Masses a week before, as he recounted in this letter, and for where, with the £5 that had been collected he had bought the load of corrugated iron for the roof, transporting it there himself on his name day, eating his lunch on the way back between the River Shavanowe and the River Nyakambiri. The third one to the north of St Paul's remained nameless, the 'place which was pretty inaccessible' to which he would retire. And then the Mass Stations which he had visited, as regularly as he could, are shown. Altogether not a bad record for the brief timy he had had in which to work and one which surely had justified Fr Boyle's hopes.

After this he wrote nothing more of general interest until the end of January — there had been a letter to Patrick with a legal query, and one to Rupert about Hopkins Life, but on 29 January he wrote,

29 January 1959

Just after I had posted a letter to Patrick a worthy black man in a very handsome car and clothes arrived at the Mission — a Mr Herbert Chitepo, an advocate (the only African advocate in Southern Rhodesia). He came about the famous Beer Case which is due to explode in these parts — concerning which more later.

What transpired after a short conversation was that:

(a) he had just returned from Delhi and was overwhelmed to learn that I was Mr Justice Devlin's brother (did Patrick meet him at the Conference?)

(b) he is the same Chitepo about whose poem I have written an article in 'The Month' — which should have appeared ages ago and I suppose will eventually. (59)

I must explain about the Case in which he is defending Counsel. The Native Commissioner (White) has long been at loggerheads with the hereditary chief (Black) of this reserve. As one move in the campaign the N.C. summoned all headsmen together on Christmas Eve and told them that all brewing and drinking of native beer was forbidden for 3 months from Jan 4 to April 4 in two districts of the Reserve — (the precise districts that constitute my 'kingdom') — giving no reasons for his ukase, and sweeping out when they began asking reasons. On January 5th or 6th the police swooped on some nearby villages, overturned the pots of beer and arrested five men. The Chief then slipped up to Salisbury and engaged the services of Chitepo. Chitepo is the lawyer employed by the African Congress, who of course are cashing in on this, telling the people to go on drinking because they will be protected etc; this is bad because hitherto the Chief has been the great bulwark against Congress. Any way Chitepo arrived and began to ask the Mission Superior (Fr Davis) and a storekeeper, questions about the drunkenness in the neighbourhood and district. Fr Davis said I would know more about it than he, so that was how I was called in to see Chitepo. Then shortly after he left, the police arrived with a subpoena for Fr Davis and the storekeeper to appear as witnesses tomorrow in the district court.

30 January

Apparently it was Chitepo and not the Police who called Fr Davis as witness. On the previous day he had the N.C. for many hours in the witness box, and the N.C. had quoted Fr Davis among others as saying drunkenness in the neighbourhood was growing dangerously. So all Chitepo wanted to know was whether Fr Davis had lodged a formal complaint with the N.C. which of course he hadnt. Case goes on — verdict unknown. But the police seem to have been very impressed with Chitepo — not only a very clever man, they said, but a gentleman. Nevertheless it will be a bad thing if he wins the case — but perhaps no less bad if he loses. We were peaceful till now, but it is over unnecessary aggravations like these that trouble starts.

17 February

Madly exciting about Pope John and the new Council.

(59) It appeared in 'The Month' of March 1959.

I am wondering whether you have received the Hopkins volumes yet. According to Philip Caraman they should have been sent out (the gift copies) in early January. The only interest I have (in the publication date) is a basely utilitarian one: I am wondering whether any hard cash may accrue to me, enough to get a 2nd hand Land-rover, for my present ancient vehicle (which I rely on completely for my apostolic chores) is utterly on its last legs and is in any case not much use in this wet weather without 4-wheel drive.

26 February
Rhodesia is in the news now, not very pleasantly. The N.C. has just been telling us with gusto how the Congress members round here were arrested — chained hand and foot, chucked into lorries and shackled to the cross-bar. I kept very quiet. Not that I have any sympathy with the Congress who are mostly rats; they are certainly well out of the way and it was most expeditiously done; but it does mark sharply the difference between the British Tradition (officially repudiated by our Prime Minister) which prevails in Northern Rhodesia and Nyasaland, where all the trouble is, and the 'baaskap' rule which really prevails here in Southern Rhodesia. It is surprising the number of quite simple Africans who have no sympathy with Congress yet know enough to be surprised that people can be sentenced without being charged and tried. It will be interesting historically to see the outcome: whether the action will justify itself by its success (as I expect the like has done in the Portuguese possessions) or whether it will provoke the trouble which does not as yet exist.

30 March, Easter Monday
I am all of a dither! On Wednesday heard a stray mention of Mr Justice Devlin on the *B.B.C.* (60) (They are deliberately disregarding the Commission in this country.) Then I had to go off for my Holy Week. Returned last night to find your letter — but with no dates of his arrival or length of stay. Also a letter from Kitten saying they had begged him to come and stay if possible. That would really be the best idea, if he and I could stay together at Government Lodge for a day or two. They really are *very* nice and kind.
Tremendous crowds at my mountain village. 600 Communions and 400 confessions.
Would it be better if P. came to stay *after* the enquiry is over?

Remembering how Christopher had longed to see Billy in the war it is easy to understand how he looked forward to seeing Patrick now. Ten days after the B.B.C. announcement he met him at Salisbury airport. Thereafter he pinioned on paper his excitement and pleasure sending it, post haste through the air to us at home. He went into Salisbury on 10 April and stayed at Campion House from where he wrote,

(60) The announcement that Patrick was to be Chairman of the Nyasaland Inquiry Commission.

185

10 April: 4 p.m.
I arrived in great state in the Governor's car at 12 at the airport.
Alas! Flight delayed till 5.15. But now I have just rung up and heard
that it is 4.59. So the Governor's car is coming round in a few
minutes to bear me once more to the Airport. So will continue this
letter after the great event has happened.

10.30 p.m.
And now it has happened and I am too sleepy to give more than
the merest details. 5.p.m. saw, the plane arrive. Fought my way
through a mob of big-wigs in time to seize P. before he was pushed
into a commissionarial car. Everything then of course vanished
before immediate family privacy. Long conversation while he was in
the bath, then wonderful dinner at 'Meikles' (the Salisbury Hotel,
— really very good.)
Saw all the coloured 'stills' and have now just returned to
Campion House laden with a great parcel I havent yet had time to
explore (including socks and a missive from Timothy).

13 April: from Musami.
We met again for breakfast on Saturday morning and then parted
at 10 at which time a car was due to take them to the airport. I
should say that P., though very tired, was extremely cheerful; he
finds his fellow commissioners extremely pleasant and seems quite
on top of the job. It struck me with increased force after 3 years —
what an extremely *Good* man he is!
It was all very enjoyable looking at the coloured photos — and
the socks are quite marvellous — thank you very much indeed.

19 April:
I thought I had safely avoided the photographers at the airport, as
the only photo in our press was the one I sent you. So I hope the
Times one is not too bad. I look forward to seeing it — also any
more Hopkins reviews. The last ones you sent (by P.) were
extremely good — couldnt have been better.

20 April:
Big News — Just heard from Kitten on the phone. A letter to her
from P. suggesting a week-end visit — and he is coming *next*
Saturday (25th, Frances's birthday!) and staying till Monday and so
I have been bidden to come and so of course I will. She says they
have a party of long-standing on Sunday afternoon so P. and I can
slope off during that time — Perhaps we might pay a visit here!
(Musami)

27 April:
I did a letter yesterday at Governor's Lodge, but had no stamps
and the paper was too thick any way, so will start again.
I think the best way will be just to give a timetable:

25 April: Saturday
11 a.m.
Called for at Musami by Governor's car and driver! On the way
arranged to say Mass at Nazareth House, a nearby convent, next day.

1 p.m.
Luncheon at Gov. Lodge. Guests included Lord Dulverton (heir of Wills) who directs a Rhodesian Trust of untold millions. Wished I could have touched him for a thousand.

2.45
Set off for the airport with a Comptroller called 'Buster' to meet 'Mr Richardson', plane due 3.15

3.05
Arrived in time to see P. emerging from aircraft – 10 minutes early. P. armed with large suitcase and bulging brief case. P. said hotel at Zomba all right if you were on a climbing holiday, (food good and plentiful) but not very pleasant when you had to stay in all day interviewing etc. Had misty weather there.

3.45
Tea at Gov. House.

4.0 till 6.0
Walked, sat on lawn: pleasant weather. 'Buster' hovered solicitously round the whole time asking questions and volunteering information. Apologised to me afterwards but said he found it so absorbingly interesting. I found it quite interesting too. P. told good tales of crazy evidence-givers which I expect you will hear later.

6.0
Dark. Drink. P. departed for much longer for 'proper' bath.

7.30
A few private words with P. about plans for tomorrow.

8.0
Dinner: only Peveril and Kitten present. Very pleasant.

11.0
Plans for tomorrow: private lunch for P and me (P, having to avoid big-wigs at luncheon party) and then Peveril (incredibly kind *and humble* in himself) said he would drive himself P. and me to Musami, where I said I would remain – since Prime Minister coming informally to dinner: better for me to skip (Whitehead)

26 April: Sunday
7.30
Having said Mass privately and returned, was finishing breviary in garden when heard click: P. had risen early and was taken photographs.
Peveril and Kitten passed us on way to church having breakfasted upstairs.

8.0
Breakfast. 2 dishes, each with 2 eggs and bacon inside. P. refreshed by good sleep said 'You take one and I'll take the other.' (dish). Did so. Slight hiatus when ADC and Lady-in-waiting arrived and had to wait while more was cooked!
(Actually household is run superbly by catholic African butler,

my firm friend, of course. ADC is nephew of Evelyn Waugh — son of Alec.

9.0 till 11.30
P. resolutely found chair and shady place and became completely absorbed in arrears of work

11.30
Sir Roy Welensky (61) arrived. — enormous girth. K. called me to see vista down the garden with P. sunk in one cane chair and Sir R. overflowing from another but equally sunk in deep confab. Peveril took telescope lens photo of the scene. — perhaps historic!!?

1.0
P and I had private but palatial lunch upstairs —reminiscent of certain situations at West Wick when you were holding fort below.

2.0
Set out for Musami in Peveril's Rolls, no flag flying. P. next to Peveril, I behind. At the sight of Musami hills P kept jumping out to take photos.

4.0
Arrived at Musami, unheralded of course, so no one around. Saw the river and a few other things and had a private tea.

5.0
Time for Peveril and P. to depart — Sir Edgar Whitehead coming to dinner. Before departing P. said he hoped to manage another occasion before May 23rd when he hopes to meet you in ROME.
Meanwhile will get this off with love to all.

8 May
No word of P. since I last wrote but I didnt expect any. A public word, though, there was; that they will be down in Bulawayo next week, 13th, interviewing Dr Banda etc, but I dont think they will go by Salisbury. He was hoping he might get a day off *during* the Commission.
But he was quite definite that he would go straight back — and quite right too — immediately after it was over.

From 8 May until 22 Christopher had no more news to send of Patrick. On the 10th, however he wrote to his nephew Gilpatrick, who had by now finished his Military Service, about half of which, just over a year — he had done in Cyprus, and on Whit-Sunday, 17 May he was going to Liverpool to be confirmed by the Archbishop, Archbishop Heenan.

10 May
I fear the stealthy march of time has caught me unawares, and that this may be too late to give you my heartiest congratulations

(61) Sir Roy Welensky was Prime Minister Of the Federation from 1956-63. Sir Edgar Whitehead was Prime Minister of S. Rhodesia.

188

best wishes and prayers for the great event in Liverpool. (62)

I have a sombre feeling that we have not corresponded for about three years, shortly after I came here. A lot of water — seas and oceans in fact — have flown since then. You have become a seasoned warrior in Cyprus and your Da has visited 3 continents.

I was reading a story called 'Death Stalks in Cyprus' but it was not about recent events — only a peaceful murder among the American Colony, written with that atmosphere of 'unendurable suspense' which becomes so boring after the first few chapters.

I expect you felt the same as I did when I was in Greece in 1944-45 — such wonderful opportunities but such awkward situations.

Do you realise that I once met old Grivas? He was head of the lousy X-ites who started shooting it out with the vile ELAS-ites the day we arrived. (63)

I had 2 wonderful days here with Da. He took a lot of photographs I do hope they come out — but I fear there is a grave suspicion that something went wrong with the spool.

Then there were two more notes about Patrick's visit:

22 May
Just a hasty note written in a bad light. P. as I expect you know is coming to Salisbury on Saturday (tomorrow) staying the week-end and flying back (via Rome?) either Monday or Tuesday. But one fixed point is that I go in tomorrow for lunch tomorrow to see what is afoot.

1 June
I suppose Patrick touched down in Rome a day earlier that you had been told?

Tell him that the other day Sir Edgar Whitehead assured the House that he was doing all he could to get the office of Governor scrapped (merged with Gov-General) as soon as Sir P.W.P. retired, because it would save so much money. I thought it rather a rotten send-off for Peveril who has always stood up for them most loyally. I cant avoid thinking that these Rhodesians have all the vices of Colonials and Welfare State combined — a horrid combination!

It really was wonderful seeing P. so relatively much. I never thought things would work out so satisfactorily.

The excitement being over 'of my brother hovering in the air' as Christopher had expressed it in a letter to Fr Philip Caraman explaining why he was behind hand with a review for 'The Month', correspondence returned to the gentler pace of the last two years. On 22 June he apologised for a short letter saying that his headpiece was not in very good working order owing to various distractions.

I do not mean that I have actually gone insane — only the well-known creeping uncertainty as to relative positions of head and

(62) Gilpatrick's confirmation.
(63) See p. 79.

189

heels. A vile custom of a new department that I have to teach in is to have half-yearly exams, so they had to be set and now corrected. Then by a strange mischance there has been a positive confluence of crazy letters. One from a Pole who wants to get out and come to England to write a thesis on Hopkins and Scotus (Urrh!) addedly crazy because it assumes that a letter written from Poland in December reached me, which it didnt, — sinister(?) — but I suppose one ought to try to help any one from that unfortunate country. Then a boy in Bulawayo with a long list of difficulties such as 'Was there Mass in the B.C.?' varied with obvious quotations from an anti-papist tract — 'would not the money spent on lavish displays be better devoted to the poor and needy?' The letter begins 'Yours could draw up the best attentions of Ideas to my last probles', and ends 'If there is any way, however small, in which I can be of help, Please let me know'.

A month later came the laconic remark,

24 July
Perverse of the Government to disagree with the Report. (64) But I suppose it is Macmillan's principle to stick to his ministers through thick and thin.

He wrote about it again on 31 July and then nearly a month later, on 26 August.

I thought the 'Observer's' reaction and comments rather fine. I should think it's fairly safe to guess that the Report will be remembered long after Lennox-Boyd has disappeared into the anonymity of 'the Colonial Secretary'. It is said to be a best-seller here — but no royalties I suppose, for P. — for the Govt instead, insult to injury! Rhodesian reactions were of course as expected (though more guarded) because they depart from the arm-chair pioneer principle that 50 African lives are a small price to pay to avoid the risk of one European. They make no bones about a threat to beat or kill, or even just to insult being little different from an organized massacre plot. — both mortal sins — so why worry? But it is rather sad to see respectable English papers endorsing this view that the distinction is quibbling and academic.

26 August
One way in which I think the report is so valuable, almost unique, is as a historical document: all the available evidence collected and sifted in the nick of time, before the whole affair vamoosed into the realms of myth and counter-myth. At some future date I think the Conservatives will be sorry not to be able to take the credit for it.

In September there was only one letter; it is of little interest, but on 8 October a letter to Timothy speaks of Christopher's latest activity.

(64) The Tory Government of the day, on the eve of an election, rejected the Nyasaland Commission's Report; the actions of the next Tory Government, elected that year, only make sense on the assumption that the Report was in fact acceptable.

Your 'fort' (hut) seems to have reached majestic proportions. What about illustrating the walls if they are white-wash or plaster? That is my latest craze which I must tell you about. It is WALL-PAINTING, and it is threatening to take up all my available time. The idea came to me when I couldnt get any decent pictures for the walls of my village churches. I suddenly thought 'Why not paint some yourself? They cant be any worse than some of the things in pious shops and repositories.' Then I found it was really quite easy to make a life-size drawing with a thick soft pencil of some conventional religious subject, e.g., I have done Our Lady kneeling before the manger, Our Lord at the Last Supper, using firm flowing lineṣ as far as possible. Then I found that you can get powder (tempera paint) fairly cheap, about 4/- a tin, in any number of different colours, and very fine colours too. There is stuff called water-glass, used for preserving eggs, a sort of treacly substance with a fish-like smell. If you mix this with water it causes the paint to stick quite well on plaster or white-wash. So you just have different saucers of this mixed water for different colours, sprinkle some of the powder in another saucer or on the lid of the tin, dip the brush in the water and then in the powder – and lay on. Dab the powder into a pretty firm paste on the brush, otherwise coloured water will run down the wall. It is very good fun. I make the figures dark-skinned and African-looking and use bright colours. When I have finished the ones I am doing now, I hope that the people themselves will do the others.

Those in contemplation are; a Mary Magdalen, a St Michael lancing a demon in the place where people are baptized so that they can kick the devil when saying 'I renounce Satan'; a fine St Sebastian with arrows and blood spurting all over the place; and a St Cecilia with a gleaming necklace to show where her head was cut off and bracelets where the fetters were.

Great excitement here, this morning, at Musami and some distraction from schools; a dead crocodile was brought in to be burnt. It is a young one a year old, about 5½ feet long; it was danced around with much savage glee because its parents have been a great menace in that particular place.

In Christopher's next letter home, which is dated 20-23 October there is the last of his delightful tales of Africans;

I have just had the greatest success with a sermon since the coin-throwing one at Mondoro – and this was a coin-throwing one too. I was explaining the tribute to Caesar Gospel, and having outlined the great dilemma and its possible applications I made a circle of left thumb and forefinger, like the Italians do, and went on: 'So he said, "whose picture is on this coin?". They said "Caesar's". He said "All right – " ' (with a sudden pitching motion) – ' "Give it back to Caesar then . . . But to GOD –" ' (slapping my heart) ' "Give back what is his" – your heart – ' There was a great exclamation of 'A-ah! A-ah!' So I hastily finished off with: 'And after *that* no man durst ask him any more questions.'

But – as I am slowly discovering – it is very easy to impress these people superficially, and very difficult to impress them profoundly; they appear to have built up a sort of shock-absorbing mechanism over the ages to resist or defer sudden and alarming innovations.

Then Christopher added, rather inconsequentially

By the way it is amusing to see the way the Report is gradually seeping through into the shape of an accepted norm of judgment.

But shortly before this letter he had decided to write the new Superior, Fr Corrigan (65) to tell him of his feelings of frustration at Musami. He had of course been thinking of doing so for a very long time, and presumably he did so now, on 15 October, because he felt that he had done as much work as was possible for him to do in the bush whilst he was tied by his teaching and really did not want to spend another school year, the year beginning in January 1960, at it, if he could be given another task. He wrote,

Have you any alternative to Musami for me? I like the place, but am not needed here except in the capacity of teacher, and, alas, my spiritual life is not strong enough to stand this teaching business any more.
    It is not that the work is particularly onerous but —
    (a) I am in a purely stoodge capacity which gives almost no scope for interest or initiative.
    (b) I am really rather a bad teacher though I do try fairly conscientiously. My results last year were decidedly poor; almost all the failures (66) were due to English alone, or to English and History (my subjects). Someone with less knowledge of these subjects and a more equable temperament, and perhaps a higher salary, would do the job better and be more acceptable.
    I know that mid-term at the end of a school-year is not the ideal time to review one's attitude to teaching. But actually I am quite cold-blooded about the affair. I know very well that I might find a worse job in a worse place. I have no desire to jump out of the frying pan into the. fire, but only cautiously to enquire: Is there any alternative ·man to do my job, and if so what would be the alternative job for me?

The Superior indeed had plans in which Christopher was to be given an important task especially suited to what he called Christopher's 'extraordinary talents', but feeling that Christopher might be turbulent and that his plan for him was not entirely in line with what he knew Christopher had always wanted — and wanted even more by now because he had become overshadowed by a distrust of authority, he wished to approach him with caution so as to get his whole-hearted support. Indeed, when told, Christopher was hesitant and it was not until the first week in December that the matter was

(65) Fr Terence Corrigan, S.J., remained Superior of the Mission in Rhodesia until he succeeded Fr John Coventry in 1964 as Provincial of the English Province.
    (66) i.e. failure in examination results.

finally settled and Christopher welcomed his 'alternative job'.

Meanwhile he had written, on 23 November, a letter to Patrick which deserves a place here.

A peculiar experience which I have lately undergone is responsible for the lateness of this birthday letter. I was suddenly coopted onto a board of examiners and had to transport myself to an American Methodist Mission near MTOKO where I and my co-examiners were incarcerated for six days from Monday morning the 16th to Saturday mid-day the 21st. The Education Department had decided that too many children were passing a certain standard with defective English, so the exam was made a public one, set and marked by the Department, but with a Methodist and a Catholic coopted who would be held up as shields against ensuing complaints. The Catholic got ill just beforehand and I had to take his place in correcting 515 English Compositions. I had been deluded by false information that there were only 240 papers to be done, so set off at crack of dawn on Monday with Waugh's *Knox* and other books and a packet of airmails to fill in what I imagined would be the leisure hours. But there were no leisure hours. I hadnt realised I was joining a company of slaves: 7.30 a.m. to 5 p.m. were the fixed hours, but you were also expected to work for an hour or two after supper till the lights went out at 9.30.

Naturally *I* didnt work all those hours — I thought it well to make it clear from the start that I had come as a matter of courtesy, with nothing to gain or lose, and that since no facilities were available for my saying daily Mass (I was sharing a small bedroom in a crowded Methodist household) I would have to find my own time and place for so doing — Consequently any spare time I had or seized was spent in discovering Catholic natives in the neighbourhood who of course demanded more than just Mass.

Fortunately the Lord and Saint Christopher were with me in the matter of the old car which came and went valiantly on every journey, also in the matter of the rains which always just enabled me to say Mass outside, it being almost physically impossible to say it inside a native hut.

At the cost of considerable suffering at both ends head and tail, I did 100 papers the first day and thereafter 150 each day, (we worked in common of course), finishing my chore on Thursday.

Then the Inspector gave me one of those enormous ghastly new-fangled papers, innumerable questions in tiny print with smudged pictures to be identified and marked in ½s and ¼s; each question paper was a book of ten pages, and of course all the candidates did the questions in a different order. I tried one paper and my spectacles kept falling off as I peered to and fro between the pages. I took the whole pile back to the Inspector.

'Mr So and So,' I said, 'I will sweep the floor, if you like, I will clean out the P.K. (Rhodesian word for lavatory) — and it badly needs it — I will do almost anything within reason, but I will not correct any more of these papers. . ' Fortunately this was taken in good part as were also my apostolic excursions during hours — at least I hope they were.

The Methodists were very kind and bonhomous, but pretty clearly this was in spite of my being a priest, which I found odd, papists being so generally acceptable in the U.S.A. I was never asked to say grace at a meal; even when only women were present, some old pussy asked the blessing.

Though the other catholic schools did well, Musami did extremely badly so I was the bearer of bad news on my return and had little comfort at either end there too, returning as I did to more exam papers here.

All this to explain, my dear Patrick, why this letter is late, and to excuse me to Madeleine for not having written.

There was also a letter he wrote on December 11th. In this he did not explain the new plans and the letter alarmed us mildly — it also explains, perhaps, something that lay behind some of his discontent;

Our term and school year have ended at last, and I am at present resting in a supine position as much as possible, for I may have to have a minor operation for piles (internal) at the beginning of January. It is very uncertain and depends on various things: whether they are bad enough or get better with present treatment, whether there is a bed in the hospital, etc. Also my own future next year, for I may be leaving Musami at the end of the year since other teachers with better qualifications than me are available. But it is all rather tied up with the proposals for returning in the second half of 1960 to do the Hopkins book; I mean there wouldnt be much point in taking on a new job and then having to leave it after a few months. So what I am waiting for, after the false alarm of last time, is some definite official information.

.   .   .

The job Fr Corrigan had asked Christopher to do was to go to Harari, the native township of Salisbury and to live there with the native priests. Up to this time no white priest had done so and it may be remembered that when in August 1956 Christopher had gone there to supply he supplied for both native priests who were on holiday at the same time. He was to do mission work there of course but also he was to write and to lecture in Salisbury in an attempt to bridge the 'great divide'.

Once this had been proposed it had taken Christopher a little while to master his prejudices about living in the town, but he did so as he began to realise that if he was to play an effective part — as he had always been anxious to do — in breaking down apartheid, both outside and inside the Church, he could best do it from this township and that, even if he preferred the unsophisticated black people who lived in the isolated places, it was the minority who lived in the townships who turned to politics. Once the conviction came he fully agreed to the pivotal job to which he was assigned, and, indeed, must have worried a little over the possibility of being called home in 1960 to do the Hopkins Life.

194

But worry was needless. He was not to take up either project. Providence, as had happened before, stepped in and Christopher's next letter was written on Monday afternoon 14 December from hospital. It was headed

St Anne's Hospital (Blue Nuns) Salisbury.
(I get visited frequently every day)
This is going to be rather a disgusting letter but I have become quite hospital-minded in my 2 days here. On Saturday after I had sent you my last letter, I got a terrific haemorrhage lasting from 2 to 6 p.m. Strange to say apart from the embarrassment, I found it very pleasant getting rid of all that blood. But at the end I was too weak to get off the bed, so it was a great mercy of God that it didn't happen on Sunday when I should have been out in the bush saying Mass. As it was the doctor arrived at 6 p.m., and, with some shots of morphia, I was despatched in a semi-conscious but quite blissful condition to this excellent hospital where I have the luxury of a private room and the nun-nurses are of course wonderful. All that night and Sunday morning I had intra-venous infusions etc. and by 2 p.m. my blood-pressure was returned to normal. The surgeon who has a reputation for great competence and devotion is going to do an exploration tomorrow — there appears to be a growth in the bowel higher up than the piles — but I am not sure what will follow after that. So I will keep the rest of this airmail to report briefly on further developments.

15 December
Well, my dear Madeleine, unless I have lost the use of my wits (and that is indeed quite probable for I find it difficult to distinguish between dreaming and waking) but if I am still compos then Providence has clicked fairly audibly. Mr Honey, the surgeon, says that an operation is necessary BUT if it were himself or his wife in question he would advise going back to England for it — as they haven't quite got the necessary skills here. He says that it *can* be performed quite successfully.
I had a letter to Joan Mary long overdue — so I have informed her, but less dramatically!
Honey says I have a very good bowel and it can easily be snipped across.

And to Fr Philip Caraman he wrote briefly saying that Fr Corrigan was arranging for him to be flown back on 20 December, and asking whether the periodical 'Rhodesia' could reprint an article from 'The Month'. He also wrote to Rupert Hart-Davis giving him Farm Street as his address and apologising for his handwriting which was bad, due, he said, not to weakness but to the angle at which he had to write, he added, for good measure, as a postcript, 'My health is rude.'

PART FIVE

HOME

1

A Jesuit Provincial serves for a term of six years and Fr Boyle had been succeeded by Fr John Coventry. It was Fr Coventry who phoned to say that Christopher, gravely ill, was being flown home that day. We had not heard from him since his letter of 11 December, for those written from Hospital were caught up in the Christmas mails, and had not yet arrived. Patrick was away on Assize — it was the 21 December — and could not get free for another two days; he told me to ask the Provincial if I might meet the plane.

As I had seen him go — so I met him on his return; the meeting was equally inconsequential. His plane had been delayed; it was many hours late in leaving Salisbury. Fr Corrigan had waited with him at the airport, becoming increasingly alarmed as the drugs, with which Christopher had been filled for the journey, began to wear off — but not Christopher. Airborne he denied that *he* was the sick man whom the sympathetic air-hostess had been warned to expect, and he thoroughly enjoyed the journey, his first flight since 1946. He had to change planes in Rome; it was still daylight when he flew on and once more he knew the delight of seeing the Alps below him. And so to Heathrow. He was lighting his pipe as he came through the barrier; he said he was pleased to be met; the plane was so late he had feared that there might be no public transport available.

He was allowed to spend the night at Gray's Inn. The flat was already overcrowded as all the children had returned for the holidays and we had been due to leave for West Wick; the welcome his nephews and nieces gave him was heart-warming. Next day the surgeon who was to operate said that he could come to Wiltshire for Christmas.

In his Christmas sermon he embodied the theme of his letter of January 1958 — that unexpected solutions are something very much to be believed in.

To Joan Mary he wrote from Hospital on 27 December — he was to be operated on on the next day,

I had a lovely 2 or 3 days at West Wick. Dialogue Mass every morning for all the children, 2 guests (Gwyns) and a servant.

Now I am preparing for the operation.

The 'Gwyns' were Julian who was to marry Clare, and his sister, Caroline. Christopher knew their father well as he was an exact contemporary of Patrick's at Stonyhurst.

On the 28th, the Feast of the Holy Innocents, the operation took place. When it was over — after four hours, it was for cancer of the bowel and involved a colostomy which would be permanent — warning was given me that the cancer might just possibly have already spread, to the liver, in which case, probably, surgery could do no more. His Superiors when I told them, said in view of the uncertainty and since he was well-prepared for death at any time — he should be told of the possibility only if he asked. Christopher did not think about his health more than was necessary; he never asked.

Twelve days after the operation he wrote to Joan Mary,

10 January 1960

All the prayers have certainly stood me in good stead for I have come through very well. I can go to the bath now every day and that will greatly help the wound. It has really been a wonderful experience getting inside the Hospital World and feeling the Holy Spirit working over-time, so to speak, 'lava quod est sordidum' etc. (1)

And to Fr Philip Caraman four days later,

I have a great hankering for Poetry. Could you send me the old Auden Anthology — if you still have it — Not all the volumes, of course, but those which include Shakespeare (and Southwell) in the 16c and stretch to Christopher Smart in the 18c — must have the Song of David. If you havent got the Auden Anthology then something on those lines. Perhaps I might have the 19c too?

By 22 January he confessed in a birthday letter to Joan Mary, to 'doing well' but to being at the 'weariness in well-doing stage'.

During the three weeks that had passed since the operation he had suffered greatly, and his suffering was added to, one might say fortuitously, for he caught one of the devastating bugs that can haunt a hospital; it manifested itself in carbuncle after carbuncle. He remained sanguine through each trial living up to his belief as once expounded in a letter to Charlie Meade:

Health and sickness *as facts* are impersonal, but according to the use we make of them we can enter into more personal communication with Our Lord — I mean a closer awareness of his presence and care. And it does seem de facto that illness and misfortune do provide often a more satisfactory channel for that than good health and

(1) From the 'Sequence of the Mass for Pentecost', Veni, Sancte Spiritus.

197

good fortune. But not necessarily and not always. It is useless to speculate and important to trust. Trust transcends health.

We have to pass through a process of lonely purification in order to attain full happiness. 'He that loses his soul shall find it . .' and in so far as illness is a rehearsal for death it would be an obvious help to this process of purification, but depending of course on the use we make of it.

There is something still further to be said, 'Did it not behove the Son of Man to suffer and so enter into his glory?' Suffering, especially by the sympathy of others can be irradiated by a foretaste of glory: but it remains an evil in itself, something to be passed through.

Many of his Jesuit brethren came to cheer him with their visits and many friends did too. Charlie came, and above all there was Rupert Hart-Davis. Rupert not only made the time-consuming journey to the hospital, which was outside London, but on his visit suggested that Christopher should write a book for him to publish; though at the time he suspected that Christopher might be too ill to finish it, he did not care so long as the idea gave Christopher an immediate interest. Write, he said, on anything you like, only please don't make it a religious book. The coming weeks and months were 'irradiated' by this offer; even on the worst days there was the book to plan and read for, and then to write. Rupert, as the days went by, at considerable cost in both time and money, was to bring or post many of the books Christopher needed to consult. Dear friendship could hardly have gone further. Christopher had not hesitated over the subject; this was to be 'poor Kit Smart' the eighteenth century poet who had suffered from bouts of madness and about whom Christopher had long hoped to find time to write.

On 1 February — it was exactly four years since he had set sail for Africa — refusing the surely greater comfort of an ambulance, he came by car to West Wick. Soon work on the book would begin.

He explained the move to his American correspondent, Miss Moseley writing to her on 21 February,

Our Provincial, a very kind and liberal man, said it would be death for me to stay in a Jesuit house, and was only too glad to grant the request of my brother and sister-in-law that I stay with them (looked after daily by the local doctor) until my main wound is healed and I am more or less able to look after myself.

Last Sunday (one week ago) after much practice I was able to say Mass — a wonderful joy — and have been doing so ever since. Apart from that and an occasional stroll, I still spend most of the time in bed because the wound is not yet healed and I *cant* sit down — so bed is really the best place if you *have* to lie down!

For weeks Christopher only left his bedroom to say Mass in the room opposite, which was temporarily arranged as a chapel; his 'strolls' were confined to crossing the passage. How he managed to write the scholarly highly successful little book is a mystery; it seemed sometimes, as though he conjured it — like some act of Prospero's — out of the air. Research for it had to be contrived in devious ways; much of it could be done from the books he asked Rupert to send him, and much from those he asked the Public Library to obtain and post. He instructed Clare in his methods and she gave him what time she could, often diving into the Record Office in her lunch hour, and, sometimes with Julian's help, searching elsewhere. If Clare did not come to the country for the week-end Christopher wrote to say what he needed, for example,

6 March 1960
Many thanks to you and Julian for exploration into Bedlam on my behalf. There is a book in the British Museum I want consulted, it is not in the London Library. 'Arcana Microcosmi' by Alexander Ross, 1652. The chapter that 'Fishes are cunning docible creatures.' But it would take too long on paper to explain its possible connection with Smart.
We have written for 'The Hoxton Madhouses' (2). O'D (3) throws out incidentally that it was there that Charles and Mary Lamb were confined.

Clare was very successful in finding what was needed, but she had too little time to give to the task — she was reading Law at London University — and so further research was fitted in by a professional, who was already engaged on mammoth research work, to whom Christopher wrote his needs. Actually the last necessary fragments were gathered in by her *mother*, who, as it chanced, lived not too far from Barnard Castle where they were to be found. (4)

And so the months passed not too slowly since Christopher had this work to do. He also wrote to his pupils in Africa quite frequently, often in Shona which he did not want to forget; he received shoals of letters from them in return, some in English, some in Shona and some in a mixture of both languages. He kept them all. The refrain of those in English is always 'when shall we see you again?' and 'thank you for all you did for me.' They are very touching. For instance, Blandina wrote in January 1960,

I wish I could win £30,000 and fly to see you and your family . . . ;

and a little later Susanna wrote,

Why were you taken suddenly ill; I was told about it and I trembled . . . ;

(2) 'Hoxton Madhouses' by Dr Arthur Morris.
(3) O'Donoghue, Rev. J., 'History of Bethlem Hospital' (London 1911).
(4) Mrs Stokes, who was Professor Aspinall's assistant, whilst working on Sir Lewis Namier's 'History of Parliament', and her mother, Mrs Edington.

and from George there came,

I loved the way you taught history and I wish we had you now. May God keep you in moral goodness. Pray for Africa . . . ;

and from Peter,

Dearest Father, Will you send me your picture if you have one? . . . ;

and from Gertrude

I see you in my imagination overcoming pain bravely . . . ;

and from a Susanna, with a beautiful handwriting,

Sometimes school life gets so hard that my mind gets no peace . . . ;

and from Isabella

I beg you not to forget this mission and especially my school St Stephen's, Rota. Many Catholics there are crying for you . . . ;

and from 'your loving pupil Timothy',

We wish we would see you again in Rhodesia. How are we going to learn English and History? We have got used to your teaching . . . ;

and from Clemence,

Pray that I may be a good boy. How is your brother? Give him my love. Has he any daughters or sons? If he has I send them my love too . . . ;

and from Mary,

Thank you with my whole heart for teaching me to pray . . . ;

One could go on and on. They told him about 'the splendid new buildings at Musami' and 'the magnificent swimming pool' which only the boys were allowed to use. And much else besides all of which he enjoyed very much, and sent them various things, photos, maps, post cards and books in return. Not that he neglected other school boys; in May he wrote his nephew Timothy,

I have thought of a good holiday task for you and Matthew. The carpet in this bedroom has got several ink and other stains. You could set to sork with ink and other things and stain it all over so as to make a fine dappled pattern.

On one of his visits the Provincial brought Henry Wardale, the scholastic from Musami, to see Christopher — he was finishing his studies at Heythrop and would very soon be returning to Rhodesia.

To return to Africa was still Christopher's burning hope. By Whitsun he was well enough for me to leave him and Patrick and I went for a holiday. He wrote us on 10 June,

Virginia has been looking after me terribly well. The weather has been very good, lovely at first, then storms, but always streaks of sunshine. I have a good many meals downstairs. Joe has come every day.
I have finished Chapter 4 What we thought was a semi-swarm of Bees has turned into a full-blown Martins' nest. Three Goldfinches are all around the garden now, especially on the cornflowers (big blue daisies?) Joe, the family Doctor, Dr Byrne, was immensely kind. Christopher once wrote of him,

his goodness is so much a part of him with its fussiness etc that you take it for granted, yet it is so genuinely beneficent, like the sun, spreading its goodness. Bonum est diffusivum sui.

Chapter 4 of course referred to the progress he was making with 'Kit Smart'. It seemed strange then and does so still, that he was ignorant about flowers whilst noticing them for their colours. His habit of putting capitals for the names of birds, and often of animals, had begun at Stonyhurst, was never abandoned.
On 2 July he wrote a letter of some interest to Fr Rea S.J., once his colleague — he was the Senior History Master at Beaumont and had followed Christopher out to Rhodesia teaching first of all at St George's College and later at the University in Salisbury, where indeed he still is. Christopher wrote,

It is a long time since we corresponded last and I wonder how you have been getting on. As you may cynically guess it is a request to be asked of you which has touched off this letter.
Francis Cowper, editor of 'Graya', the Gray's Inn Journal, wants an article on Henry Walpole. I told him you were the authority so he asked me to ask you . . .
I have been a long time convalescing, having been somewhat mucked-up in hospital after the operation. But I am now definitely on the mend, and beginning to burst right out of all available clothes and expect to be seconded to one of our houses next month.

And 'next month' he went to Garnet House at Wimbledon, where, at that time the Provincial and his staff lived. He wrote to us from there on 12 August,

The garden reaches down to the golf-course — extremely pleasant. The Czech, ('Maminka') cultivates bits of it, besides doing the cooking etc., but most of it has inevitably gone to seed; there are lots of birds, flocks of Bullfinches, also Jay, Magpie, Woodpecker. 'Maminka' is a woman of unbounded energy. 'Jan' the Czeck man is very willing but limp and absent-minded, finds Maminka too much

for him. ('Good wife — but not for husband.')!
Fr Clarke is benevolence itself. I think this is quite the most suitable S.J. house that could have been picked for me.

31 August, from Garnet House
I have finished C. Smart — all except the loose ends — Afraid I have found my interest flagging sadly towards the end. But I think that is quite a good way to feel about a book.
I shall see you on Sept 8.

It was with some trepidation that Christopher had gone to Garnet House; normal living could never be very convenient for him again and he feared that living in a community he might be a nuisance to others. At the end of September he was, as he put it, 'trapped into hospital', this time at Hammersmith, as the wound had been troublesome, but he escaped within a very few days 'bursting with health', he said, and a month later he was delighted to be given some work to do. He felt that it had been proved that he could live a more or less normal life and he welcomed the job as the first step on the road back to Africa. He was sent as Chaplain to the Ursuline School at Westgate-on-Sea. He was very happy there; he found the nuns

Very natural and friendly — no scurrying, muttering, grimacing, etc.
There have been one or two lovely days and very pleasant walking.
A phenomenon — last Friday or Saturday a flock of martins appeared flying round the house. My old nun-waitress said she also saw swallows, but she might be confusing the two. (5)

and he wrote to Joan Mary,

I am very well established here. There is a fine sea-wall within easy reach, about 10 minutes walk. It's been mostly rain so far, as I suppose everywhere, but occasionally when a stiff sea-breeze blows the clouds away it is most invigorating to totter along the front. In fact, I am told, that if you were to take the wings of a bee — a good sturdy bee, I suppose — you would reach the North Pole without meeting any land in between — However I have no desire to try.
My duties are not onerous, so I have time for writing. I have just been tidying up the Smart MS and am now doing a pamphlet on Robert Southwell for Fr Caraman's 'Impressa'. (6)

.   .   .

The Christmas holidays Christopher spent at West Wick, just as he had done so many times before and, just as before, he supplied for the Parish Priest. He was to remain at Westgate until Easter and wrote to tell Joan Mary so. He longed for Africa but as he said several times on different occasions when he was there, quite cold-

(5) 7 November, from Westgate to Madeleine.
(6) 12 November, from Westgate to Joan Mary.

202

bloodedly. He did not want to return unless he could do a job for which he was specially needed and he did not want to be a trouble there because of his disabilities. His future, he told Joan 'was unknown',

I had hoped to go back to Africa after Easter; but there seems little chance of that now. Perhaps the Provincial when he returns from his visit there will be able to tell me whether there is any need of me (quâ me) as opposed to a younger and healthier man. If there were no doubt the doctors' objection could be overcome; if not I would be more of a burden than a help. (7)

He said something of the same thing when back at Westgate he answered a letter from Lady Acton who had written to ask whether he would return to Rhodesia as her chaplain, he wrote,

I have a feeling the Provincial is going to say 'unless Devlin (including his disabilities) is urgently needed for a job which cannot remain in England.'
One plan was that I should operate from Mbebe in the neighbouring reserve. If that were proved to be impracticable, I dont know whether I would come back to Rhodesia just as your chaplain. The longer I stay in England the more involved I get and everything combines to say 'Africa is finished for you'. So I cant honestly say for example, that I will do my utmost to persuade the Provincial to send me back as your chaplain', — though I would come like a shot if I were sent. (8)

Fr Corrigan wrote later on to say that he had heard of Christopher's reply and that he felt that there was a possibility of someone who knew Shona 'working up the neighbourhood and really making quite a centre of it' whilst being a chaplain as suggested. (9) And so far as his family ever knew Christopher's desire to return to Africa never wavered, though it is easy to understand how he was getting involved with writing.

On his return to Westgate, at the beginning of the spring term, Christopher wrote to Joan Mary,

In spite of having to waste a good deal of time because of circumstances over which as yet I have but imperfect control, I have got through a good bit of writing in these last three months. Besides amending and adding to 'Kit Smart', (which has gone to the Printers) I have done my 10,000 word pamphlet on Southwell — and just corrected the proofs — and an article for the Gray's Inn Journal called 'Hunter and Hunted' on Topcliffe and Henry Walpole who were both members of Gray's Inn!
I have also written two long articles on the Mashona — their

(7) 30 December 1960, from West Wick.
(8) 22 February 1961, from Westgate.
(9) 8 April 1961, from Salisbury, S.R.

203

history from Silviera martyred 15 March 1561, to the present day which will appear in 'The Month' for March and April.

It is a great blessing to have the ability and taste for writing because another year seems to be the verdict in regard to me and Africa. (10)

When he sent these Mashona articles (11) to 'The Month' Christopher wrote to Fr Philip Caraman that they were

terribly compressed, really the nucleus of a book I would like to write if I could find an opening for it.

His notes for this book of the history of the Shona people are copious.

Perhaps Christopher's time in Rhodesia might also be described as 'terribly compressed'; it had lasted only 46 months and we know something of what he achieved in the bush and elsewhere. He never wrote the book he had planned. The notes for it had been made from the time he arrived, particularly whilst he was learning the language at Musami but to a lesser extent all the while; (he checked and added to them sometimes when he could get to the library of the School for African Studies on his visits to London from Westgate); he used them for the three articles he wrote for 'The Month', the first, the 'Shona Eclogue', written whilst he was still in Africa was, in addition to being a review of a lovely poem 'a peg for an article on the nature of the people'; but the real value of these nots is not either historical or literary; their value lies in what he achieved, amongst the Ma-Shona, in their gathering. They were his passport to them; his 'open sesame'. They gave Christopher a second approach. Other missionaries had, also, sometimes a second approach — notably Fr Michael Hannan who studied the Shona language, a language 'essentially pastoral and peasant', until he understood the riches of its vocabulary, a vocabulary in which words have infinite shades of meaning, and was able to translate the bible into it. (He also compiled a dictionary.) Christopher's way, if less spectacular, was profoundly important. In his approach he used precisely the same gifts as he had used when he set about writing 'Robert Southwell', or got into the skin of Hopkins; it was exactly the same gift as he had used in his tenderness towards the children of Liverpool, in his teaching at Beaumont, or with the airmen on active service; it was the gift that made his friendships, whether with the scholastics he taught, or with his own contemporaries, or with those, like Charlie and Aileen, older than himself, so succesful and so dear. It

(10) 23 January 1961, from Westgate.
(11) 'The Mashona and the Portuguese', 'The Month', March 1961. 'The Mashona and the British', 'The Month', April 1961.

was the Ignation 'going in at others' doors'. It was that deep sympathy which enabled him to enter into and understand the lives of others, and whether he met people face to face, or whether they had died a few or several hundred years before he was born — whether they were of his own race or of another — it seemed to make no difference to him.

In Rhodesia he used this extraordinary gift, and the others it brought in its train, to the full. He was enabled to understand the Africans without sentimentality; he saw, sharp and clear, the difficulties of these Black Rhodesians in the mass, thirsting for education, with too little land in the Native Reserves to gain a proper standard of living; and in the towns having too few jobs open to them, which were in any event too badly paid, so that often to support themselves they made ends meet in undesirable ways. He saw them, as they were, caught between their ancestral past and the industrial future and knew the problems and tensions this engendered. He understood the great promise and sensitivity of the best of them and what education could do, not only for them but for myriads if they could get a chance of it. And because he could enter these African lives with naturalness and sympathy he was able to become friends with many, who in their turn, were able to be friends with him — both sides on equal terms —friend with friend.

This was his achievement, and he left behind the memory of a common basis on which 'two people in one country' could build if ever communication, broken now as it had been between them for some years, is restored. In any event he is yet so well remembered it is not too much to hope that in the hearts of those he served the fruit of his brief ministry will last and multiply — for the Glory of God and the Good and Peace of Mankind.

As for Christopher himself; he had 'made his soul', which was the reason Patrick had attributed to Fr Boyle at the time when we, too, wondered why he had been sent to the Missions; he had made it amongst the African people, listening and talking to them; and alone, sitting on the tall purple granite boulders above Musami, gazing out on the unspoilt country, bush all around as far as eye could see; gazing into the 'Vast Inane'.

. . .

Fr Coventry returned from Rhodesia and he was very willing to send Christopher back there to do any work of which he might be capable. He thought his work could still be valuable and that even if it happened that he had not long to live he would yet be happier

205

working in Rhodesia to the end. He came to West Wick to see him and chanced on a very bad day when movement was difficult and came to the decision that sending him back could only add intolerably to his suffering — and so he spoke instead of a posting to Farm Street. But before this there really had been hope. Movement was not always difficult and there were times when Christopher felt that if only the wound would heal he would be quite fit. Once a month, much to his annoyance, he had to go to London to be examined by his surgeon. By this time they did not get on very well. The surgeon thought that Christopher should behave as a sick man; Christopher could not think of himself as such. The visits became more and more frigid.

On one of these days in town he arranged in addition to visit Aileen and Charlie at their London house, as of old; as of old this was a happy time. Afterwards he wrote to them,

It was a terrific pleasure to bridge the gap of the years in such a pleasant manner and to find you so unquenched by the waters of tribulation that have flowed there under. A pretty metaphor.

and to us on the same day, '21 February, Feast of Robert Southwell', he said,

I enjoyed yesterday in London very much. Aileen was much better, hardly any cough and was in good form. Coney was there, she helps them a lot. They have a squat Bass-Italian maid called Rafaella who cooks very well and looks at them in a proprietary manner.

On 31 March, having left the Convent, Christopher once more stayed at Garnet House. He wrote to Joan Mary,

The Provincial has more or less taken me off Westgate, though he will probably ask me to do a stand in there in May or June. After that I dont know. I should think there is a chance of my being stationed at Farm Street for a bit and doing work on 'The Month' etc. If so, and if all the operational work is cleared up, that would be a good time for me to come and stay with you. Our Provincial is very anxious to do all he can for me so there will be no difficulty on that side.

On 10 April Clare married Julian at St Etheldreda's, the thirteenth century church in Holborn. Christopher who had baptised her twenty-one years earlier, now offered her Nuptial Mass, performed the marriage ceremony and preached the sermon which he had most carefully prepared and polished till it was a thing of beauty. Exhausting as it had been for him, as soon as he got back to Garnet House that night he wrote to Joan Mary. (12)

(12) Joan Mary's Order is enclosed and she would not have been allowed to come to the wedding.

I have just returned from the wedding and the reception. It went off quite perfectly, not a hitch, both bride and groom behaving very well and naturally. Timothy and Matthew assisted and served the nuptial mass and there were many comments on how nicely they did it. Gil and Dominick were ushers. Patrick was very pleased with the whole thing. Billy proposed the health of the bride at the reception. Virginia enjoyed herself very much as bridesmaid.

The reception in Gray's Inn Hall was an extraordinary amalgam of relatives and friends I had not seen for ages and who were completely unknown to each other. I did not stay very long; but I was sorry I missed two people I had been looking for — Diana Devlin and Ruth Fermoy. (13) It was a great blessing the weather kept fine, it would have been a disaster otherwise, as St Etheldreda's is no church for parking.

Among the Crombie gathering whom I met were: Harvey and his wife, Kitten and Peveril with Jean, Johanna, Merlyn and Morrice and twins, Anne and Gordon and sons. (14)

I go into hospital tomorrow — the Westminster — Franklin is still to do the operation but I am under the care of Frank D'Abreu who has a fine post-operational team. It is a very small affair, But I imagine the after-care is important.

Madeleine has been thoughtful in the midst of all the wedding cares. She will keep you informed.

He was right; the after-care was very important for the successful operation was followed suddenly by complications which happily Frank D'Abreu overcame for the operation was to give Christopher a brief spring of delight. Both the distinguished surgeons — the D'Abreu brothers, were contemporaries of Patrick and Christopher at Stonyhurst. We had asked Fr Coventry whether there might be a second opinion on Christopher — it had confirmed the first but that is how Frank came into the picture.

It was while Christopher was in Westminster Hospital that he answered Fr Corrigan's letter about the suggestion of going back to Rhodesia as Lady Acton's chaplain. He had received it a few days before Clare's wedding. He made fairly light of the ordeal through which he had just been and said he was now feeling fine 'though still confined to bed' and added 'The Future? Vaguer than ever.' (15) Ten days later he wrote Joan Mary from Gray's Inn,

D'Abreu and the Provincial conspired to get me out of hospital and sent here where I have been looked after by District Nurses from whom Madeleine has learnt to take over.

I am so much better that we are off to BRAEMAR tomorrow, for

(13) Diana, Billy's daughter and Ruth, Lady Fermoy, 'the cousin with corn-coloured hair, (p. 12).

(14) Jean, la Baronne de Boulemont, Harvey and Kitten's sister (Uncle Jim's children) Johanna, Aunt Joan, Uncle John's widow, and her daughter Mary Lindsay (Merlyn) who had married Morrice Henderson, and Anne, her daughter who had married Gordon Maclean, and the grandchildren.

(15) Letter of 26 April, from Westminster Hospital to Fr Corrigan.

10 days —Pat, Madeleine and I. I wont be able to walk about but it will be lovely just to see the old places again. The whole thing was Pat's idea, and it was he who arranged it. We come back on May 29th and I hope to visit you early in June.

The time at Gray's Inn was memorable for two things. Christopher had permission to say Mass in the flat; it seems likely, and it would not be unfitting, if his was the first Mass said there after 370 years. The flat is probably only a stone's throw — a good throw — from where Swithin Well's house had stood in Gray's Inn Fields, it is presumed opposite and slightly to the east of where Verulam Buildings stand today. There in 1591 the pursuivants, headed by Richard Topcliffe, (16) who on any view was an infamous member of the Inn, had broken in whilst Fr Edmund Gennings had been saying Mass; his host (who was martyred at Tyburn for harbouring him and who regretted not having been present at the celebration) was away but one of Robert Southwell's pupils in Rome was there, Fr Polydore Plasden; he also was seized on this occasion and hanged, drawn and quartered at Tyburn. Fr Gennings himself underwent that fate actually in Gray's Inn Fields — all three died on the same day. Actually a couple of hundred yards to the south and four years earlier, in 1587, another priest on the English Mission had said Mass in the Irish Rents which stood in the south-east corner of what is now South Square — he too was hanged drawn and quartered. Christopher said Mass in the flat in Gray's Inn Square several times and his thoughts must have turned to these men as he did so.

His own sufferings must be described as acute but at least, though finely borne, they were borne in private and not inflicted because of his Faith. (17)

And the other matter for which these days was memorable: Christopher had written,

Two things only did I take away from school, the friendship of a master . . .

Fr Martin D'Arcy's friendship had indeed stood the test of years. He came to dinner in the flat before he left to lecture in America and whilst Christopher was still confined to bed. Of all his brothers in Religion probably Fr D'Arcy was the dearest to Christopher. It was, then, also fitting that he was the last one Christopher saw.

A week later we left for Deeside, putting the car on the train as far as Perth. Christopher did not feel very well during the journey

(16) As is recorded by Christopher in 'Life of Robert Southwell', p. 238.
(17) For the geography of sixteenth century Gray's Inn and some of the information, I am indebted to Frances Cowper himself & to his book, 'A Prospect of Gray's Inn'.

but he had no sooner set foot on his native land than a great change came over him. He seemed well at last. When we stopped for a picnic lunch he jumped a gate. Arrived at the Invercauld Arms at Braemar he sent Joan Mary a card,

It is wonderful being here — terribly cold, but the hotel is extremely comfortable. Said Mass for you.

He went out daily before breakfast to say Mass 'in the lovely old parish church where the Farquharsons and Macdonalds had kept the Faith ever since St Machar brought it' (18) where he had planned to say it in August 1941 and had been foiled by his call-up; and

on the purple moor with its green blaeberry tufts and silver birch trees; between the shadow of Morrone and the sheen of the River Dee

for which he had confessed his love when he was fourteen. He felt so restored that Africa seemed to him — and to us — just around the corner. He could walk two or three miles; he ate lustily — the years slipped away and I was an onlooker as he and Patrick went over the familiar ground of their childhood. As he wrote to Joan Mary from Gray's Inn after we had returned,

We had a lovely time at Braemar — enough fine days to see all the old places. Callater and Quoich remained the favourites; we had time for two long trips, one to Strathdon, one to Goval. We invited Canon Kear (the parish priest) and his housekeeper (Miss Farquharson, the Queen's hairdresser at Balmoral) to dinner and had a great sederunt about old times.

This was written on 1 June.

2

       In Maiden's eyes, in Maiden's eyes,
          All wisdom I descry
      My books and my academies
          My deep divinity.
      This is my faith and in it I
          Profoundly hope to die.

       In Maiden's eyes, in Maiden's eyes,
          True loveliness I spy,
      The lovely bridge of Paradise
          That spans infinity
      This is my faith and in it I
          Profoundly hope to die.

(18) p. 37.

In Maiden's eyes, in Maiden's eyes,
All shadows I deny
Except the shadowy depth where lies
The Blessed Trinity;
This is my faith and in it I
Profoundly hope to die.

Back in London Christopher appeared to be very well indeed, so well that when he saw Frank D'Abreu, Frank just hesitated — could this be one of the rare cases where the cancer had been arrested and, for no known reason, was clearing away? —He thought not, probably, and said, 'Wait one more month before taking up your duties at Farm Street.'

From West Wick there were to be gay expeditions, tracing Roman roads near Devizes, visiting early sixteenth century priories — but only for a little while. Before the month was out troubles arose and his strength began to fail. He wrote to Joan Mary, she too was ill and had written him well-knowing how frustrated he must feel,

Many thanks for your letter. Yes it is a disappointment and makes one wonder how it is all going to end. I find it best just to live from day to day. And I have my blessings to count in the process — chief among them is the Daily Mass. (19)

But he showed no sign of wondering and it became increasingly difficult to know what to say.

At the end of August 'Poor Kit Smart' came out. It was so called from a remark of Dr Johnson's, 'I'd as lief pray with Poor Kit Smart as any one else.' At once, most gratifyingly, it was greeted with good reviews and Ruth Simon, who worked with Rupert and was soon to be his wife, telephoned to say that it was to be the subject of a talk on the wireless. Could, she asked, Christopher go to London to be interviewed during the programme? Alas, he did not feel well enough to go. Instead on his nephew Matthew's tape-recorder he did a mock interview with Patrick as the interviewer; he was light-hearted and gay and both of them were excruciatingly funny in their mockery. 'Ah,' said Christopher, 'if only one could gag all the time.'

On 7 September he wrote Joan Mary a brief note to wish her a happy day on the 8th which is celebrated as the feast of Our Lady's Nativity, it was brief because he had 'collected a bit of a temperature'.

The time now seemed fast approaching, as he had written his mother, just after ordination 'when the earthly altar would give place to the heavenly one;'. Soon I felt I would have to tell him what he had never asked, now that there was not even the slenderest thread of doubt. And so one day I told him.

(19) 7 July 1961, from West Wick.

210

'What shall we do?' he asked,
'Do?'
'Shall I go to hospital?'
'Do you want to?'
'No.'
'Well we just go on.'
'But you will have a corpse on your hands.' The matter was not referred to again except that I asked if he wanted any one to know. 'Only the Provincial,' he said and seemed relieved when I replied that the Provincial already knew.

But silently he begged for release. One morning as he was getting up a robin flew in through the window. I thought he would be pleased but he said 'I only want my freedom' and chided it for coming. I knew I ought to understand but I did not and did not like to ask. Indeed I *should* have known that Christopher would be facing death with thought moulded in Elizabethan verse; what else was in his mind but:

> Call for the robin-redbreast and the wren
> Since o'er shady groves they hover
> And with leaves and flowers do cover
> The friendless bodies of unburied men. (20)

The bird had come too soon.

In the last week of September Christopher, to his great bewilderment, went once more through the Dark Night. 'I can't pray', he said, 'I can't pray and I have always been so close, so close; I don't understand.'

His devotion had truly 'been born of close union with a personal saviour' and nourished 'on the great heights of revelation'. (21) But now all was obscure. But not for long. With the coming of October 'a dawn wind stirred', the mists parted and the Dark Night of the senses gave way.

Let me kiss him with the kiss of his mouth . . .

Thus he thought Southwell had prayed in the Tower,

My dove in the clefts of the rock, in the hollow places of the wall, show me thy face, let thy voice sound in my ears.

On the eve of the feast of the Guardian Angels — and he had great devotion to the angels — Christopher made one last determined walk

(20) Peter Levi whom I asked about it long afterwards said 'surely you knew' and at once quoted the lines from Webster's 'The White Devil'.
(21) 'True devotion to be born requires close union with a personal saviour; but to be nourished it must be able to move at ease on the great heights of revelation.' 'Sermons and Devotional Writings of G.M.H.', p. 114.

right round the garden. Then, on the Feast itself, 2 October, he offered Mass for the last time. There was not too long to wait.

On the morning of the 5th Billy came, with Meriel, his wife and of whom Christopher was extremely fond. Together Christopher and Billy searched in the 'Oxford Book of Verse' for a loved quotation which they failed to find. Soon afterwards Billy and Meriel went away. A little later Patrick, who had been lecturing in the United States, arrived home and was gaily greeted. By the end of the afternoon Christopher had lost his voice, which he thought rather silly, — but he could still laugh. Towards evening he waved us a shy apologetic Blessing, and then, towards midnight, once again he spoke, 'Don't worry', he said, 'I'm all right.' I felt that he already saw

Those mighty angelic beings whom we should see if our senses corresponded perfectly with our intellect. (22)

and, still before midnight that Thursday, smilingly, he died. 'With a sweep of my plumes I galloping go', he had written in a gay poem whilst at Heythrop. He 'lightly stepped across', Patrick said. It was the last page — just as he had written it in 'Robert Southwell' —

It was not yet too difficult for them to see the heavens opened and a ladder of angels ascending to the Son of Man.

(22) From notes of a Long Retreat Christopher gave at Manresa to the Scholastics when he was teaching there. Found among his papers, but the notes were made by Fr John Harriott.